417

A BOOK OF
SCOTTISH
VERSE

Oxford University Press, Amen House, London E.C.4

GLASGOW NEW YORK TORONTO MELBOURNE WELLINGTON
BOMBAY CALCUTTA MADRAS KARACHI KUALA LUMPUR
CAPE TOWN IBADAN NAIROBI ACCRA

INTRODUCTION

THIS anthology contains poems ranging in date from the end of the thirteenth century to the beginning of the twentieth century, but does not include the work of any author now living. Nor does it include specimens of the work of writers like Andrew of Wyntoun and Sir David Lindsay, whose verse, though invaluable to the student of Scottish History, is almost negligible as poetry.

Most of the poems are printed in their entirety; omissions have been indicated in the notes. The spelling of the earlier poems has been modernized where there seemed no risk that the altered form might disguise the original sound of the word; but all obsolete words, and obsolete inflections like final *-and* indicating the present participle, and final *-is* or *-ys* indicating the plural of the noun, have been retained. The modern equivalents of the obsolete words, however, have been given in footnotes. It should be noted that final *-e* was not sounded in Middle Scots; that final *-is*, *-ys*, and *-es* were treated as separate syllables when added to monosyllables and to dissyllables with a final accent; and that the vowel in final *-it* or *-yt*, indicating the past indicative or past participle, was sounded.[1] Neglect of these rules will work havoc with the rhythms of Dunbar and Henryson.

In this collection Scottish verse has been taken

---

[1] For a full description of the characteristics of Middle Scots see the Introduction to *Specimens of Middle Scots* by G. Gregory Smith (W. Blackwood & Sons).

to include verse written in English by Scottish authors. To narrow the definition to verse written in Scots—the Vernacular, as it is sometimes loosely called—would lead to absurdities like the exclusion of writers as thoroughly Scottish as Sir Walter Scott and Drummond of Hawthornden, to say nothing of practically all that is original and vital in the work of more recent Scottish poets. For the Scots of Burns has become a foreign language to the educated, as to the uneducated, Scot: he may understand it, but he does not think in it; consequently his experiments in the vernacular are usually mere pastiche.

Originality, in fact, has not been a distinguishing feature of the Scottish poets of any age. They seldom innovate, seldom write poetry as startling and unaccountable as the *Shepherd's Calendar* or *Absalom and Achitophel* or *The Lyrical Ballads*. In *The Kingis Quair*—the earliest considerable Scottish poem with the exception of Barbour's *Brus*, a rhyming chronicle which once or twice quickens into poetry—the debt to Chaucer's *Knight's Tale* is obvious. But the poem is more than a mere imitation: the King's remembered woe and present rapture revivify the Chaucerian phrases. And the cry of the birds in the castle garden:

Away, winter, away!
Come, summer, come, the sweet season and sun,

echoes through Scottish poetry down to the present day, for, *pace* Mr. John Buchan, the twentieth-century Scot still grows weary of his protracted winters, is still tantalized by the treacherous and long-delaying northern spring.

The debt of Robert Henryson (1425?–1506?)

is equally unmistakable; he even ventures to write a sequel to *Troilus and Cressida*. Henryson is not Chaucer: he is less subtle, more of a moralist, than his master. But *The Testament of Cresseid* is not unworthy of the place that the early printers of Chaucer gave it, immediately after *Troilus*: it has a chilling and terrible beauty, like the stars by the light of which the stricken Cressida moves to her doom. So in the *Fables* Henryson owes much to the author of *The Nonne Prestes Tale*. But the background of the *Tale of the Uponlandis Mous and the Burges Mous* is as Scottish as the setting of the story of Chauntecleer and Pertelote is English. And we find in Henryson's fable that identification of the narrator with the animal characters in his story, that mouse-eye view of the world, which we shall encounter again in Burns.

Henryson's *Robene and Makyne* is something quite new—a pastoral which, unlike the better remembered *Shepherd's Calendar*, owes nothing to Theocritus or Virgil—a little rural comedy, with two genuine rustics for actors, played on some whin-clad Lowland pasture. In Henryson, too, we get for the first time that accurate observation of the spare Scottish landscape, that shivering consciousness of the unkindly Scottish climate, which we shall find again and again in later poets.

William Dunbar (1460?-1520?) makes no secret of his debt to Chaucer. His elaborate, carefully wrought allegories like *The Golden Targe* clearly owe much to the Chaucer who wrote *The Parlement of Foules* and translated the *Roman de la Rose*. But to call Dunbar 'the Scottish Chaucer' is to do both the Scottish and the English poet an injustice. In the technique of versification Dunbar out-distances his master. He is an innovator who delights in discovering new measures and in getting new effects out of old ones, an experimenter who, finding the vernacular inadequate, enriches it with the plunder of three languages to give us poems which are jets and cascades of glittering words. But he possesses as little of Chaucer's amused and sympathetic understanding of humanity as he does of his narrative gift. Dunbar's is the narrower mind, introverted, embittered by poverty and the vain wait for preferment, darkened by the fear of death. Sometimes his discontent seeks relief in wild invective, sometimes in lubricity, sometimes in a repetition of the commonplaces of philosophy or religion. He flits from mood to mood, from theme to theme, with disconcerting ease: an Easter hymn or a description of a royal amour, it is all the same to him; each is done with the same gusto, the same conscientious craftsmanship. But his versatility is more apparent than real: the skill with which he plays his parts blinds us to the fact that there are only three or four of them.

At times we hear in Dunbar's verse something that seems to be an echo, not of Chaucer, but of Villon. As we read, phrases from the *Ballade des Dames du Temps Jadis* weave themselves into *The Lament for the Makaris*. It cannot be proved, however, that the resemblance is due to imitation, conscious or unconscious. Dunbar does not use Villon's favourite ballade form or repeat his phrases. It can be accounted for on the hypothesis that two poets, similar in temperament, reacted in the same way to similar experiences. Not till we come to Andrew Lang shall we find a Scottish poet who writes ballades and rondeaux. Contrary to common belief, the debt of Scottish poets to France is almost infinitesimal.

As Henryson anticipates the Elizabethan pastoral poets, so Gavin Douglas (1475?–1522) anticipates the great succession of Elizabethan translators. His translation of the *Aeneid* was written in the fourteen months before the battle of Flodden, while he was Provost of St. Giles' Church in Edinburgh. After Flodden came promotion to the see of Dunkeld, then exile and death in England. One must not expect from Douglas Virgil's 'ocean roll of rhythm', but by a happy chance, in his rendering of the Sixth Book, the harsh, labouring verse suits the grim and terrible theme. More interesting than the actual translations are the prologues with which he prefaces the various Books. He complains in the Prologue to Book I that the vernacular alone will not serve his turn—

> So me behuvit whilom, or than[1] be dumb
> Some bastard Latin, French, or English use.
> Where scant war[2] Scots I had na other choice,
> Nocht for our tongue is in the selfin[3] scant
> Bot for that I the fowth[4] of language want.

In other words he is forced to compound a 'synthetic Scots'. But 'fowth of language' would seem to be what he needs least, for he piles up a 'vast confusion and wild heap' of words till the lines seem to creak and groan under their weight. Still, his descriptive passages are effective, for

[1] then. [2] was. [3] same. [4] abundance.

though he overcrowds his canvas, it is because his vision of the external world is too vivid, because to him every detail is just as important as every other detail.

With Flodden ends this brief efflorescence of Scottish poetry, this spring without a summer. Two and a half centuries have to pass before a poet of the calibre of Dunbar or Henryson appears in Scotland, and when he arrives the work of those older makars has been almost completely forgotten. An easy explanation offers itself—the Reformation and the spirit of Calvin. In the words of Andrew Lang, 'to Scotland in general the New Learning came not as a key to the garden of the Muses, not as "a magic casement opening on the foam of perilous seas" haunted by Circe and the sirens, but merely as a light on the Bible and on the disputes of theologians. Scotland, like Hamilton, her first martyr, received the Reformation without the Renaissance. The revival of the world of Greece brought to her not beauty, not joy in life, but a sword and ill will to men.' But Scotland was not compelled, except by her own nature, to accept the Reformation without the Renaissance. Calvinism was not imposed on Scotland from without. It was accepted because it was congenial to the national temperament.

While it is true that the Reformed Church was hostile to music and to secular poetry, there is nothing to show that it succeeded in silencing any poet of the first order. There is no trace, in Scottish prose literature of the sixteenth and seventeenth centuries, of anything like the pamphlets of Milton or the sermons of Donne;

anything to show a great poetical imagination deflected from its true end. In reality the influence of the Kirk did not go quite as deep as is supposed. The stream of popular song flowed almost as freely after the Reformation as before: the reformers might circulate their *Gude and Godlie Ballatis* 'changed out of prophane sanges for avoyding of sinne and harlotrie'; the profane originals survived their pious parodies. The courtier or country gentleman of literary tastes shrugged his shoulders at the frowning ministers and went his own way. Alexander Scott, for example, wrote love poetry worthy to rank, for its grace and felicity, beside the best work of the minor Elizabethans. But we cannot place him beside Spenser or Marlowe. And we see in his work the first warning signs of that blight that later was to overspread Scottish vernacular literature—sentimentalism.

Least of all did the Reformation harm the ballads. In fact most of our finest ballads came into existence or assumed their present form in the century following the Reformation. In them we discover something that had vanished from Scottish poetry for two centuries: the joy in sturt and strife, known to Barbour but unknown to Dunbar and Henryson, and something completely new, the faint, disturbing sound of elfin music—

> About the middle o' the night
> She heard the bridles ring;
> This lady was as glad at that
> As any earthly thing.

One deadly blow, however, the Reformers did strike at Scottish vernacular literature. By intro-

ducing the English Bible, an English metrical
psalter, and even for a time the English Book of
Common Prayer, they hastened the degradation
of Scots to the level of a dialect. Scots for every-
day matters, English for serious concerns, became
the rule. We see it exemplified in Drummond of
Hawthornden (1585–1649), the first of the long
line of Scottish poets who write wholly in English.

Though Drummond owes nothing to his
Scottish predecessors, he is not a pioneer. He is
rather a belated Elizabethan; one, too, who
draws much of his material from French and
Italian poetry. But his 'slow-endeavouring art'
builds up new shapes of beauty from what he
has borrowed. And again and again, as in his
sonnet on the Baptist, his scholarly, meditative
verse blazes up into unexpected splendour.
Drummond had no successor in the seventeenth
century: Montrose preferred to live his epic. But
all through the Civil War, the Cromwellian
occupation, and the Killing Times the old,
simple songs and ballads were repeated and new
songs and ballads composed. Few of their
authors have been identified; we may suspect
that to most of them, as to Lady Grizel Baillie,
authoress of *Werena my heart licht I wad dee*,
inspiration came once, and once only.

It is difficult at this time of day to understand
the vogue of *The Gentle Shepherd* of Allan Ramsay
(1686–1758) with its sentimentalized scenes from
rural life that suggest the kailyard novel of the
'nineties. Ramsay is important, not because he
points forward, but because he points back;
because he rediscovered the work of the older
Scottish poets, and collected and preserved many

evanescent ballads and songs. Still, we owe to him two delightful love songs, and, in a translation from Horace, an impressionistic sketch of a Scottish winter that is more effective than the crowded canvases of Douglas or James Thomson.

Though James Thomson wrote only in English, though he strove to be more Miltonic than Milton, it is of Gavin Douglas that one is reminded as one reads *The Seasons*. Here is the same accurate observation, the same accumulation of detail, and the same sensitiveness to the harsher moods of Nature. But the languid beauty of *The Castle of Indolence* and the wit and grace of the lines *To Fortune* would have been alike beyond the heavy-handed art of the earlier poet.

The town-bred Fergusson (1750–74) is, like Thomson, primarily a descriptive poet, intent, however, not on the 'intricate device of days and seasons', but on the doings of his fellows. Eighteenth-century Edinburgh, dirty and pretentious, drunken and pious, lives again in his pages. And there are some who prefer the direct, sincere rendering of the thing seen in *The Farmer's Ingle* to the sentimentalism masquerading as realism of the more famous *Cotter's Saturday Night*.

Burns (1759–96) would have been of their number. 'Having twenty times the abilities of Allan Ramsay and of Fergusson,' says Scott, 'he talked of them with too much humility as his models.' His indebtedness to his predecessors was real enough. He borrows not only from Ramsay and Fergusson, but from scores of innominate poets, and he attempts nothing that has not been attempted before. To say this is not to disparage his genius. He is the river into

which all streams run, the city to which all
roads tend. Not only does he resume in himself
the achievements of his predecessors: what was
merely promise in them becomes fulfilment in
him. He seems to know what the older song-
writers wanted to say better than they did themselves: one has only to compare his *Auld Lang
Syne* with Allan Ramsay's, or his *Ca' the Yowes*
with Isobel Pagan's, or *Were my Love yon Lilac
fair* with the earlier *O gin my Love were yon
Red Rose*, given in the *Border Minstrelsy*, to see
that he can transmute silver into gold. He shows
as keen an awareness of the varying moods of
Nature as Douglas or Thomson, but he uses
a more effective method than the laborious
accumulation of detail—one or two strokes, and
the picture is complete—

> One night as I did wander
>   When corn began to shoot,
> I sat me down to ponder
>   Upon an auld tree-root:
> Auld Ayr ran by before me
>   And bickered to the seas;
> A cushat crooded o'er me
>   That echoed through the braes.

Within the limits that his predecessors have
imposed on him he displays a marvellous variety.
He reminds one of writers as different from himself and from each other as Chaucer and Browning in his power of escaping from himself and
looking on the world through another man's, or
through a woman's eyes. He finds in humanity
nothing alien to himself but cruelty and pretence.

There are, it is true, certain elements in the
works of his predecessors which we do not find in
Burns. He never seeks to enter the twilight land

of ghosts and fairies, beloved of the balladists. Unlike Dunbar, he is not tormented by horror of the all-encompassing night. With these reservations, we may say that in Burns Scottish vernacular poetry reaches the perfection of which it is capable. Thus it is difficult for a modern poet who would use the vernacular not to write imitation Burns: writers as antipathetic to him as Stevenson and Andrew Lang speak in his idiom and use his measures when they attempt verse in Scots.

The ballad reaches its fulfilment, not in Burns, but in Scott. In fact, were it not for the existence of the unique and inimitable *Tam o' Shanter*, one might be tempted to declare that the storyteller's gift was altogether denied to Burns. 'Reaches its fulfilment' is used in a double sense, for the whole of the splendid ballad of *Kinmont Willie*, and many of the finest passages in other famous ballads, are substantially the work of Scott. In the narrative verse to which he put his name Scott seldom achieved anything quite as good as the lines, fashioned from material supplied to him by Hogg, which he interpolated in *The Battle of Otterbourne*—

> 'My nephew good,' the Douglas said,
> 'What recks the death of ane!
> Last night I dreamed a dreary dream,
> And I ken the day's thy ain.
>
> My wound is deep; I fain would sleep;
> Take thou the vanguard of the three,
> And hide me by the bracken bush,
> That grows on yonder lilye lee.
>
> O bury me by the bracken bush,
> Beneath the blooming brier,
> Let never living mortal ken,
> That ere a kindly Scot lies here.'

We do indeed come across passages in his longer
poems that stir the blood like

> a blast of that dread horn
> On Fontarabian echoes borne,

but he cannot maintain a strong even flight; his
muse is as slipshod and temperamental as Mr.
Masefield's. Hence comes the paradox that we
must look for the most perfect work of the
greatest Scottish narrative poet not among his
narrative poems but among his lyrics. But
though they display Scott as conscious craftsman
at his best, they are the utterance of a man who
rarely gives himself away—whose songs, like
Browning's, are always dramatic lyrics.

Almost the whole of nineteenth-century vernacular verse—that couthy, pawky, or tearful
stuff that swells out anthologies like *Whistle
Binkie*—is dilute Burns, just as most of the verse
written in English by Scottish authors is dilute
Scott, or later, dilute Tennyson. But sometimes
a miracle happens, and a versifier for a moment
becomes a poet. One would think, for example,
that there was nothing in the diffuse metrical
romances of James Hogg (1770–1835) to justify
his boast that he was King of the Mountain and
Fairy School, till one discovers the magical opening lines of *Kilmeny*, and the equally wonderful
close. There is nothing in W. B. Scott's pleasant
Tennysonian stanzas to prepare one for the black
magic of *The Witch's Ballad*; nothing in the lus-
cious verses of Alexander Smith at all comparable
with his *Glasgow*, that grim vision of a new Scotland from which his contemporaries averted
their eyes.

Three or four later nineteenth-century writers

deserve more than a passing mention. It would be unfortunate if the decline in the vogue of Stevenson's self-conscious, mannered prose led to the neglect of his verse. It is true that at times he seems to be struggling with an unfamiliar medium, and that he is at his ease only in the simplest measures; but he does succeed in compelling the stubborn words to do his will, in making the conventional measures seem fresh and new. The hard, bare verse attracts. It has a quality of the spare landscapes, the high, clear skies, the chill, pure winds of Fife and the Lothians. There is little pose and pretence here. We get poem after poem which rings absolutely true, which has been fashioned by one who has not allowed his vision of a very queer world to be distorted by sentimentalism or meretricious romance.

Andrew Lang—Stevenson's 'dear Andrew of the brindled hair'—shows a greater mastery of the technique of the craft in his graceful, neatly rounded verse. For all its lightness and grace it is the verse of a scholar, full of echoes from Homer, Ronsard and his brethren of the Pleiade, and the French Romantics, suffused with the scholar's melancholy. It is a melancholy learned more from books than from experience, and only Lang's humour and fastidious taste keep it from degenerating into sentimentalism.

The verse of James Thomson the Second stands away from the main stream of Scottish tradition, equally untouched by the pawkiness and by the sentimentalism of the nineteenth-century minor poet. New sentimentalism is but old Calvinism writ small. The Scot turns affrighted from 'the horror of the shade' to take refuge in imitation emotions and passions. Shaw has explained how Barrie, 'too tender-hearted to break our spirits with the realities of a bitter experience, coaxed a wistful pathos and a dainty fun out of the fairy cloud land that lay between him and the empty heavens'. Thomson refuses to evade reality, and his spirit is broken. But though his sombre and terrible verses owe little to previous Scottish writers, his debt to De Quincey and Swinburne is evident.

Of the later nineteenth-century poets John Davidson is the only one who makes a clean break with tradition. His technique is uncertain, and his range narrow, but what he gives us is his own. Like the older Scottish poets, he sings of escape into the sunlit woods. It is an escape, however, not from the prison-house of winter, but from the prison-house of London and the labyrinth of his own tormenting thoughts. He seems to have escaped too, from the prison-house of Calvinism. He glories in the discovery that the heavens are empty, that there is nothing higher than Man in the universe. Then a new terror replaces the old: the individual can enjoy fullness of life only at the cost of his fellow mortals; human greatness must always rest on a basis of cruelty and injustice. The fetter that the poet loosed from his right foot is now fixed firmly on his left: the great man in all his vileness is God, and cruelty and injustice are once more enthroned in the heavens.

From this brief survey some disconcerting conclusions emerge. Of the poems assembled here— the salvage of six centuries—none is conceived on a grand scale. The Scot does not write odes and epics: he writes songs and ballads; he can achieve perfection only when he works within narrow limits. Even this perfection seems usually to be the result not of conscious art, but of some happy accident; Allan Ramsay is not the only Scottish poet of repute who scores one hit to half a hundred misses. This *naïveté* extends to the substance of the verse; the Scottish poet is seldom subtle or profound; he lives a life of sensations, not of thoughts. Thus in spite of the supposed pre-occupation of the Scot with philosophy and religion, Scotland has not produced any great religious poetry, though in George MacDonald's diffuse, pietistic verse we are occasionally arrested by a fragment which, with its mingled sincerity and fantasy, recalls the work of the seventeenth-century English mystical poets. Similarly, when he writes of love the Scottish poet does not, like Donne, attempt to sound all the depths and shoals of passion: his love poems are the simple expression of desire, or frustration, or disillusionment.

This is not said to deter the reader. He would court only disappointment if he looked for Alpine splendours in the 'honest gray hills' to which Scott gave his heart. But if he can forget the 'mountains, ice, and eyries of the Stars', if he can be content with Stevenson's poet

> 'To gang thinking whaur ye gang linking,
> Hermiston burn, in the howe,'

to ride over the brown moorlands with the 'Auld, auld Elliotts, clay-cauld Elliotts, dour, bauld Elliotts of auld', he will find much to delight him in the pages that follow.

ACKNOWLEDGEMENTS for permission to use copyright poems are due to Mrs. John Davidson and Mr. Grant Richards for 'Vivian's Speech' (from *Holiday and other poems*), 'I haunt the hills' (from *The Testament of a Man Forbid*), 'Like savage wood-nymphs' (from *The Testament of a Prime Minister*), and 'The Last Journey' (from *The Testament of John Davidson*), by John Davidson; to Mr. Lloyd Osbourne, the Authors' Society, and Charles Scribner's Sons, for 'Blows the wind to-day', 'It is the season now to go', 'The House Beautiful', and 'In the Highlands', by R. L. Stevenson; to Messrs. John Lane and Messrs. Dodd, Mead & Co. for 'From a Ballad of the Making of a Poet', 'London', 'In Romney Marsh' (from *Ballads and Poems*), and 'Good Friday' (from *Fleet Street Eclogues*), by John Davidson; to Messrs. Longmans, Green & Co. and the Andrew Lang Trustees, for nine poems by Andrew Lang; to Dr. Greville MacDonald, Messrs. A. P. Watt, and Messrs. Chatto & Windus, for the ten poems from *Poems by George MacDonald*; to Mrs. Harold Monro for 'Midnight Lamentation', by Harold Monro; to the Logie Robertson trustees for 'Hughie's Advice to Dauvit', and 'Hughie seeks to console a Brother Shepherd', by J. Logie Robertson; to the author's executors for 'The River', by Sir Ronald Ross; to Messrs. W. C. Henderson & Son for 'Moonlight North and South' and 'For Scotland', by R. F. Murray; and to the Scottish Text Society for permission to use their texts as a basis for the modernized versions of medieval poems.

CONTENTS

WILLIAM DRUMMOND OF HAWTHORNDEN, 1585–1649

SIR ROBERT AYTON, 1570–1638

JAMES GRAHAM, MARQUIS OF MONTROSE, 1612–50

CONTENTS

ANON.

Cantus

QWHEN Alexander our kynge was dede,
   That Scotland lede in lauche and le,[1]
Away was sons[2] of alle and brede,
   Off wyne and wax, of gamyn and gle.
Our golde was changit into lede.
   Crist, borne into virgynyte,
Succoure Scotlande and ramede,
   That is stade[3] in perplexite.

> (The earliest extant piece of Scottish verse.
> Quoted in *The Original Chronicle* of Andrew
> of Wyntoun, completed about 1420.)

JOHN BARBOUR
1320?–1395

Freedom

AH! Freedom is a noble thing!
Freedom makes man to have liking;
Freedom all solace to man gives;
He lives at ease that freely lives!
A noble heart may have nane ease,
Na elles nocht[4] that may him please,
Gif[5] freedom fail; for free liking
Is yharnit[6] owre all other thing.
Na[7] he that aye has livyt free,
May nocht knaw weill the property,

---

[1] law and peace.   [2] abundance.   [3] beset.   [4] nor
anything else.   [5] if.   [6] yearned for.   [7] nor.

The anger, na the wretched doom
That is couplit to foul thraldom.
But gif he had assayit it,
Than all perquer[1] he suld it wit,
And suld think freedom mair to prize
Than all the gold in world that is.

(*The Bruce*, Book I, ll. 225-40.)

The Battle of Bannockburn

THERE was the battle stricken weill;
So great dinning[2] there was of dyntis
As wapnys[3] upon armour stintis,[4]
And of spearis so great bristing,[5]
With sic thrawing[6] and sic thristing,[7]
Sic girning,[8] granyng,[9] and so great
A noise, as they can other beat,
And cryit ensenyeis[10] on everilk side,
Gifand[11] and takand woundis wide,
That it was hideous for till[12] hear
All four the battles,[13] wicht[14] that were,
Fechtand in-till ae front wholly.[15]

Almichty God! Full douchtely[16]
Sir Edward the Bruce and his men
Amang their fais contenyt them[17] then,
Fechtand into sa good covyne[18]
So hardy, worthy, and so fine,

---

[1] then all by heart.   [2] striking.   [3] weapons.   [4] stop.
[5] breaking.   [6] throwing.   [7] thrusting.   [8] grimacing.
[9] groaning.   [10] battle-cries.   [11] giving.   [12] to.
[13] companies.   [14] strong.   [15] Fighting together on one front.
[16] valiantly.   [17] demeaned themselves.   [18] to such good
purpose.

That their avaward[1] rushit was
And, maugre theiris,[2] left the place,
And to their great rout[3] to warrand[4]
They went, that then had upon hand
So great not,[5] that they were effrayit,[6]
For Scottis men them hard assayit,[7]
That then war in ane schiltrom[8] all.
Wha happnit in that ficht to fall,
I trow again he suld not rise.
There men micht see on mony wise
Hardiment eschevit[9] douchtely,
And mony that wicht were and hardy
Doun under feet lyand all dede,
Whar all the field of blood was red.
Armouris and quyntis[10] that they bare
With blood was swa[11] defoulit there,
That they micht nocht discrivit[12] be.

Ah! Michty God! wha than micht see
The Steward Walter and his rout[13]
And the good Douglas that was stout
Fechtand into the stalwart stour[14]
He suld say that till all honour
They war worthy, that in that ficht
Sa fast pressit their fais micht[15]
That they them rushit whar they yeid[16]
There micht men see full many a steed
Fleand on stray,[17] that lord had nane.
Ah! lord! qha than good tent had tane[18]

---

[1] vanguard.   [2] in spite of them.   [3] main army.
[4] for safety.   [5] employment.   [6] afraid.   [7] attacked.
[8] one serried mass.   [9] valiant deeds achieved.
[10] armorial devices.   [11] so.   [12] described.   [13] company.
[14] conflict.   [15] the might of their foes.   [16] went.   [17] flee-
ing astray.   [18] who then had taken good heed.

To the good Earl of Murreff,[1]
And his, that swa great routis[2] gaf,
And faucht so fast in that battale,
Tholand[3] sic pain and sic travail,
That they and theiris made sic debate,
That where they come, they made them gait![4]
Then men micht hear ensenyeis cry,
And Scottis men cry hardely,
'On them! On them! On them! they fail!'
With that so hard they can assail,
And slew all that they micht owre-ta,[5]
And the Scottis archers alsua[6]
Shot amang them so sturdely,
Ingrevand them so gretumly,[7]
That what for them that with them faucht,
And swa great routis to them raught,[8]
And pressit them full eagerly,
And what for arrows that felly[9]
Mony great woundis can them ma,[10]
And slew fast of their horse alsua,
That they vandist[11] a little way;
They dread so greatly then till dee,[12]
That their covyne was war than ere
For they that with them fechtand were
Set hardyment, and strength, and will,
With heart and courage als there-till,[13]
And all their main and all their micht,
To put them foully to the flicht.

(*The Bruce*, Book XIII, ll. 152–224.)

---

[1] Moray.   [2] blows.   [3] enduring.   [4] made a passage for
themselves.   [5] overtake.   [6] also.   [7] annoying them so
greatly.   [8] dealt.   [9] cruelly.   [10] make.   [11] retreated.
[12] die.   [13] also thereto.

KING JAMES THE FIRST OF SCOTLAND
1394–1437
From *The Kingis Quair*

(i)

BEWAILING in my chamber thus alone,
   Despaired of all joy and remedye,
For-tirit[1] of my thought, and woebegone,
   Unto the window gan I walk in hye,[2]
   To see the warld and folk that went forby;
As for the time, though I of mirthis food
Might have no more, to look it did me good.

Now was there made fast by the touris wall
   A garden fair, and in the corners set
Ane herbere[3] green, with wandis long and small
   Railit about, and with treis set
   Was all the place, and hawthorn hedgis knet[4]
That life was nonë walking there forby
That might within scarce ony wight aspy.

So thick the bewis[5] and the leavis green
   Beshadit all the alleyes that there were.
And middis every herbere might be seen
   The sharpë, greenë, sweetë Junipere
   Growing so fair with branchis here and there,
That, as it seemit to a life[6] without,
The bewis spread the herbere all about;

And on the smallë greenë twistis[7] sat
   The little sweetë nightingale, and song
So loud and clear, the hymnis consecrat

---

[1] wearied.   [2] haste.   [3] garden plot.   [4] twined.
[5] boughs.   [6] creature.   [7] twigs.

Of loves use, now soft, now loud among,
   That all the garden and the wallis rong[1]
Right of[2] their song, and of the copill[3] next
Of their sweete harmony, and lo the text:

Cantus

'Worshippë, ye that loveris been, this May,
   For of your blisse the Kalendis are begun,
And sing with us, away, Winter, away!
    Come, Summer, come, the sweet seasoun and
      sun!
    Awake for shame! that have your heavenis
      won,
And amorously lift up your headis all;
Thank Love that list you to his mercy call.'

When they this song had song a little thraw,[4]
   They stent[5] a while, and therewith unafraid,
As I beheld and cast mine eyne a-law,[6]
    From bough to bough they hippit[7] and they
      played,
    And freshly in their birdis kind arrayed
Their featheris new, and fret them[8] in the sun,
And thankit love, that had their makis[9] won.

This was the plainë ditee of their note,
   And therewithal unto myself I thought,
'What life is this, that makis birdis dote?
    What may this be, how cometh it of ought?[10]
    What needeth it to be so dear ybought?
It is nothing, trow I, but feignit cheer,
And that men list to counterfeiten cheer.'

---

[1] rung.	[2] with.	[3] verse, stanza.	[4] time.
[5] stopped.	[6] down.	[7] hopped.	[8] adorned
themselves.	[9] mates.	[10] aught.	

Eft[1] wald I think: 'O Lord, what may this be,
  That Love is of so noble might and kind,
Loving his folk: and such prosperitee,
  Is it of him, as we in bookis find?
  May he our hertes setten and unbind?
Hath he upon our hertes such maistrye?
Or all this is but feignit fantasye?

For gif he be of so great excellence,
  That he of every wight has cure and charge,
What have I guilt to him[2] or done offence?
  That I am thrall, and birdis gone[3] at large,
  Sen him to serve he might set my corage?[4]
And gif he be noght so, than may I seyne,[5]
What makis folk to jangle of him in vain?

Can I nought elles find, but gif that he
  Be lord, and as a lord may live and reign,
To bind and loose, and maken thrallis free,
  Than wold I pray his blissful grace divine
  To hable me unto[6] his service digne;
And evermore to be one of tho[7]
Him truly for to serve in weal and woe.

And therewith cast I doun mine eye again,
  Where as I saw, walking under the tour,
Full secretly new cummyn her to pleyne,[8]
  The fairest or the freshest younge flour
  That ever I saw, methought, before that hour,
For which sudden abate,[9] anon astert[10]
The blood of all my body to my hert.

---

[1] again.   [2] How have I sinned against him.   [3] go.
[4] heart.   [5] say.   [6] qualify me for.   [7] those.
[8] play.   [9] surprise.   [10] started.

And though I stood abased tho a lyte,
  No wonder was; for-why[1] my wittis all
Were so owre-come with pleasance and delight,
  Only through latting of mine eyen fall,
  That suddenly my heart became her thrall,
For ever, of free will; for of manace,
There was no token in her sweetë face.

And in my head I drew right hastily,
  And eft-soonës I leant it forth again,
And saw her walk, that very womanly,
  With no wight mo, but only women twain.
  Than gan I study in myself and seyne,
'Ah sweet! are ye a warldly creature,
Or heavenly thing in likeness of nature?

Or are ye God Cupidis owin princess,
  And cummyn are to loose me out of band?
Or are ye very Nature the goddess,
  That have depainted with your heavenly hand
  This garden full of flouris, as they stand?
What sall I think, alas! what reverence
Sall I minister to your excellence?

Gif ye a goddess be, and that ye like
  To do me pain, I may it naught astert[2];
Gif ye be warldly wight that doth me sike,[3]
  Why lest[4] God mak you so, my dearest hert,
  To do a silly prisoner thus smert
That loves you all,[5] and wot of naught but woe?
And therefore mercy, sweet, sen it is so!'

When I a little thraw had made my moan,
  Bewailing mine infortune and my chance,
Unknowing how or what was best to done,
  So far I fallen was in loves dance,

  [1] because.   [2] escape.   [3] causes me to sigh.   [4] pleased.
  [5] wholly.

That suddenly my wit, my countenance,
My heart, my will, my nature, and my mind,
Was changit right clean in another kind. . . .

(stanzas 30–45.)

(ii)

To reckon of every thing the circumstance,
  As happnit me when lessen gan my sore
Of my rancour and all my woeful chance,
  It war too long; I lat it be therefore.
  And thus this Flour, I can say you no more,
So heartly has unto my help attendit,
That from the death her man she has defendit.

And eke[1] the goddis merciful wirking,
  For my long pain and true service in love,
That has me given halely[2] mine asking,
  Which has my heart for ever set above
  In perfect Joy, that never may remove,
But only death: of whom, in laud and prise[3]
With thankful heart I say richt in this wise:—

'Blissit mot[4] be the heye goddis all,
  So fair that glittern in the firmament!
And blissit be their might celestial,
  That have convoyit hale, with one assent,
  My love, and to so glad a consequent!
And thankit be Fortunys axletree
And wheel, that thus so weel has whirlit me.

'Thankit mot be, and fair and love befall
  The nichtingale, that with so good intent,
Sang there of love the notes sweet and small
  Where my fair hertis lady was present,
  Her with to glad, or that she further went!

[1] also. [2] wholly. [3] praise. [4] may.

And thou, geraflour!¹ mot y-thankit be
All other flouris for the love of thee.

'And thankit be the fairë castle wall,
  Where as I whilom lookit further and lent!
Thankit mot be the sanctis Marciall,²
  That me first causit hath this accident!
  Thankit mot be the greenë bewis bent,
Through whom, and under, first fortunit me
My heartis heal,³ and my confort to be!'

For to the presence sweet and delitable,
  Richt of this flour that full is of pleasance,
By process and by meanis favourable,
  First of the blissful goddis purveyance,
  And syne through long and true continuance
Of very faith in love and true service,
I come am, and yet further in this wise.

Unworthy, lo, but only of her grace,
  In Loves yoke, that easy is and sure,
In guerdon eke of all my loves space,
  She hath me tak, her humble creature.
  And thus befell my blissful aventure,
In youth of love, that now, from day to day,
Flourith aye new; and yet further, I say

Go, little treatise, naked of eloquence,
  Causing simplese and poverty to wit;⁴
And pray the reader to have patience
  Of thy default, and to supporten it,
  Of his goodness thy brukleness⁵ to knit,
And his tongue for to rulen and to steer,
That thy defaultis healit may been here.

---

¹ gilly flower.   ² of the month of March (the month
in which he was captured).   ³ healing.   ⁴ making
known your simplicity and poverty.   ⁵ feebleness.

Alas! and gif thou comest in presence,
 Whereas of blame fainest thou wald be quit,
To hear thy rude and crooked eloquence,
 Who sall be there to pray for thy remit?[1]
 No wicht, but gif her mercy will admit
Thee for good will, that is thy guide and steer,[2]
To wham for me thou pitously requere.

And thus endeth the fatal influence,
 Causit from Heaven, where power is commit
Of governance, by the magnificence
 Of him that hiest is in the Heaven sitt;
 To Whom we thank that all our life hath writ,
Who couth it read, agone syne mony a year,
'Hich in the heavens' figure circulere.'[3]

Unto the impnis[4] of my maisteris dear,
 Gower and Chaucer, that on the steppis sat
Of rhetoric, while they were livand here,
 Superlative as poets laureate
 In moralitee and eloquence ornate,
I recommend my book in linis seven,
And eke their saulis unto the bliss of Heaven.

(*The Kingis Quair*, stanzas 187–97.)

ROBERT HENRYSON
1425?–1506?

Robene and Makyne

ROBIN sat on gude green hill,
 Keepand a flock of fe[5]:
Merry Makyne said him till
 'Robin, thou rue[6] on me;

---

[1] remission. [2] control. [3] a repetition of the opening
line of the poem. [4] hymns, poems. [5] sheep. [6] have pity.

I have thee lovit loud and still[1]
Thir yearis two or three;
My dule in dern but gif thou dill,[2]
Doubtless but dreid[3] I dee.'

Robin answerit, 'By the Rood,
Nathing of love I knaw,
But keepis my sheep under yon wid,[4]
Lo where they rake on raw![5]
What has marrit[6] thee in thy mood[7]
Makyne, to me thou shaw.
Or what is love, or to be lo'ed?
Fain wald I lear that law.'

'At lovis law gif thou wilt lear
Tak there ane A B C :
Be heynd,[8] courtass, and fair of feir,[9]
Wise, hardy, and free;
So that no danger do thee dear,[10]
What dule in dern thou dree;[11]
Press thou with pain at all poweir,[12]
Be patient and previe.'[13]

Robin answerit her again,
'I wat nocht what is love;
But I have marvel in certain
What makis thee thus wanrufe[14]:
The weddir is fair and I am fain,
My sheep gois haill above;
And[15] we wald play us in this plain
They wald us baith reprove.'

---

[1] openly and secretly.   [2] unless thou assuagest my
secret sorrow.   [3] without doubt.   [4] wood.   [5] wander
in a row.   [6] marred.   [7] mind.   [8] gentle.
[9] demeanour.   [10] disdain harm thee.   [11] whatever sorrow
thou sufferest in secret.   [12] strive earnestly to the best of
your ability.   [13] discreet.   [14] unhappy.   [15] if.

'Robin, tak tent unto my tale,
And wirk all as I rede,[1]
And thou sall have my hairt all haill,
Eke and my maidenheid.
Sen God sendis boot for bale,[2]
And for mourning remeid,
In dern with thee but gif I daill,[3]
Doubtless I am but deid.'

'Makene, to-morn this ilk a tide,[4]
An[5] ye will meet me here,
Peraventure my sheep may gang beside,[6]
Till we have liggit[7] full near;
But maugre have I and I bide,
Fra they being to steer;[8]
What lyis on hairt I will nocht hide;
Makyne, than mak gude cheer.'

'Robin, thou reivis me rufe[9] and rest;
I love but thee alone.'
'Makyne, adieu, the sun gois west,
The day is near hand gone.'
'Robin, in dule I am so drest,
That love will be my bone.'[10]
'Ga love, Makyne, wherever thou list,
For leman[11] I love none.'

'Robin, I stand in sic a styll[12];
I sich,[13] and that full sair.'
'Makyne, I have been here this while;
At hame God give I were!'

---

[1] counsel.   [2] comfort for sorrow.   [3] unless I deal
with thee in secret.   [4] at this same time.   [5] if.
[6] stay near.   [7] lain.   [8] But I shall be ill at ease if I
stay after they begin to move.   [9] deprivest me of ease.
[10] bane.   [11] mistress.   [12] plight.   [13] sigh.

'My honey, Robin, talk ane while,
Gif thou will do na mair.'
'Makyne, some other man beguile,
For hameward I will fare.'

Robin on his wayis went,
As licht as leaf on tree;
Makyne mournit in her intent,[1]
And trowit him never to see.
Robin braid attour the bent;[2]
Than Makyne cryit on hie,
'Now may thou sing, for I am shent![3]
What ailis love at me?'

Makyne went hame withoutin fail,
Full weary efter couth[4] weep:
Than Robin in a full fair dale
Assemblit all his sheep.
By that some pairt of Makynis ail
Out through his hairt could creep;
He fallowit her fast her till assail,
And till her took gude keep.[5]

'Abide, abide, thou fair Makyne,
A word for ony thing!
For all my love it sall be thine,
Withoutin depairting.[6]
All haill thy hairt for till have mine[7]
Is all my coveting;
My sheep to-morn till houris nine
Will need of no keeping.'

'Robin, thou has heard sung and say,
In gestis[8] and storeis auld,
The man that will nocht when he may
Sall have nocht when he wald.

---

[1] thought.   [2] hurried over the grass.   [3] undone.
[4] she did.   [5] heed.   [6] division.   [7] to have thy heart
wholly mine.   [8] tales.

I pray to Jesu every day
Mot eke[1] their cairis cauld,
That first pressis with thee to play,
Be firth,[2] forest, or fauld.'[3]

'Makyne, the nicht is soft and dry,
The wedder is warm and fair,
And the green wood richt near us by
To walk attour all where;
There may na janglour[4] us espy.
That is to love contrair;
Therein, Makyne, baith ye and I
Unseen we may repair.'

'Robin, that warld is all away
And quite brocht till ane end,
And never again thereto perfay
Sall it be as thou wend[5];
For of my pain thou made it play,[6]
And all in vain I spend[7];
As thou has done, sa sall I say,
Mourn on, I think to mend.'

'Makyne, the hope of all my heal,
My hairt on thee is set,
And evermair to thee be leal,
While I may live but let[8];
Never to fail, as otheris fail,
What grace that ever I get.'
'Robin, with thee I will nocht deal;
Adieu, for thus we met.'

---

[1] may increase.   [2] coppice.   [3] enclosed field, en-
closure.   [4] tell-tale.   [5] thoughtest.   [6] made game.
[7] spent.   [8] without hindrance.

Makyne went hame blithe aneuch,
Attour the holtis hair[1];
Robin mournit, and Makyne leuch[2];
She sang, he sichit sair;
And so left him, baith woe and wretch,[3]
In dolour and in care,
Keepand his herd under a heuch,[4]
Amangis the holtis hair.

The Abbey Walk

ALONE as I went up and doun,
In ane abbey was fair to see,
Thinkand what consolatioun
Was best into adversitie,
On case[5] I kest on side mine ee,
And saw this written upon a wall:
'Of what estate, man, that thou be,
Obey, and thank thy God of[6] all

'Thy kingdom and thy great empire,
Thy royalty, nor rich array,
Sall nocht endure at thy desire,
But as the wind will wend away;
Thy gold and all thy gudis gay,
When fortune list will fra thee fall;
Sen[7] thou sic[8] samples sees ilk[9] day,
Obey, and thank thy God of all.

'Job was maist rich in Writ we find,
Tobie[10] maist full of cheritie:
Job wox puir, and Tobie blind,
Baith temptit with adversitie.

---

[1] gray thickets.   [2] laughed.   [3] woeful and wretched.
[4] cliff.   [5] by chance.   [6] for.   [7] since.   [8] such.
[9] every.   [10] Tobit.

Sen blindness was infirmitie,
And poverty was natural,
Therefore richt patiently baith he and he[1]
Obeyit and thankit God of all.

'Though thou be blind, or have ane halt,
Or in thy face deformit ill,
Sa it come nocht through thy default,
Na man suld thee repreif by skill[2]
Blame nocht thy Lord, sa is his will;
Spurn nocht thy foot aganis the wall;
But with meek heart and prayer still
Obey, and thank thy God of all.

'God of his justice mon correct,
And of his mercy pity have;
He is ane Judge to nane suspect.
To punish sinful man and save.
Though thou be lord attour the lave[3]
And efterward made bound and thrall,
Ane puir beggar, with scrip and staff,
Obey, and thank thy God of all.

'This changing and great variance
Of erdly[4] statis up and doun
Is nocht but casualty and chance,
As some men sayis, without reasoun,[5]
But by the great provisioun
Of God above that rule thee sall;
Therefore ever thou mak thee boun[6]
To obey, and thank thy God for all.

---

[1] the one and the other. [2] with reason. [3] above the rest. [4] earthly. [5] i.e. is not, as some men say without reason, merely casualty and chance. [6] ready.

'In wealth be meek, heich[1] not thyself;
Be glad in woeful povertie;
Thy power and thy warldis pelf
Is nocht but very vanitie.
Remember Him that deit on tree,
For thy sake tastit the bitter gall;
Wha heis law and lawis hie;[2]
Obey and thank thy God of all.'

The Taill of the Uponlandis Mous and the Burges Mous

AESOP, mine Author, makis mentioun
Of twa myis, and they were sisteris dear,
Of wham the eldest dwelt in ane borrous toun,[3]
The other wynnit uponland,[4] weill near,
Solitar, while under busk,[5] while under breir,
Whilis in the corn, in other mennis skaith,[6]
As outlawis does and livis on their waith.[7]

This rural mous into the winter tide
Had hunger, cauld, and tholit[8] great distress,
The other mous that in the burgh can bide
Was gild brother and made ane free burgess;
Toll free als,[9] but custom mair or less,[10]
And freedom had to ga wherever sho list,
Among the cheese in ark,[11] and meal in kist.[12]

Ane time when sho was full and unfootsair,
Sho took in mind her sister uponland,
And langit for to hear of her weelfare,
To see what life sho had under the wand[13]:

[1] exalt.   [2] who raises the low and humbles the high.
[3] burgh.   [4] landward.   [5] bush.   [6] to other men's
hurt.   [7] hunting.   [8] suffered.   [9] also.   [10] exempt
from both the Great and the Petty Customs.   [11] box.
[12] chest.   [13] in the open.

Barefoot, alone, with pikestaff in her hand,
As puir pilgrim sho passit out of toun,
To seek her sister baith owre dale and doun.

Furth mony wilsome[1] wayis can sho walk,
Through moss and muir, through bankis, busk,
   and breir
Sho ran cryand till sho come to ane balk[2]:
'Come furth to me, my awin sister dear;
Cry peep anis!' With that the mous cryit 'Here!'
And knew her voice, as kennisman will do,
Be very kind;[3] and furth sho come her to.

The heartly cheer, Lord God, gif ye had seen,
Beis kith[4] when that thir sisteris met;
And great kindness was shawin them between,
For whiles they leuch,[5] and whiles for joy they gret,[6]
While kissit sweet, whilis in armis plet,[7]
And thus they fure,[8] till soberit was their mind.
Syne foot for foot into the chalmer wend.

As I heard say, it was ane sober wane,[9]
Of fog[10] and fern full febillie was made,
Ane silly shiel[11] under ane steadfast stane,
Of whilk the entres was not hie nor braid;
And in the samin they went but mair abade,[12]
Without fire or candle birnand bricht,
For commonly sic pickers loves not licht.

When they were lodgit thus, thir[13] silly mice,
The youngest sister in her buttery glide,
And brocht furth nuttis and candle instead of
   spice;
Gif this was gude fare, I do it on them beside.[14]

---

[1] wild.   [2] bank.   [3] nature, instinct.   [4] is shown.
[5] laughed. [6] cried. [7] folded. [8] fared. [9] dwelling. [10] moss.
[11] poor hut. [12] without more delay. [13] these. [14] I leave
it to them.

The burgess mous prompit[1] furth in pride,
And said, 'Sister, is this your daily food?'
'Why not,' said she, 'is not this meat richt gude?'

'Na, be my saull, I think it but ane scorn.'
'Madam,' quod sho, 'ye bee the more to blame;
My mother said, sister, when we were born,
That I and ye lay baith within ane wame[2]:
I keep the rate and custom of my dame,
And of my living into poverty,
For landis have we nane in property.'

'My fair sister,' quod sho, 'have me excusit,
This rude diet and I can not accord;
To tender meat my stomach is aye usit,
For whiles I fare as weel as ony lord;
Thir widderit peas and nuttis, or they be bored,
Will brek my teeth and mak my wame[3] full
    slender,
Whilk was before usit to meatis tender.'

'Weel, weel, sister,' quod the rural mous,
'Gif it please you, sic thingis as ye see here,
Baith meat and drink, harberie[4] and house,
Sall be your awin, will ye remain all year;
Ye sall it have with blithe and merry cheer,
And that suld mak the messes that are rude,
Amang freindis, richt tender and wonder gude

'What pleasure is in the feastis delicate,
The whilkis are gevin with ane glowmand[5]
    brow?
Ane gentle heart is better recreate
With blithe courage, than seethe to him ane
    cow:

---

[1] moved.   [2] womb.   [3] stomach.   [4] lodging.
[5] frowning.

Ane modicum is mair for till allow,
Swa that gude will be carver at the dais,
Than thrawit[1] will and mony spicit mess.'

For all her merry exhortatioun,
This burgess mous had little will to sing,
But heavily sho cast her browis doun,
For all the dainties that sho could her bring.
Yet at the last sho said, half in hething,[2]
'Sister, this victual and your royal feast
May weel suffice unto ane rural beast.

'Lat be this hole, and come unto my place;
I sall to you shaw be experience
My Gude Friday is better nor your Pace[3];
My dish weshingis is worth your hail expence;
I have houses enow of great defence;
Of cat nor fall-trap I have na dreid.'
'I grant,' quod sho, and on togidder they yeid.

In skugry aye,[4] through rankest girss and corn,
And wonder sly, full privily couth[5] they creep,
The eldest was the guide and went beforn,
The younger to her wayis took gude keep.
On nicht they ran, and on the day can sleep;
Till in the morning, or[6] the laverock sang,
They fand the toun, and in blithly could gang.

Not far fra thine[7] unto ane worthy wane
This burgess brocht them soon where they suld
    be;
Without 'God speed' their herberie was tane,
Into ane spence[8] with victual great plentie;

---

[1] distorted.   [2] derision.   [3] Easter.   [4] by secret
ways ever.   [5] did.   [6] before.   [7] thence.   [8] larder.

Baith cheese and butter upon their skelfis[1] hie,
And flesh and fish aneuch, of fresh and salt,
And seckis full of meal and eek of malt.

Efter when they were disposit for to dine,
Withouten grace they wesh and went to meat,
With all coursis that cookis could divine,
Mutton and beef stricken in tailyeis[2] great;
Ane lordis fare thus couth they counterfeit,
Except ane thing, they drank the water clear
Instead of wine, but yet they made gude cheer.

With blithe upcast and merry countenance,
The eldest sister sperit at[3] her guest,
Gif that sho be reason[4] fand difference
Betwix that chalmers[5] and her sarie[6] nest.
'Yea, dame,' quod sho, 'how lang will this lest[7]?'
'For evermair, I wait, and langer too.'
'Gif it be swa,[8] ye are at ease,' quod sho.

Till eke their cheer ane subcharge[9] furth sho
    brocht,
Ane plate of groatis,[10] and ane dish full of meal;
Thraf[11] cakis als I trow sho sparit nocht,
Abundantly about her for to deal;
And mane[12] full fine sho brocht instead of geill,[13]
And ane white candle out of ane coffer stall,[14]
Instead of spice to gust[15] their mouth withal.

Thus made they merry till they micht na mair,
And 'Hail, Yule, hail!' cryit upon hie.
Yet after joy ofttimes comes care,
And trouble after great prosperitie.

---

[1] shelves.   [2] cuts, portions.   [3] asked.   [4] for
good reason.   [5] chamber.   [6] sorry.   [7] last.   [8] so.
[9] additional cause.   [10] grain.   [11] unleavened.   [12] fine
bread.   [13] jelly.   [14] stole.   [15] give relish to.

Thus as they sat in all their jollitie,
The spenser[1] come with keyis in his hand,
Openit the door, and them at denner fand.

They tarryit not to wesh, as I suppose,
But on to ga wha that micht foremost win.
The burgess has ane hole, and in sho goes;
Her sister had na hole to hide her in:
To see that silly mous it was great sin,[2]
So desolate and will of ane gude reid;[3]
For very dreid sho fell in swoon near deid.

But, as God wald, it fell ane happy case;
The spenser had na leisure for to bide,
Neither to seek nor search, nor scare nor chase,
But in he went, and left the door up wide.
The bauld burgess his passing weel has spied;
Out of her hole sho come and cryit on hie,
'How fare ye, sister? Cry peep, wherever ye be!'

This rural mous lay flatling on the ground,
And for the death sho was full sair dredand,
For till her heart straik[4] mony woeful stound,
As in ane fever sho trimbillit fute and hand;
And whan her sister in sic ply her fand,
For very pity sho began to greet,
Syne confort her with wordis humble and sweet.

'Why lie ye thus? Rise up, my sister dear,
Come to your meat, this peril is overpast.'
The other answerit her with heavy cheer,
'I may not eat, sa sair I am aghast;
I had lever[5] thir forty dayis fast,
With water kail[6] and to gnaw beanis and peis,
Than all your feast in this dread and disease.'

---

[1] steward.　　　[2] pity.　　　[3] at a loss for what to do.
[4] struck.　　[5] rather.　　[6] broth made without meat.

With fair treaty yet sho gart her[1] uprise,
And to the burde they went and togidder sat,
And scantly had they drunken aince or twice,
When in come Gib Hunter, our jolly cat,
And bade God speed; the burgess up with that,
And till the hole sho went as fire on flint:
Baudrons the other be the back has hint.[2]

Fra foot to foot he kest her to and fra,
Whiles up, whiles doun, as cant[3] as ony kid;
Whiles wald her rin under the stra,
Whiles wald he wink, and play with her buk heid.[4]
Thus to the silly mous great pain he did,
Till at the last, through fortune and gude hap,
Betwix ane burde and the wall sho crap.

And up in haste behind ane parraling[5]
Sho clam so hie, that Gilbert micht not get her,
Syne be the cluke[6] there craftily can hing,
Till he was gane, her cheer was all the better.
Syne doun sho lap when there was nane to let[7]
      her,
And to the burgess mous loud can sho cry:
'Farewell, sister, thy feast here I defy!

'Thy mangerie is mingit[8] all with care,
Thy goose is gude, thy gansell[9] sour as gall;
The subcharge of thy service is but sair,
Sa sal thou find hereefterwart may fall.
I thank yon curtain and yon perpall[10] wall
Of my defence now fra ane cruel beast.
Almichty God, keep me fra sic ane feast.

---

[1] caused her to.   [2] caught.   [3] lively.   [4] hide and seek.
[5] partition.   [6] claw.   [7] prevent.   [8] feast is mingled.
[9] garlic sauce.   [10] partition.

'Were I into the kith[1] that I come fra,
For weal nor woe suld I never come again.'
With that sho took her leave and furth can ga,
Whiles through the corn, and whiles through the
    plain;
When sho was furth and free, sho was full fain,
And merrily markit[2] unto the muir:
I cannot tell how weel therefter sho fure.

But I heard say sho passit to her den,
As warm as wool, suppose it was not great
Full beinly[3] stuffit, baith but and ben,[4]
Of beanis and nuttis, peas, rye, and wheat;
Whenever sho list, sho had aneuch to eat;
In quiet and ease, withouten ony dreid,
But to her sisteris feast na mair sho yeid.

Moralitas

Freindis, ye may find, and[5] ye will tak heed,
Into this fable ane gude moralitie;
As fitchis[6] myngit are with noble seed,
Swa interminglit is adversitie
With eirdlie joy; swa that na estate is free,
Without trouble and some vexatioun:
As namely[7] they whilk clymmis up maist hie,
That are not content with small possessioun.

Blissit be simple life withouten dreid;
Blissit be sober feist in quietie:
Wha has aneuch, of na mair has he need,
Though it be little into quantitie.

---

[1] country.   [2] found her way.   [3] well   [4] both in
the outer and in the inner room.   [5] if.   [6] vetch.
[7] especially.

Great abundance and blind prosperitie
Oftimes makis ane evil conclusioun;
The sweetest life, therefore, in this countrie
Is sickerness,[1] with small possessioun.

O wanton man! That usis for to feed
Thy wame, and makis it ane god to be,
Look to thyself: I warn thee weel, but dreid,
The cat comes, and to the mous has ee:
What vaillis than thy feast and royaltie,
With dreadful heart, and tribulatioun?
Best thing in eird therefore, I say, for me,
Is blitheness in heart, with small possessioun.

Thy awin fire, my freind, sa it be but ane gleid,[2]
It warmis weel, and is worth gold to thee;
And Solomon says, gif that thou will read,
'Under the heaven there can no better be,
Than aye to be blithe and live in honestie.'
Wherefore I may conclude be this reasoun[3]:
Of eirdlie joy it bearis maist degree,
Blitheness in heart, with small possessioun.

The Testament of Cresseid

(i) *Prologue*

ANE doolie[4] season to ane careful dyte[5]
Suld correspond, and be equivalent.
Richt sa it wes when I began to write
This tragedy; the wedder richt fervent,
When Aries, in middis of the Lent,
Showeris of hail can fra the north descend,[6]
That scantly fra the cauld I micht defend.

---

[1] security.   [2] ember.   [3] declaration.   [4] dull.
[5] sorrowful poem.   [6] did bring down from the north.

Yet, nevertheless, within mine oratur[1]
I stood, when Titan had his beamis bricht
Withdrawin doun, and sylit[2] under cure,[3]
And fair Venus, the beauty of the nicht,
Upraise, and set unto the west full richt
Her golden face, in oppositioun
Of God Phoebus, direct descending doun.

Through out the glass her beamis brast[4] sa fair
That I micht see on every side me by.
The northin wind had purifyit the air,
And shed[5] the misty cloudis fra the sky;
The frost freisit, the blastis bitterly
Fra pole Arctic come whistling loud and schill,[6]
And causit me remove aganis my will.

For I traistit that Venus, Lovis Queen,
To whom some time I hecht[7] obedience,
My faded heart of love sho wald mak green;
And thereupon, with humble reverence,
I thocht to pray her high magnificence;
But for great cauld as than I lattit[8] was,
And to my chalmer to the fire can pass.

Thoch love be hait,[9] yet in ane man of age
It kindles nocht sa soon as in youthheid,
Of whom the blude is flowing in ane rage,
And in the auld the corage doif[10] and deid,
Of whilk the fire outward is best remeid;
To help be physic where that nature failit,
I am expert—for baith I have assailit.[11]

---

[1] oratory.　　[2] hidden.　　[3] cover.　　[4] pierced.
[5] swept.　　[6] shrill.　　[7] promised.　　[8] prevented.
[9] hot.　　[10] dull.　　[11] tried.

I mend the fire, and beikit¹ me about,
Than took ane drink my spreitis to comfort,
And armit me weel fra the cauld thereout
To cut the winter nicht, and mak it short,
I took ane quair,² and left all other sport,
Written by worthy Chaucer glorious,
Of fair Cresseid and worthy Troilus. . . .

(ll. 1–42.)

*(The Gods have assembled in Council and pronounced
sentence on Cressida)*

(ii)

This duleful sentence Saturn took on hand,
And passit doun where careful³ Cresseid lay,
And on her heid he laid ane frosty wand;
Than lawfully on this wise can he say:
'Thy great fairness, and all thy beauty gay,
Thy wanton blude, and eek thy golden hair,
Here I exclude fra thee for evermair.

'I change thy mirth into melancholy,
Whilk is the mother of all pensiveness;
Thy moisture and thy heat in cauld and dry;
Thine insolence, thy play and wantonness
To great disease⁴; thy pomp and thy riches
In mortal need; and great penurity
Thou suffer sall, and as ane beggar die.'

O cruel Saturn! fraward⁵ and angry,
Hard is thy doom, and too malicious:
On fair Cresseid why hes thou na mercy,
Whilk was sa sweet, gentle, and amorous?

---

¹ warmed.   ² book.   ³ sorrowful.   ⁴ discomfort.
⁵ froward.

Withdraw thy sentence, and be gracious
As thou was never; so shawis thou thy deed,
Ane wraikful¹ sentence given on fair Cresseid.

Than Cynthia, when Saturn passed away,
Out of her sait² descended down belyve,³
And read ane bill on Cresseid where sho lay,
Containing this sentence definitive:
'Fra heat of body I thee now deprive,
And to thy seikness sall be na recure,⁴
But in dolour thy dayis to endure.

'Thy crystal een minglit with blude I mak;
Thy voice sa clear, unpleasand, hoir and hace⁵;
Thy lusty lyre⁶ owre spread with spottis black,
And lumpis haw⁷ appeirand in thy face;
Where thou cummis, ilk man sall flee the place;
Thus sall thou go begging fra house to house
With cup and clapper like ane lazarous.'⁸

This doolie dream, this ugly vision
Brocht to ane end, Cresseid fra it awoke,
And all that court and convocatioun
Vanished away; than raise sho up and took
Ane poleist glass, and her shadow could look⁹;
And when sho saw her face sa deformait,
Gif sho in heart was wa aneuch, God wait!¹⁰

Weeping full sair, 'Lo, what it is,' quod she,
'With fraward langage for to move and steer
Our crabbit Goddis, and sa is seen on me!
My blaspheming now have I bocht full dear;

¹ vindictive.   ² seat.   ³ straightway.   ⁴ recovery.
⁵ rough and hoarse.   ⁶ complexion.   ⁷ livid.   ⁸ leper.
⁹ did look at.   ¹⁰ God knows if she was sad enough.

All eirdlie[1] joy and mirth I set arear[2]
Alas, this day! alas, this woeful tide!
When I began with my Goddis for to chide.'

Be this was said, ane child come fra the hall,
To warn Cresseid the supper was ready;
First knockit at the door, and syne could[3] call,
'Madam, your father bids you come in hy,
He has marvel sa lang on grouf[4] ye lie,
And says your prayers been too lang some deal,[5]
The Goddis wait[6] all your intent full weel.'

Quod sho, 'Fair child, ga to my father dear
And pray him come to speak to me anon.'
And sa he did, and said, 'Douchter, what cheer?'
'Alas!' quod sho, 'Father, my mirth is gone.'
'How sa?' quod sho, and sho can all expone,[7]
As I have tauld, the vengeance and the wrack,[8]
For her trespass, Cupid on her could tak.

He lookit on her ugly lipper[9] face,
The whilk before was white as lily flower;
Wringand his hands, ofttimes he said, alas,
That he had levit to see that woeful hour;
For he knew weel that there was na succour
To her seikness, and that doublit his pain;
Thus was there care aneuch betwix tham twain.

When they togidder mournit had full lang,
Quod Cressid, 'Father, I wald not be kenned;
Therefore in secret wise ye let me gang
Unto yon hospital at the tounis end;
And thidder some meat for cheritie me send,
To live upon; for all mirth in this eird
Is fra me gane—sic is my wicked weird.[10]

---

[1] earthly.   [2] away.   [3] then did.   [4] grovelling.
[5] are somewhat too long.   [6] know.   [7] explain.
[8] punishment.   [9] leper.   [10] fate.

Then in ane mantle and ane bawer[1] hat,
With cup and clapper, wonder privily
He opnit ane secret yett, and out thereat
Convoyit her, that na man suld espy,
Unto ane village half ane mile thereby;
Deliverit her in at the spittal hous,[2]
And daily sent her part of her almous.[3]

Some knew her weel, and some had na knawledge
Of her, because she was so deformait
With bylis[4] black owrespread is her visage,
And her fair colour faidit and alterait.
Yet they presumit for her hie regrait,[5]
And still murning, sho was of noble kin:
With better will therefore they took her in.

The day passit, and Phoebus went to rest,
The cloudis black owrewhelmit all the sky:
God wait gif Cresseid was ane sorrowful guest,
Seeing that uncouth fare and harbery![6]
But[7] meat or drink sho dressit her to lie
In ane dark corner of the house alone;
And on this wise, weeping, sho made her moan.

The Complaint of Cresseid

'O sop of sorrow, sunken into care!
O catiff Cresseid! for now and evermair
Gane is thy joy, and all thy mirth in eird;
Of all blitheness now art thou blaiknit bare[8];
There is na salve may save thee of thy sair.[9]

---

[1] beaver.　[2] hospital.　[3] alms.　[4] boils.　[5] great
sorrow.　[6] lodging.　[7] without.　[8] blackened without hope.　[9] heal thee of thy disease.

Fell is thy Fortune, wicked is thy weird;
Thy bliss is banished, and thy bale on breird[1];
Under the earth God give I graven were,[2]
Where nane of Greece nor yet of Troy might
heird.[3]

'Where is thy chalmer wantonly beseen,
With burely bed and bankouris browderit bene,[4]
Spicis and wine in thy collatioun,
The cupis all of gold and silver sheen,
The sweet meatis, servit in plaittis clean,
With saipheron[5] sauce of ane gude seasoun,
Thy gay garmentis with mony gudely goun,
Thy pleasand lawn prinnit[6] with golden preen?[7]
All is arear, thy great royal renown.

'Where is thy garden with thir greissis gay,
And fresh flowris, whilk the Queen Floray
Had painted pleasantly in every pane,
Where thou was wont full merrily in May
To walk and take the dew be it was day,
And hear the merle and mavis[8] mony ane,
With ladies fair in carolling to gane,[9]
And see the royal rinkis[10] in their array,
In garmentis gay, garnished on every grain.[11]

'Thy great triumphand fame and hie honour,
Where thou was callit of eirdlie wichtis flour—
All is decayit, thy weird is welterit[12] so,
Thy hie estait is turnit in darkness dour.
This lipper lodge[13] tak for thy burely bour,[14]

---

[1] increasing. [2] were laid in my grave. [3] hear it.
[4] with handsome bed and tapestries embroidered beautifully.
[5] saffron. [6] pinned. [7] pin. [8] blackbird and
thrush. [9] go. [10] folk. [11] in every colour. [12] fortune
is reversed. [13] leper lodging. [14] handsome bower.

And for thy bed tak now ane bunch of stro;
For waillit[1] wine and meatis thou had tho,
Tak mowlit[2] breid, perry, and cider sour;
But cup and clapper, now is all ago.

'My clear voice and courtly carolling,
Where I was wont with ladies for to sing,
Is rawk[3] as rook, full hideous, hoir and hace;
My pleasand port, all otheris precelling[4]—
Of lustiness[5] I was hald[6] maist conding[7]—
Now is deformit the figure of my face—
To look on it na leid[8] now liking hes:
Sowpit in syte,[9] I say with sair siching,[10]
Lodgeit amang the lipper leid, alas!

'O ladies fair of Troy and Greece attend
My misery, whilk nane may comprehend,
My frivoll fortoun, my infelicity,
My greit mischief, whilk na man can amend;
Be war in time, approachis near the end,
And in your mind a mirror mak of me;
As I am now, peradventure that ye,
For all your micht, may come to the same end,
Or ellis war,[11] gif ony war may be.

'Nocht is your fairness but ane fading flower,
Nocht is your famous laud and hie honour
But wind inflat[12] in other mennis earis;
Your roseing[13] red to rotting sall retour.[14]
Exempill mak of me in your memour,
Whilk of sic thingis woeful witness bearis,
All wealth in eird away as wind it weiris[15];
Be war, therefore, approachis near the hour:
Fortune is fickle, when sho beginnis and steiris.'

---

[1] choice. [2] mouldy. [3] raucous. [4] excelling.
[5] amorousness. [6] held. [7] excellent. [8] person.
[9] drenched in sorrow. [10] sighing. [11] worse.
[12] blown. [13] rosy. [14] return. [15] wastes.

Thus chydand with her dreary destiny,
Weeping, sho woke the nicht fra end to end;
But all in vain; her dule, her careful cry,
Micht not remeid, nor yet her mourning mend.
Ane lipper lady raise, and till her wend,
And said, 'Why spurnis thou aganis the wall,
To slay thyself, and mend nathing at all.

'Sen thy weeping doubillis but thy woe,
I counsel thee mak virtue of ane need;
Go leir[1] to clap thy clapper to and fro,
And live efter the law of lipper leid.'
There was na boot, but furth with them she
     yeid,[2]
Fra place to place, till cauld and hunger sair
Compellit her to be ane rank beggar.

That samin time of Troy the garnisoun,
Whilk had to chieftain worthy Troilus,
Through jeopardy of weir[3] had stricken doun
Knichtis of Greece in number marvellous:
With great triumph and laud victorious
Again to Troy richt royally they rade,
The way where Cresseid with the lipper bade.

Seeing that company, they come all with ane
     stevin[4];
They gave ane cry, and shook cuppis gude
     speed;
Said, 'Worthy lords, for Goddis love of heaven,
To us lipper part of your almous deed!'[5]
Than to their cry noble Troilus took heed,
Having pity, near by the place can pass
Where Cresseid sat, not witting what sho was.

     [1] learn.   [2] went.   [3] war.   [4] cry.   [5] give of
your charity.

Than upon him sho cast up baith her een,
And with ane blenk it come into his thocht
That he sometime her face before had seen;
But sho was in sic plye[1] he knew her nocht;
Yet than her look into his mind it brocht
The sweet visage and amorous blenking[2]
Of fair Cresseid, sometime his awin darling.

Ane spark of love than till his heart could spring,
And kendlit all his body in ane fire,
With het fever ane sweit and trimbling
Him took, till he was ready to expire;
To bear his shield his breist began to tire;
Within ane while he changit mony hue,
And, nevertheless, not ane another knew.

For knichtlie pity and memorial
Of fair Cresseid, a girdle can he tak,
Ane purse of gold, and mony gay jowall,
And in the skirt of Cresseid doun can swak[3]:
Than raid away, and not ane word he spak,
Pensive in heart, till he come to the toun,
And for greit care oft syis[4] almaist fell doun.

The lipper folk to Cresseid than can draw,
To see the equal distribution
Of the almous; but when the gold they saw,
Ilk ane to other privily can roun,[5]
And said, 'Yon lord has mair affectioun,
However it be, unto yon lazarous
Than to us all; we knaw by his almous.'

'What lord is yon,' quod sho, 'have ye na feill,[6]
Has done to us so greit humanitie?'
'Yes,' quod a lipper man, 'I knaw him weill;
Sir Troilus it is, gentle and free.'

---

¹ plight.   ² glances.   ³ throw.   ⁴ often.
⁵ whisper.   ⁶ knowledge.

When Cresseid understood that it was he,
Stiffer than steel there stert ane bitter stound
Throughout her heart, and fell doun to **the**
  ground.

When sho, owrecome with sighing sair and **sad**,
With mony careful cry and cauld 'Ochane!
Now is my breist with stormy stoundis stad,[1]
Wrappit in woe, ane wretch full will of wane.'[2]
Than swoonit sho oft or sho could refrain,
And ever in her swooning cryit sho thus:
'O false Cresseid! and true knicht Troilus!

'Thy love, thy lawtie,[3] and thy gentleness,
I countit small in my prosperity,
Sa elevat I was in wantonness,
And clam[4] upon the fickle wheel sa hie;
All faith and love I promissit to thee
Was in the self [5] fickle and frivolous;
O, false Cresseid! and true knicht Troilus!

'For love of me thou kept gude continence,
Honest and chaste in conversatioun,
Of all wemen protector and defence
Thou was, and helpit their opinioun[6]:
My mind in fleshly foul affectioun
Was inclinit to lustis lecherous:
Fie, false Cresseid! O, true knicht Troilus!

'Lovers, beware, and tak gude heed about
Whom that ye love, for whom ye suffer pain;
I lat you wit, there is richt few thereout
Whom ye may trust to have true love again;

---

  [1] beset.   [2] devoid of hope.   [3] loyalty.   [4] climbed.
[5] in itself.   [6] aided their reputation.

Prove when ye will, your labour is in vain;
Therefore, I rede ye tak them as ye find,
For they are sad[1] as widdercock in wind,

'Because I know the great unstableness,
Bruckle[2] as glass, into myself I say,
Trusting in other as great unfaithfulness,
As unconstant, and as untrue of fay[3];
Thoch some be true, I wait richt few are they;
Wha findis truth, lat him his lady ruse[4]:
Nane but myself, as now, I will accuse.'

When this was said, with paper sho sat doun,
And on this manner made her testament:
'Here I beteiche[5] my corpse and carrioun
With wormis and with taidis[6] to be rent;
My cup and clapper, and mine ornament,
And all my gold, the lipper folk sall have,
When I am deid, to bury me in grave.

'This royal ring, set with this ruby reid,
Whilk Troilus in drowrie[7] to me send,
To him again I leave it when I am deid,
To mak my careful deid[8] unto him kend:
Thus I conclude shortly, and mak ane end;
My spreit I leave to Diane, where sho dwells,
To walk with her in waste woodis and wellis.[9]

'O Diomede! Thou has baith brooch and belt,
Whilk Troilus gave me in takning[10]
Of his true love'—and with that word sho swelt[11];
And soon ane lipper man took off the ring,
Syne buryit her withouten tarrying:
To Troilus forthwith the ring he bare,
And of Cresseid the deith he can declare.

---

[1] steadfast. [2] brittle. [3] faith. [4] extol.
[5] deliver. [6] toads. [7] courtship. [8] sorrowful
death. [9] fountains. [10] token. [11] died.

When he had heard her great infirmitie,
Her legacie and lamentatioun,
And how sho endit in sic povertie,
He swelt[1] for woe, and fell doun in ane swoun;
For great sorrow his heart to brist was boun[2]:
Siching full sadly, said, 'I can no more;
Sho was untrue, and woe is me therefore.'

Some said he made ane tomb of marble gray,
And wrait her name and superscriptioun,
And laid it on her grave, where that sho lay,
In golden letteris, containing this reasoun[3]:
'Lo, fair ladies, Cresseid of Troyis toun,
Sometime countit the flower of womanheid,
Under this stane, late lipper, lyis deid.'

(*The Testament of Cresseid*, ll. 309–616.)

The Praise of Age

INTIL ane garth, under ane reid rosere,[4]
Ane auld man and decrepit heard I sing;
Gay was the note, sweet was the voice and clear:
It was great joy to hear of sic ane thing.
And to my doom,[5] he said in his ditting,[6]
'For to be young I wald nocht, for my wis[7]
Of all this warld to mak me lord and king:
The more of age the nearer heavenis bliss.

'False is this warld, and full of variance,
Owreset with syt[8] and other sinnis mo;
Now truth is tint,[9] guile has the governance,
Wrechitness has wrocht all wealthis weal to woe;

---

[1] fainted.   [2] was ready to break.   [3] declaration.
[4] rose-tree.   [5] in my opinion.   [6] singing.   [7] wish.
[8] overwhelmed with sorrow.   [9] lost.

Freedom is flemyt[1] all the lordis fro,
And covetice is all the cause of this;
I am content that youthhead is ago[2]:
The more of age the nearer heavenis bliss.

'The state of youth I repute for na gude,
For in that state great peril do I see;
Can nane gainstand[3] the raging of his blood,
Na yet be stable until he aged be;
Than in the thing that maist rejoicit he
Nathing remains for to be callit his;
For-why[4] it was but very vanitie:
The more of age the nearer heavenis bliss.

'This wrachit warld may na man trow,[5] for why
Of erdly joy aye sorrow is the end;
The state of it can na man certify
The day a king; the morn na thing to spend.
What have we here but grace us to defend?
The whilk God grant us till amend our miss,
That till[6] his joy he may our saulis send:
The more of age the nearer heavenis bliss.'

WILLIAM DUNBAR
1460?–1520?

From *The Tua Mariit Wemen and the Wedo*

(i)

UPON the midsummer even, merriest of nichtis,
I movit furth alane, near as midnicht was past,
Beside ane goodlie green garth, full of gay flouris,
Hedgeit, of ane huge hicht, with hawthorn trees;

---

[1] put to flight.　　[2] gone.　　[3] withstand.　　[4] because.
[5] believe, trust.　　[6] to.

Whereon ane bird, on ane branch, so birst out
    her notis
That never ane blithefuller bird was on the beuch
    heard:
What through the sugarit sound of her sang glaid,
And through the savour sanative[1] of the sweet
    flouris,
I drew in dern[2] to the dyke to dirken efter
    mirthis;[3]
The dew donkit[4] the dale, and dynnit[5] the foulis.
I heard, under ane hollyn[6] heavenly green hewit,
Ane hie speech, at my hand, with hautand[7]
    wordis;
With that in haste to the hedge so hard I
    inthrang[8]
That I was heildit[9] with hawthorn, and with
    heynd[10] leavis:
Through pykis[11] of the plet thorn I presandlie
    luikit,
Gif ony person wald approach within that
    pleasand garden.
I saw three gay ladies sit in ane green arbour,
All graithit[12] into garlandis of fresh gudlie
    flouris;
So glitterit as the gold were their glorious gilt
    tresses,
While all the gressis did gleam of the glaid
    hewis;
Kemmit[13] was their clear hair, and curiously
    shed,[14]

---

[1] health-giving.   [2] secret.   [3] to lie still in search
of amusements.   [4] made dank.   [5] made a din.
[6] holly.   [7] proud.   [8] pressed.   [9] concealed.
[10] sheltering.   [11] prickles.   [12] arrayed.   [13] combed.
[14] parted.

Atour their shulders doun shyre,[1] shining full
    bricht;

With curches,[2] cassin[3] them abune, of kirsp[4] clear
    and thin:

Their mantles green were as the gress that grew
    in May seasoun,

Fetrit[5] with their white fingeris about their fair
    sidis:

Of ferliful[6] fine favour were their faces meek,

All full of flourist fairheid,[7] as flouris in June;

White, seemly, and soft, as the sweet lilies;

New upspread upon spray, as new spynist[8] rose,

Arrayit royally about with many rich wardour,[9]

That Nature, full nobillie, enamelit fine with
    flouris

Of alkin[10] hewis under heaven, that ony heynd[11]
    knew;

Fragrant, all full of fresh odour finest of smell.

Ane marble table coverit was before thai three
    ladies,

With royal cuppis upon rawis full of rich wines:

And of thir fair wlonkes,[12] with twa that weddit
    war with lordis,

Ane was ane widow, I wist, wanton of laitis.[13]

And as they talkit at the table of mony tale
    fund,

They wauchtit at[14] the wicht[15] wine, and waris
    out[16] wordis;

And syne they spak more speedily, and sparit
    no matteris.

                      (ll. 1–40.)

---

  [1] sheer, wholly.   [2] kerchiefs.   [3] cast.   [4] lawn.
[5] fastened.   [6] wonderful.   [7] beauty.   [8] blossoming.   [9] verdure.   [10] every kind of.   [11] person.
[12] beauties.   [13] manners.   [14] quaffed.   [15] strong.
[16] dispense.

(ii)

Thus drave they out that dear night with dances
  full noble,
Till that the day did up daw, and dew donkit the
  flouris;
The morrow mild was and meek, the mavis[1] did
  sing,
And all removit the mist, and the mead smellit;
Silver shouris doun shook, as the sheen crystal,
And birds shouted in shaw,[2] with their schill
  notis;
The golden glitterand gleam so gladit their
  heartis,
They made a glorious glee amang the green
  bewis.
The soft souch[3] of the swyr,[4] and soun of the
  streamis,
The sweet savour of the sward, and singing of
  foulis
Micht confort ony creature of the kin of Adam;
And kindle again his courage though it were
  cauld slocknit.[5]
Than raise thir royal roses, in their rich
  weedis,
And rakit[6] hame to their rest, through the ryce
  bloomis;[7]
And I all privily passes to a pleasand arbour,
And with my pen did report their pastance[8]
  most merry.

(ll. 511–26.)

---

[1] thrush.   [2] grove.   [3] whisper of the wind.
[4] hollow.   [5] cold and extinguished.   [6] went.
[7] blossoms of the thicket.   [8] pastime.

The Golden Targe[1]

RIGHT as the stern of day[2] begouth[3] to shine,
When gone to bed were Vesper and Lucine,[4]
   I raise, and by a rosere[5] did me rest;
Up sprang the golden candle matutine,[6]
With clear depurit beames crystalline,
   Glading the merry foulis in their nest;
   Or[7] Phoebus was in purpur cape revest[8]
Up raise the lark, the heaven's minstrel fine
   In May, in till a morrow mirthfullest.

Full angellike thir birdis sang their houris
Within their curtains green, into their bouris,
   Apparralit white and red, with bloomes sweet;
Enamelit was the field with all colouris,
The pearly droppis shake in silver shouris,
   Till all in balm did branch and leavis fleet[9];
   To part fra Phoebus did Aurora greet,[10]
Her crystal tearis I saw hing on the flouris,
   Whilk he for love all drank up with his heat.

For mirth of May, with skippis and with hoppis,
The birdis sang upon the tender croppis,
   With curious note, as Venus chapel clerkis:
The roses young, new spreading of their knoppis,[11]
War powderit bricht with heavenly berial[12]
     droppis,
   Through bemes red, birnand as ruby sparkis;
   The skyes rang for shouting of the larkis,
The purpur heaven owre skailit in silver sloppis[13]
   Owregilt[14] the treis, branchis leavis and barkis.

---

[1] The golden shield of Reason.   [2] day star (sun).
[3] began.   [4] the morning star and the moon.   [5] rose-tree.
[6] of the morning. [7] before. [8] clad. [9] float. [10] weep.
[11] birds. [12] beryl. [13] the rosy sky covered over with silver
clouds like scales, i.e. the mackerel sky.   [14] gilded over.

Doun through the ryce[1] a river ran with streamis,
So lustily again thai lykand leamis,[2]
　　That all the lake[3] as lamp did leam of licht,
Whilk shadowit all about with twinkling gleamis;
That bewis bathit were in second beamis[4]
　　Through the reflex of Phoebus visage bricht;
　　On every side the hedges raise on hicht,
The bank was green, the brook was full of
　　　　breamis,[5]
　　The stanneris[6] clear as stern in frosty nicht.

The crystal air, the sapphire firmament,
The ruby skyes of the orient,
　　Kest berial beamis on emerant bewis green;
The rosy garth[7] depaint and redolent,
With purpur, azure, gold, and gules gent
　　Arrayed was, by dame Flora the queen;
　　So nobily, that joy was for to seen;
The roch[8] again the river resplendent
　　As lowe[9] enlumynit all the leaves sheen.

What through the merry foulis harmony,
And through the riveris soun richt ran me by,[10]
　　On Flora's mantle I sleepit as I lay,
Where soon in to my dreames fantasy
I saw approach again the orient sky,
　　A sail, as white as blossom upon spray,
　　With merse[11] of gold, bricht as the stern of day;
Whilk tendit to the land full lustily,
　　As falcon swift desirous of her prey.

---

　　[1] bushes.　　　　[2] So delightfully against these pleasing
gleams.　　　[3] water.　　　[4] That the bows were bathed in
secondary beams from the reflection of the bright visage of
Phoebus.　　[5] little rapids.　　[6] pebbles.　　[7] rose garden.
[8] rock.　　[9] flame.　　[10] the sound of the river (which)
ran past me.　　[11] top.

And hard on board unto the bloomit meads,
Amang the greene rispis[1] and the reedis,
   Arrivit she, whar fro anon there landis
Ane hundred ladies, lusty into weedis,[2]
As fresh as flouris that in May upspreadis,
   In kirtillis grene, withouten kell[3] or bandis:
     Their bricht hairis hang glittering on the strandis
In tressis clear, wyppit[4] with golden threadis;
     With pappis white, and middlis small as wandis.

Discrive[5] I wald, but who could weel endite
How all the fieldis with thai lilies white
   Depaint were bricht, whilk to the heaven did glete[6]:
Nocht thou, Homer, as weel as thou could write,
For all thine ornate style so perfyte;
   Nor yet thou, Tullius, whose lippis sweet
     Of rhetoric did into termes fleet:
Your aureate tongis both been all too lyte,
   For to compile that paradise complete.

There saw I Nature, and as dame Venus queen,
The fresh Aurora, and lady Flora sheen,
   Juno, Apollo, and Proserpina,
Diane the goddess chaste of woodis green,
My lady Clio, that help of makaris[7] been,
   Thetis, Pallas, and prudent Minerva,
     Fair feignit Fortune, and leamand Lucina,
Thir michty queenis in crounis micht be seen,
   With beamis blithe, bricht as Lucifera.

---

   [1] coarse grass.   [2] pleasant to look upon in their garments.   [3] cap.   [4] bound.   [5] describe.   [6] glitter.
[7] poets.

There saw I May, of mirthful monethis queen,
Betwix Aprile and June, her sisteris sheen,
   Within the garden walking up and doun,
Wham of the foulis gladdith all bedene[1];
Sho was full tender in her yearis green.
   There I saw Nature present her a goun,
   Rich to behald, and noble of renoun,
Of every hue under the heaven that been
   Depaint, and broud[2] be gude proportioun.

Full lustily thir ladies all in fere[3]
Enterit within this park of most plesere,
   Where that I lay owre-helit[4] with leavis ronk;
The merry foulis, blissfullest of cheer,
Salust[5] Nature, me thocht, on their manere,
   And every bloom on branch, and eke[6] on bonk,
   Opnit and spread their balmy leavis donk,
Full low inclining to their queen so clear,
   Wham of their noble nourishing they thonk.

Syne to Dame Flora, on the samyn wise,
They saluse, and they thank a thousand syse;
   And to Dame Venus, loves michty queen,
They sang ballattis in love, as was the guise,
With amorous notis lusty to devise,[7]
   As they that had love in their heartis green;
   Their honey throatis, opnyt fro the spleen,
With warbles sweet did pierce the heavenly skies,
   Till loud resownyt the firmament serene.

Ane other court there saw I consequent,[8]
Cupid the king, with bow in hand aye bent,
   And dreadful arrowis grunden **sharp** and
      square:

---

[1] quickly.   [2] embroidered.   [3] company.   [4] covered
over.   [5] saluted.   [6] also.   [7] pleasant to remark.
[8] following.

There saw I Mars, the god armipotent,
Awful and sterne, strong and corpulent[1];
   There saw I crabbit Saturn auld and hair,
   His look was like for to perturb the air;
There was Mercurius, wise and eloquent,
   Of rhetoric that fand the flouris fair;

There was the god of gardens, Priapus;
There was the god of wilderness, Phanus[2];
   And Janus, god of entree delightable;
There was the god of floodis Neptunus;
There was the god of windis Eolus,
   With variand look, richt like a lord unstable;
   There was Bacchus the gladder of the table;
There was Pluto, the eldritch incubus,
   In cloak of green, his court usit no sable.

And every one of thir, in green arrayit,
On harp or lute full merrily they playit,
   And sang ballettis with michty notis clear:
Ladies to dance full soberly assayit,
Endlang the lusty river so they mayit:
   Their observance richt heavenly was to hear;
   Than crap[3] I through the leavis, and drew
     near,
Where that I was richt suddenly affrayit,
   All through a look, which I have bocht full
     dear.

And shortly for to speak, by Lovis Queen
I was espiet, sho bade her archeris keen
   Go me arrest; and they no time delayit;
Than ladies fair let fall their mantles green,
With bowis big in tressit hairis sheen,[4]
   All suddenly they had a field arrayit;

---

[1] large of body.   [2] Faunus.   [3] crept.   [4] The
bows had bowstrings of bright plaited hair.

And yet richt greatly was I nocht affrayit,
The party was so pleasand for to seen;
  A wonder lusty bicker[1] me assayit.

And first of all, with bow in hand aye bent,
Come Dame Beauty, richt as sho wald me shent[2];
  Syne followit all her damoselis in fere,
With mony diverse awful instrument,
Unto the press, Fair Having with her went,
  Fine Portraiture, Pleasance, and Lusty Cheer.
  Than come Reason, with shield of gold so
    clear,
In plate and mail; as Mars armipotent
  Defendit me that noble chevalier.

Syne tender Youth come with her virgins ying,
Green Innocence, and shameful Abaising,
  And quaking Dread, with humble Obedience;
The Golden Targe harmit they no thing;
Courage in them was nocht begun to spring;
  Full sore they dread to done a violence:
  Sweet Womanhood I saw come in presence,
Of artilye[3] a warld she did in bring,
  Servit with[4] ladies full of reverence.

Sho led with her Nurture and Lawliness,
Continuance, Patience, Gude Fame, and Stead-
    fastness,
Discretion, Gentrice, and Considerance,
Leful Company, and Honest Business,
  Benign Look, Mild Cheer, and Soberness:
  All thir bure ganyeis[5] to do me grevance;
But Reasoun bure the Targe with sic constance,
Their sharp assayes micht do no duress
  To me, for all their awful ordinance.

---

[1] attack.   [2] destroyed.   [3] weapons.   [4] handled
by.   [5] arrows.

Unto the press pursuït Hie Degree,
Her followit aye Estate and Dignitee,
   Comparisoun, Honour, and Noble Array,
Will, Wantonness, Renown, and Libertee,
Richesse, Freedom, and eek nobilitee;
   Wit ye they did their banner hie display;
   A cloud of arrowis as hail shower lowsit[1] they,
And shot, till wastit was their artilye,
   Syne went aback aboytit of[2] their prey.

When Venus had perceivit this rebute,[3]
Dissimilance[4] sho bade go mak pursuit,
   At all powere to pierce the Golden Targe;
And sho that was of doubleness the root,
Askit her choice of archeris in refute.[5]
   Venus the best bade her go wale[6] at large;
   Sho took Presence, plicht anchor[7] of the barge,
And Fair Calling that weel a flayn[8] could shoot,
   And Cherishing for to complete her charge.

Dame Hameliness sho took in company,
That hardy was, and hend[9] in archery,
   And brocht Dame Beauty to the field again;
With all the choice of Venus' chivalry
They come, and bickerit unabaisitly[10]:
   The shower of arrowis rappit on as rain;
   Perilous Presence, that mony sire has slain,
The battle brocht on border hard me by,[11]
   The 'sault was all the sairer, sooth to sayn.

Thick was the shot of grunden[12] dartis keen;
But Reason with the Shield of Gold so sheen,
   Warly[13] defendit who so ever assayit;

---

[1] loosed.   [2] driven back from.   [3] repulse.   [4] Dissimulation.   [5] defence.   [6] choose.   [7] sheet-anchor.
[8] arrow.   [9] skilful.   [10] battered without any fear.
[11] brought the battle to a frontier close beside me.
[12] sharpened.   [13] cautiously.

The awful stour[1] he manly did sustain
Till Presence kest a powder in his een,
  And than as drunken man he all forvayit[2]:
When he was blind the fool with him they playit,
And banist him amang the bewis green;
  That sorry sicht me suddenly affrayit.

Than was I wounded to the death weel near,
And yolden[3] as a woeful prisonere
  To Lady Beauty; in a moment space;
Me thocht sho seemit lustier of cheer,[4]
Efter that Reason tint[5] had his een clear,
  Than of before, and lovelier of face:
Why was thou blindit, Reason? Why, alas!
And gert[6] ane hell my paradise appear,
  And mercy seem, where that I fand no grace.

Dissimulance was busy me to sile,[7]
And Fair Calling did oft upon me smile,
  And Cherishing me fed with wordis fair;
New Acquaintance embracit me a while,
And favourite me, while men micht go a mile,
  Syne took her leave; I saw her nevermair:
  Than saw I Danger toward me repair,
I could eschew her presence by no wile,
  On side[8] sho lookit with ane fremyt fare.[9]

And at the last Departing could her dress,[10]
And me deliverit unto Heaviness
  For to remain, and sho in cure[11] me took;
By this the Lord of Windis, with wodeness,[12]

---

  [1] conflict.   [2] went astray.   [3] yielded.   [4] more
pleasant of countenance.   [5] lost.   [6] made.   [7] beguile.
[8] askance.   [9] strange behaviour.   [10] did make herself
ready.   [11] keeping.   [12] madness.

God Aeolus, his bugle blew, I guess;
 That with the blast the leavis all to-shook,
 And suddenly, in the space of a look,
All was hine went,[1] there was but wilderness,
 There was no more but birdis, bank, and
  brook.

In twinkling of ane ee to ship they went,
And swyth[2] up sail unto the top they stent,[3]
 And with swift course atour the flood they
  frak[4];
They firit guns with powder violent,
Till that the reek[5] raise to the firmament,
 The rochis all resounit with the rack,[6]
 For reird[7] it seemit that the rainbow brak;
With spirit afraid upon my feet I sprent[8]
 Amang the clewis,[9] so careful was the crack.

And as I did awake of my sweving,[10]
The joyful birdis merrily did sing
 For mirth of Phoebus tender beames sheen;
Sweet were the vapouris, soft the morrowing,
Halesome the vale, depaint with flouris ying[11];
 The air attemperit, sober, and amene[12];
 In white and red was all the field beseen,[13]
Through Naturis noble fresh enamelling,
 In mirthful May, of every moneth queen.

O reverend Chaucer, rose of rethoris[14] all,
As in our tongue ane flour imperiall,
 That raise in Britain ever, who readis richt,
Thou bearis of makaris the triumph riall;

---

[1] gone hence. [2] quickly. [3] stretch. [4] move
quickly. [5] smoke. [6] noise. [7] roar. [8] sprung.
[9] clefts in the rock. [10] dream. [11] young. [12] mild.
[13] arrayed. [14] eloquent writers.

Thy fresh enamellit terms celicall[1]
  This matter could illuminit have full bricht:
  Was thou nocht of our English all the licht,
Surmounting every tongue terrestrial,
  As far as Mayis morrow does midnicht?

O moral Gower, and Lydgate laureate,[2]
Your sugarit lippis and toungis aureate,
  Been to our earis cause of great delight;
Your angel mouthis most mellifluate[3]
Our rude langage has clear illuminate,
  And fair owre-gilt our speech, that imperfyte
  Stood, or your golden pennis shupe to write;
This isle before was bare, and desolate
  Of rhetoric, or lusty fresh indite.[4]

Thou little quair, be ever obedient,
Humble, subject, and simple of entent,[5]
  Before the face of every cunning wicht:
I knaw what thou of rhetoric has spent;
Of all her lusty roses redolent
  Is none in to thy garland set on hicht;
  Eshame[6] thereof and draw thee out of sicht.
Rude is thy weed, disteynit,[7] bare, and rent,
  Weel aucht thou be affeirit[8] of the licht.

To a Lady

SWEET rose of virtue and of gentleness,
Delightsome lily of every lustiness,[9]
  Richest in bounty, and in beauty clear,
  And every virtue that is held most dear,
Except only that ye are merciless.

---

[1] heavenly.   [2] crowned with laurel.   [3] flowing with
honey.   [4] writing.   [5] mind.   [6] be ashamed.
[7] stained.   [8] well mayest thou be afraid.   [9] pleasure.

Into your garth this day I did pursue,
There saw I flowris that fresh were of hue;
  Baith white and reid most lusty were to seen,
  And hailsome herbis upon stalkis green;
Yet leaf nor flour find could I nane of rue.

I doubt that Merch, with his cauld blastis keen,
Has slain this gentle herb, that I of mean;
  Whose piteous death dois to my heart sic pain
  That I wald mak to plant his root again,
So confortand his leavis unto me been.

The Dance of the Seven Deadly Sins

Of Februar the fifteen nicht,
Full lang before the dayis licht,
  I lay into a trance;
And then I saw baith Heaven and Hell:
Methocht, amangis the feindis fell,
  Mahoun[1] gart cry ane dance.

Of shrewis[2] that were never shriven,
Aganis the feast of Fastern's even,[3]
  To mak their observance;
He bad gallandis ga graith a gyiss,[4]
And cast up gambaudis[5] to the skyis,
  That last came out of France.

'Lat see,' quod he, 'now wha beginnis';
With that the foul Seven Deadly Sinnis
  Begouth to leip as anis.
And first in all the dance was Pride,
With hair wild[6] back and bonnet on side,
  Like to make wastie wanis;[7]

---

[1] The Devil.   [2] wretches.   [3] Shrove Tuesday.
[4] He bade gallants go prepare a masque.   [5] gambols.
[6] combed.   [7] waste dwellings.

And round about him, as a wheel,
Hang all in rumpillis[1] to the heel
   His kethat[2] for the nanis;
Mony proud trumpour[3] with him trippit
Through scaldand fire, aye as they skippit
   They girned with hiddous granis.

Hely harlottis on hautain wise[4]
Come in with mony sindrie guise,[5]
   But yet leuch never Mahoun;
Till priestis come in with bare shaven neckis,
Than all the fiendis leuch, and made geckis,
   Black Belly and Bawsy Broun.[6]

Than Ire come in with sturt and strife;
His hand was aye upon his knife,
   He brandeist[7] like a beir[8]:
Boasteris, braggeris, and bargaineris,[9]
Efter him passit into pairis,
   All bodin in feir of weir;[10]

In jackis,[11] and scryppis[12] and bonnettis of
    steel,
Their leggis were chenyeit[13] to the heel,
   Frawart[14] was their affeir[15]:
Some upon other with brandis beft,[16]
Some jaggit[17] otheris to the heft,[18]
   With knyvis that sharp could shear.

---

[1] folds.   [2] cassock.   [3] deceiver.   [4] proud harlots
in haughty fashion.   [5] disguise.   [6] names of witches.
[7] swaggered.   [8] boar.   [9] wranglers.   [10] arrayed in
accoutrements of war.   [11] quilted jackets.   [12] knap-
sacks.   [13] covered with chain mail.   [14] froward.
[15] bearing.   [16] struck with swords.   [17] stabbed.
[18] haft.

Next in the dance followit Envy,
Filled full of feud and felony,
 Hid malice and despite;
For privy hatrent[1] that traitor trymlit.[2]
Him followit mony freik dissymlit,[3]
 With feigneit wirdis white;

And flattereris into mennis facis;
And backbiteris of sindry racis;
 To lee that had delight;
And rownaris[4] of false leasingis[5];
Alas! that courtis of noble kingis
 Of them can never be quite.[6]

Next him in dance come Covetice,
Root of all evil and ground of vice,
 That never could be content;
Cativis, wretchis, and okkeraris,[7]
Hood-pickis,[8] hoardaris, and gadderaris,
 All with that warlo[9] went:

Out of their throatis they shot on other
Het molten gold, methocht a fother,[10]
 As fire-flaucht[11] maist fervent;
Aye as they toomit them[12] of shot,
Fiendis filled them new up to the throat
 With gold of alkin prent.[13]

Syne Sweirness, at the second bidding,
Come like a sow out of a midding,

---

[1] hatred.   [2] trembled.   [3] dissembling man.
[4] whisperers.   [5] lies.   [6] quit.   [7] usurers.   [8] misers.
[9] warlock.   [10] abundance.   [11] lightning.   [12] emptied
themselves.   [13] every kind of stamp.

Full sleepy was his grunye[1]:
Mony sweir bumbard belly huddron,[2]
Mony slut daw[3] and sleepy duddron,[4]
   Him servit aye with sounyie.[5]

He drew them furth in till a chainyie,[6]
And Belial, with a bridle reinyie,
   Ever lashed them on the lunyie[7]:
In dance they were so slaw of feet,
They gave them in the fire a heat,
   And made them quicker of counyie.[8]

Then Lechery, that laithly corse,
Come bearand[9] like a baggit horse,[10]
   And Idleness did him lead;
There was with him ane ugly sort,[11]
And mony stinkand foul tramort,[12]
   That had in sin been deid.

When they were entrit in the dance,
They were full strange of countenance,
   Like turkas birnand reid.[13] . . .

Then the foul monster Gluttony,
Of wame[14] unsatiable and greedy,
   To dance he did him dress:
Him followit mony foul drunkart,
With can and collop,[15] cup and quart
   In surfeit and excess.

---

[1] snout, face.   [2] lazy stupid greedy lump.   [3] dirty slut.   [4] sloven.   [5] excuse.   [6] chain.   [7] loin.
[8] motion.   [9] roaring.   [10] stallion.   [11] company.   [12] corpse.
[13] like red-hot pincers (three lines omitted).   [14] belly.
[15] drinking-cup.

Full mony a waistless wallydrag,[1]
With wamis unweildable[2] did furth wag,
 In creish[3] that did increase;
'Drink!' aye they cryit, with mony a gape,
The fiendis gave them het lead to lap,
 Their lovery[4] was na less.

Na menstrallis playit to them but doubt,
For gleemen there were halden[5] out,
 By day, and eke by nicht;
Except a menstrall that slew a man,
Swa till his heritage he wan,
 Entering by brief of richt.

Then cryit Mahoun for a Hieland padyane[6];
Syne ran a fiend to fetch MacFadyen,
 Far northward in a nook;
Be he the coronach had done shout
Erschemen[7] so gadderit him about,
 In Hell great room they took.

Thae tarmegantis with tag and tatter,[8]
Full loud in Ersche[9] begouth to clatter,
 And roup[10] like raven and rook:
The Devil sa deavit[11] was with their yell,
That in the deepest pit of Hell
 He smoorit[12] them with smoke.

Amends to the Tailors and Soutars

BETWIX twelve houris and eleven,
I dreamed ane angel came fra Heaven,
With pleasand steven[13] sayand on hie,
Tailyouris and Soutaris, blest be ye.

---

 [1] big-bellied person. [2] unwieldy bellies. [3] fat.
[4] allowance. [5] kept. [6] pageant. [7] Gaelic
speakers, Highlanders. [8] ragged termagants. [9] Gaelic.
[10] croak. [11] deafened. [12] smothered. [13] voice.

In Heaven hie ordained is your place,
Above all sanctis in great solace,
Next God, greatest in dignitie:
Tailyouris and soutaris, blest be ye.

The cause to you is nocht unkend,[1]
That[2] God mismaks ye do amend,
By craft and great agilitie:
Tailyouris and soutaris, blest be ye.

Soutaris, with shoon weel made and meet,
Ye mend the faults of ill-made feet,
Wherefore to Heaven your soulis will flee:
Tailyouris and soutaris, blest be ye.

Is nocht in all this fair a flyrok,[3]
That has upon his feet a wyrok,[4]
Knowll tais,[5] nor mowlis[6] in no degree,
But ye can hide them: blest be ye.

And ye tailyouris, with weel-made clais
Can mend the worst made man that gais,
And mak him seemly for to see:
Tailyouris and soutaris, blest be ye.

Though God mak ane misfashionit man,
Ye can him all shape new again,
And fashion him better be sic three[7]:
Tailyouris and soutaris, blest be ye.

Though a man have a broken back,
Have he a gude crafty tailyour—what rack?[8]
That can it cover with craftis slie:
Tailyouris and soutaris, blest be ye.

---

[1] not unknown.   [2] what.   [3] light, insignificant
creature.   [4] lump.   [5] knotted toes.   [6] chilblains.
[7] three times as well.   [8] matter.

Of God great kindness may ye claim,
That helpis his people fra crook and lame,
Supportand faultis with your supple[1]:
Tailyouris and soutaris, blest be ye.

In erd ye kith[2] sic mirakillis here
In Heaven ye sall be sanctis full clear,
Though ye be knavis in this countree:
Tailyouris and soutaris, blest be ye.

Meditation in Winter

In to thir dark and drublie[3] dayis,
When sable all the heavens arrayis,
    With misty vapouris, cloudis and skyis,[4]
    Nature all courage me denies
Of sangis ballattis and of playis.

When that the nicht does lengthen houris,
With wind, with hail, with heavy shouris,
    My dule spreit dois lurk for schoir[5];
    My heart for languor dois forloir,[6]
For lack of simmer with his flouris.

I wake, I turn, sleep may I nocht,
I vexit am with heavy thocht;
    This warld all owre I cast about,
    And aye the mair I am in doubt,
The mair that I remeid have socht.

I am assayit on every side,
Despair sayis aye, 'In time provide,
    And get some thing whereon to leif,[7]
    Or with great trouble and mischief,
Thou sall into this court abide.'

---

[1] assistance.   [2] show.   [3] dripping.   [4] shadows.
[5] hide for fear.   [6] is utterly lost.   [7] live.

Then Patience says, 'Be nocht aghast:
Hald Hope and Truth within thee fast;
 And lat Fortune wirk furth her rage,
 Whan that no reasoun may assuage,
Till that her glass be run and past.'

And Prudence in my ear sayis aye,
'Why wald thou hald that will away?[1]
 Or crave that thou may have mo space,
 Thou tending to ane other place,
A journey going every day?'

And than sayis Age, 'My friend, come near,
And be nocht strange, I thee requeir:
 Come, brother, by the hand me tak,
 Remember thou has compt to mak
Of all thy time thou spendit here.'

Syne Deid castis up his yettis[2] wide,
Saying, 'Thir open sall ye abide;[3]
 Albeit that thou were never sa stout,
 Under this lintel sall thou lout[4]:
There is nane other way beside.'

For fear of this all day I droop;
No gold in kist, nor wine in cup
 No ladeis beauty, nor loves bliss
 May lat me to remember[5] this:
How glad that ever I dine or sup.

Yet, when the nicht beginnis to short,
It dois my spreit some part confort,
 Of thocht oppressit with the shouris.
 Come, lusty summer! with thy flouris,
That I may live in some disport.

---

[1] Why would you keep what will disappear? [2] gates.
[3] you must endure these open. [4] stoop. [5] prevent
my remembering.

Lament for the Makaris

I THAT in heill[1] was and gladnèss
Am trublit now with great sickness
And feblit with infirmitie:—
    Timor Mortis conturbat me.

Our plesance here is all vain glory,
This fals world is but transitory,
The flesh is bruckle,[2] the Feynd is slee[3]:—
    Timor Mortis conturbat me.

The state of man does change and vary,
Now sound, now sick, now blyth, now sary,
Now dansand[4] mirry, now like to die:—
    Timor Mortis conturbat me.

No state in Erd here standis sicker[5];
As with the wynd wavis the wicker[6]
So wavis this world's vanitie:—
    Timor Mortis conturbat me.

Unto the deid gois all Estatis,
Princis, Prelatis, and Potestatis,
Baith rich and poor of all degree:—
    Timor Mortis conturbat me.

He takis the knichtis in to field
Enarmit under helm and scheild;
Victor he is at all mellie[7]:—
    Timor Mortis conturbat me.

That strong unmerciful tyrand
Takis, on the motheris breast sowkand,[8]
The babe full of benignitie:—
    Timor Mortis conturbat me.

---

[1] health.   [2] brittle, feeble.   [3] sly.   [4] dancing.
[5] sure.   [6] willow.   [7] mellay.   [8] sucking.

He takis the campion[1] in the stour,[2]
The captain closit in the tour,
The lady in bour full of bewtie:—
    Timor Mortis conturbat me.

He spairis no lord for his piscence,[3]
Na clerk for his intelligence;
His awful straik[4] may no man flee:—
    Timor Mortis conturbat me.

Art-magicians and astrologgis,
Rethoris, logicianis, and theologgis,
Them helpis no conclusionis slee:—
    Timor Mortis conturbat me.

In medecine the most practicianis,
Leechis, surrigianis, and physicianis,
Themself from Death may not supplee[5]:—
    Timor Mortis conturbat me.

I see that makaris[6] amang the lave[7]
Playis here their padyanis,[8] syne gois to grave;
Sparit is nocht their facultie:—
    Timor Mortis conturbat me.

He has done petuously devour
The noble Chaucer, of makaris flour,
The Monk of Bury, and Gower, all three:—
    Timor Mortis conturbat me.

The good Sir Hew of Eglintoun,
And eik[9] Heriot, and Wyntoun,
He has tane out of this cuntrie:—
    Timor Mortis conturbat me.

---

[1] champion. [2] fight. [3] puissance. [4] stroke.
[5] save. [6] poets. [7] the leave, the rest. [8] pageants. [9] also.

That scorpion fell has done infeck
Maister John Clerk, and James Afflek,
Fra ballat-making and tragedie:—
 Timor Mortis conturbat me.

Holland and Barbour he has berevit;
Alas! that he not with us levit
Sir Mungo Lockart of the Lee:—
 Timor Mortis conturbat me.

Clerk of Tranent eke he has tane,
That made the anteris[1] of Gawaine;
Sir Gilbert Hay endit has he:—
 Timor Mortis conturbat me.

He has Blind Harry and Sandy Traill
Slain with his schour[2] of mortal hail,
Quhilk Patrick Johnstoun might nought flee:—
 Timor Mortis conturbat me.

He has reft Merseir his endite,[3]
That did in love so lively write,
So short, so quick, of sentence hie:—
 Timor Mortis conturbat me.

He has tane Roull of Aberdene,
And gentill Roull of Corstorphine;
Two better fallowis[4] did no man see:—
 Timor Mortis conturbat me.

In Dunfermline he has done roune[5]
With Maister Robert Henrysoun;
Sir John the Ross enbrast has he:—
 Timor Mortis conturbat me.

---

 [1] adventures.   [2] shower.   [3] inditing.   [4] fellows.
[5] whispered.

And he has now tane, last of a,
Good gentil Stobo and Quintin Shaw,
Of quhom all wichtis[1] hes pitie:—
　　Timor Mortis conturbat me.

Good Maister Walter Kennedy
In point of deid lies verily;
Great ruth it were that so suld be:—
　　Timor Mortis conturbat me.

Sen he has all my brether tane,
He will naught lat me live alane;
On force I man[2] his next prey be:—
　　Timor Mortis conturbat me.

Sen for the deid remeid is none,
Best is that we for deid dispone,[3]
Efter our deid that live may we:—
　　Timor Mortis conturbat me.

O Wretch, beware

O WRETCH, beware! this world will wend thee
　　fro,
　　Whilk has beguilit mony great estate;
Turn to thy friend, believe nocht on thy foe,
　　Sen thou man go, be graithing to thy gait;[4]
　　Remeid in time, and rue nocht all too late;
Provide thy place, for thou away man pass
　　Out of this vale of trouble and dissait:
Vanitas Vanitatum, et omnia Vanitas.

Walk furth, pilgrim, while thou has dayis licht,
　　Dress fro desert,[5] draw to thy dwelling-place;
Speed home, for-why[6] anon comis the nicht
　　Whilk does thee follow with ane ythand[7] chase!

---

[1] wights, persons.　　[2] must.　　[3] make disposition.
[4] making ready for thy journey.　　[5] go from the
desert.　　[6] because.　　[7] busy.

Bend up thy sail, and win thy port of grace;
For and the death owretak thee in trespass,
 Then may thou say thir wordis with alas!
Vanitas Vanitatum, et omnia Vanitas.

Here nocht abidis, here standis no thing stable,
 For this false world aye flittis to and fro;
Now day up bricht, now nicht as black as sable,
 Now ebb, now flood, now friend, now cruel
  foe;
 Now glad, now sad, now weel, now into woe;
Now clad in gold, dissolvit now in ass[1];
 So dois this warld transitory go:
Vanitas Vanitatum, et omnia Vanitas.

Rorate Coeli Desuper

Rorate coeli desuper![2]
Heavens distill your balmy shouris,
For now is risen the bricht day ster,[3]
Fro the rose Mary, flour of flouris:
The clear Sun, whom no cloud devouris,
Surmounting Phoebus in the east,
Is cumin of his heavenly touris;
Et nobis Puer natus est.[4]

Archangellis, angellis, and dompnationis,
Thronis, potestatis, and martyris seir,[5]
And all ye heavenly operationis,
Ster, planet, firmament, and sphere,
Fire, erd, air, and water clear,
To him give loving,[6] most and lest,
That come into so meek mannere;
Et nobis Puer natus est.

[1] ash. [2] send down dews, ye heavens. [3] day star,
i.e. sun. [4] And unto us is born a Child. [5] various.
[6] praise.

Sinneris be glaid, and penance do,
And thank your maker hairtfully;
For he that ye micht nocht come to,
To you is cumin full humbly,
Your saulis with his blood to buy,
And lowse you of the fiendis arrest,
And only of his awin mercy,
Pro nobis Puer natus est.[1]

All clergy do to him incline,
And bow unto this barne benign,
And do your observance divine
To him that is of kingis King;
Incense[2] his altar, read, and sing
In haly kirk, with mind digest,[3]
Him honouring attour[4] all thing,
Qui nobis Puer natus est.[5]

Celestial fowlis in the air
Sing with your notis upon hicht;
In firthis[6] and in forrestis fair
Be mirthful now, at all your micht,
For passit is your dully nicht;
Aurora hes the cloudis perst,
The sun is risen with glaidsome licht,
Et nobis Puer natus est.

Now spring up flouris fra the root,
Revert[7] you upward naturally,
In honour of the blissit fruit
That raise up fro the rose Mary;
Lay out your leavis lustily,
Fro deid tak life now at the lest[8]
In worship of that Prince worthy,
Qui nobis Puer natus est.

[1] unto us is born a Child.   [2] burn incense about.
[3] well prepared.   [4] above.   [5] who was born unto us
a Child.   [6] coppices.   [7] turn.   [8] at last.

Sing heaven imperial, most of hicht,
Regions of air mak armony;
All fish in flood and fowl of flicht,
Be mirthful and mak melody:
All '*Gloria in Excelsis*' cry,
Heaven, erd, sea, man bird, and best,[1]
He that is crownit abone the sky
Pro nobis Puer natus est.

Done is a Battle on the Dragon Black

DONE is a battle on the dragon black,
Our campion Christ confoundit has his force;
The yettis[2] of hell are broken with a crack,
The sign triumphal raisit is of the cross,
The devillis trymmillis[3] with hiddous voce,
The saulis are borrowit[4] and to the bliss can go,
Christ with his blood our ransonis dois indoce[5]:
Surrexit Dominus de sepulchro.[6]

Dungen[7] is the deidly dragon Lucifer,
The cruel serpent with the mortal stang[8];
The auld keen tiger, with his teeth on char,[9]
Whilk in a wait has lyen for us so lang,
Thinking to grip us in his clawis strang;
The merciful Lord wald nocht that it were so,
He made him for to failye of that fang[10]:
Surrexit Dominus de sepulchro.

He for our sake that sufferit to be slain,
And like a lamb in sacrifice was dicht,[11]
Is like a lion risen up again,
And as gyane[12] raxit[13] him on hicht;

---

[1] beast.　[2] gates.　[3] tremble.　[4] ransomed.　[5] endorse.
[6] The Lord has risen from the grave.　[7] struck down.
[8] sting.　[9] ajar.　[10] prey.　[11] prepared.　[12] giant.
[13] stretched.

Sprungen is Aurora radious[1] and bricht,
On loft is gone the glorious Apollo,
The blissful day departit fro the nicht:
Surrexit Dominus de sepulchro.

The great victour again is risen on hicht,
That for our quarrel to the death was woundit;
The sun that wox all pale now shinis bricht,
And darkness clearit, our faith is now refoundit;
The knell of mercy fra the heaven is soundit,
The Christian are deliverit of their woe,
The Jewis and their error are confoundit:
Surrexit Dominus de sepulchro.

The foe is chasit, the battle is done cease,
The prison broken, the jevellouris fleit and
    flemit;[2]
The weir is gone, confermit is the peace,
The fetteris lowsit and the dungeon temit,[3]
The ranson made, the prisoneris redeemit;
The field is won, owrecomen is the foe,
Despoilit of the treasure that he yemit[4]:
Surrexit Dominus de sepulchro.

GAVIN DOUGLAS
1475?–1522

An Evening and Morning in June

(i)

THE licht begouth to quenschyng out and fall,
The day to dirken, decline, and devall[5];
The gummis[6] risis, doun fallis the donk rime,[7]
Baith here and there skuggis[8] and shadows dim;

---

[1] radiant.   [2] jailers terrified and put to flight.
[3] emptied.   [4] guarded.   [5] sink.   [6] vapours.   [7] mist.
[8] shades.

Up goes the bak with her peelit leddren flicht,[1]
The larkis descendis from the skyis hicht,[2]
Singand her compline sang eftir her guise,
To tak her rest, at matin hour to rise:
Out owre the swyre[3] swimmis the soppis of mist,
The nicht furth spread her cloak with sable lyst[4];
That all the beauty of the fructuous field
Was with the earthis umbrage[5] clean owreheild[6]:
Baith man and beast, firth, flood, and woodis wild
Involvit in the shadows war insylde[7]:
Still war the fowlis fleis[8] in the air
All store[9] and cattle sesit[10] in their lair;
All creature where so them likis best
Bownis[11] to tak the halesome nichtis rest,
Eftir the dayis labour and the heat:
Close waren[12] all and at their soft quiet,
But steerage[13] or removing, he or she,
Outhir beast, bird, fish, fowl by land or sea.
And shortly every thing that doth repair
In firth or field, flood, forest, earth or air,
Or in the scroggis,[14] or in the buskis ronk,[15]
Lakis, maressis,[16] or their poolis donk,[17]
Astablit[18] lyggis[19] still to sleep and restis
Be[20] the small birdis sittand on their nestis,
The little midges and the urisome fleis,[21]
As weel the wild as the tame bestial,
And every other thingis great and small,—
Out tak[22] the merry nichtingale Philomene,
That on the thorn sat singand fro the spleen.

---

[1] bat flying with wings of peeled leather. [2] height.
[3] valley. [4] border. [5] shadow. [6] covered over.
[7] enfolded. [8] birds that fly. [9] cattle. [10] tethered.
[11] prepares. [12] were. [13] movement. [14] thickets.
[15] rank. [16] marshes. [17] dank. [18] settled. [19] lies.
[20] from. [21] troublesome flies. [22] except.

Whais mirthful nottis langand[1] for to hear,
Until ane garth under ane green laurere[2]
I walk anon, and in a siege[3] doun sat
Now musing upon this, and now on that.
I see the Pole,[4] and eek the Ursas bricht
And hornyt Lucine castand bot dim licht,
Because the summer skyës shane so clear. . . .

(*Prologue to the Thirteenth Book of the Aeneid*, ll. 33–73.)

(ii)

Yonder doun dwynis[5] the even sky away,
And upspringis the bricht dawning of the day
In till ane other place, not fer in sunder,
That to behald was plesance, and half wonder.
Furth quenching gan the sternes ane be ane
That now is left bot Lucifer alane.
And furthermore, to blazon this new day,
Wha micht discryve the birdis blissful bay?
Belyve[6] on wing the busy lark upsprang
To salute the bricht morrow with her sang;
Soon owre the fieldis shines the licht clere,
Welcome to pilgrim baith and labourere:
Tyte[7] on his hines[8] gaif the grieve ane cry,
'Awake! On foot! Go till our husbandry!'
And the herd callis furth apoun his page
To drive the cattle to their pasturage;
The hynes wife clepis[9] up Katherine and Jill;
'Yea, dame,' said they, God wat, with ane good
      will.
The dewy green powderit with daisies gay
Shew on the sward ane colour dapple gray;

---

[1] longing.   [2] laurel.   [3] seat.   [4] Pole Star.   [5] sinks.
[6] straightway.   [7] quickly.   [8] hinds.   [9] calls.

The misty vapours springand up full sweet
Maist comfortable to glaid all mannis sprete;
Thereto thir birdis singis in their shawis[1]
As menstralis playis 'The jolly day now dawis'.

(*Prologue to the Thirteenth Book of the Aeneid*, ll. 163–86.)

An Evening and Morning in Winter

In this congealit season sharp and chill,
The caller air penetrative and pure,
Dazing the blude in every creature,
Made seek warm stovis and bene[2] fyris hot.
In double garment cled and wyliecoat,[3]
With michty drink, and meatis confortive,
Aganis the sterne winter for to strive,
Recreate weel, and by the chimney bekit[4]
At even betime doun on ane bed me strekit,[5]
Warpit[6] my hede, kest on claithis thrynfald
For to expel the perilous piercand cauld.
I crossit me, syne bownit[7] for to sleep,
Where lemand[8] through the glass I did tak keep[9]
Latonia the lang irksome nicht
Her subtle blenkis[10] shed and watery licht;
Full high up whirlit in her regioun,
Till[11] Phoebus richt in oppositioun,
Into the Crab her proper mansion draw
Haldand the hicht although the sun went law.
The hornit bird whilk we clepe the nicht owl
Within her cavern hard I shout and yowl
Laithly of form, with crooked camscho[12] beak,
Ugsome[13] to hear was her wild elrische[14] skreik.

---

[1] copses.   [2] comfortable.   [3] short jacket.   [4] warmed.
[5] stretched.   [6] wrapped.   [7] prepared.   [8] gleaming.
[9] observed.   [10] glances.   [11] to.   [12] bent.   [13] horrible.
[14] eldritch.

The wild geese eek clacking by nichtis tide[1]
Atour[2] the city fleand[3] hard I glide.
On slummer I slade[4] full soon, and slepyt
    sound
Till the horizon upward can rebound.
Phoebus crownit bird, the nichtis orlagere,[5]
Clappin his wingis thryis had crawin clear,
Approaching near the breaking of the day—
Within my bed I wakynnit whare I lay,
Sa fast declynnys Cynthia the moon.
And kayis keklys[6] on the roof abune;
Palamedes birdis[7] crowpand[8] in the sky,
Fleand on randoun, shapen like ane Y,
And as ane trumpet rang their vocis soun,
Whais cryis been prognosticacioun
Of windy blastis and ventositeis
Fast by my chalmer on high wisnit[9] trees
The soir gled[10] whissllis with mony ane pew,
Wharby the day was dawing weel I knew,
Bade beat[11] the fire, and the candle alicht;
Syne blissit me, and in my weedis dicht[12];
Ane shot window[13] unshut ane little on char[14]
Persavit the morning bla,[15] wan and har,[16]
With cloudy gum[17] and rack owrewhelmyt the
    air,
The sowlye[18] stiche,[19] hasard,[20] rouch and hare.[21]
Branches brattlyng,[22] and blaiknyt[23] shew the
    brayis[24]
With hirstis[25] harsk[26] of waggand wyndil strayis[27];

---

  [1] time.   [2] above.   [3] flying.   [4] slid.   [5] hour-
teller.   [6] jackdaws cackle.   [7] cranes.   [8] croaking.
[9] withered.   [10] red kite.   [11] kindle.   [12] clothed.
[13] window that can be opened.   [14] ajar.   [15] bleak.
[16] grey.   [17] vapour.   [18] soil.   [19] stiff.   [20] ashen.
[21] grey.   [22] rattling.   [23] blackened.   [24] slopes.
[25] clumps.   [26] harsh.   [27] coarse grass.

The dew droppis congealit on stibble and rind,[1]
And sharp hailstanis mortfundyit of kind,[2]
Hoppand on the thack[3] and on the causay[4] by.
The shot I closit, and drew inward in hy,[5]
Shiverand for cald, the season was sa snell,[6]
Shupe[7] with hait flambis[8] to stem the freezing
    fell.[9]

(*Prologue to the Seventh Book of the Aeneid*, ll. 91–145.)

The Entrance to Tartarus

THAN Deiphobus made this answer again:
'Beis not aggrevit, sovereign nun,[10] I pray;
I sall no langar dwell, bot go my way;
I sall complete my number furth,' quod he,
'And to dim shadows rendrit sall I be.
Pass on, pass on, our worship and renown;
Mair prosper[11] chance to hant[12] go make thee
    boun.'[13]
Thus fer spak Deiphobus, and with that saw
About turnit his pace, and gan withdraw.
Aeneas blent[14] him by, and suddenly
Under ane rock at the left side did spy
Ane wonder large castle strang and stout,
With wallis thrinfald[15] lappit round about.
Wham the grisly Tartarean Phlegeton
That ravenous flood closis environ,
With water-blasand[16] brim in fiery low,[17]
And rolland stanis rumland deep and how.[18]
The port[19] in forefront was full huge grete,
Of ferme adamant war the pillaris bete,[20]

---

[1] bark.   [2] bitterly cold by nature.   [3] thatch.
[4] street.   [5] haste.   [6] bitter.   [7] set about.   [8] hot
flames.   [9] severe.   [10] the Sibyl.   [11] prosperous.
[12] frequent, follow.   [13] ready.   [14] looked.   [15] threefold.
[16] blazing.   [17] flame.   [18] low.   [19] gate.   [20] built.

Sa that na force of men micht thame doun mine,
Nor yit the strength of Goddis with strang engyne:
Ane iron toure stood beildit wonder high,
Whilk semit for to reek[1] up in the sky:
Tisiphone that furious monster wild,
In bloody cape revestit and oversylde,[2]
Sittis kepand but[3] sleep baith nicht and day
That sorry entre and this porch alway.
Tho begouth[4] they first in this stead to hear
Mourning, gouling[5] and graning with duleful
　　bere[6]:
Fell[7] cruel strakis smiting heard they sound,
Frasing[8] of iron fetteris and chenyeis[9] round.
Aenee gan him arreist,[10] in mind within
All abasit, herkynnand[11] this fearful din.

'O holy virgin,[12] say thou furth,' quod he,
'What kind of grisly torment may this be?
In what punition, panys, and distress
Been saulis[13] yonder strenyeit, prophetess?
What means this bruit,[14] weeping and woeful
　　cryis,
With sic wailing semys fordyn[15] the skyis?'

(*Sixth Book of the Aeneid*, ll. 1120–59.)

ALEXANDER SCOTT
fl. 1547–84

A Rondel of Love

Lo! what it is to love,
Learn ye, that list to prove
By me, I say, that no ways may

---

[1] smoke.　[2] clothed and covered over.　[3] keeping
without.　[4] began.　[5] howling.　[6] sound.　[7] exces-
sively.　[8] noise.　[9] chains.　[10] stopped.　[11] listening
to.　[12] tne Sibyl.　[13] souls.　[14] noise.　[15] resound.

The ground of grief remove,
But still decay, both nicht and day:
  Lo! what it is to love.

Love is ane fervent fire,
  Kindled without desire:
Short pleasure, lang displeasure;
  Repentance is the hire;
Ane poor treasure without measure:[1]
  Love is ane fervent fire.

To love and to be wise,
  To rage with good advice,[2]
Now thus, now than,[3] so goes the game.
  Incertain is the dice.
There is no man, I say that can
  Both love and to be wise.

Flee always from the snare;
  Learn at me to beware;
It is ane pain and double train
  Of endless woe and care;
For to refrain that danger plain,
  Flee always from the snare.

Hence, heart, with her that must depart

HENCE, heart, with her that must depart,
  And hald thee with thy sovereign,
For I had lever[4] want ane heart
  Nor have the heart that does me pain;
  Therefore go, with thy love remain,
And let me live thus unmolest;
  And see that thou come not again,
But bide with her thou lovis best.

---

[1] a treasure poor beyond measure.   [2] to be mad and
yet rational.   [3] otherwise.   [4] rather.

Sen sho that I have servit lang
　　Is to depart so suddenly,
Address thee now, for thou sall gang
　　And bear thy lady company.
　　Fra sho be gone, heartless am I,
For why[1] thou art with her possest;
　　Therefore, my heart, go hence in hy,[2]
And bide with her thou lovis best.

Though this belappit[3] body here
　　Be bound to servitude and thrall,
My faithful heart is free inteir[4]
　　And mind to serve my lady at all.
　　Wald God that I were perigall,[5]
Under that redolent rose to rest!
　　Yet at the least, my heart, thou sall
Abide with her thou lovis best.

Sen in your garth the lily white
　　May not remain among the lave,[6]
Adieu the flower of haill delight!
　　Adieu the succour that may me save!
　　Adieu the fragrant balm suave,
And lamp of ladies lustiest!
　　My faithful heart sho sall it have,
To bide with her it lovis best.

Deplore, ye ladies clear of hue,
　　Her absence, sen sho must depart,
And specially, ye lovers true,
　　That wounded been with lovës dart:
　　For some of you sall want ane heart
Alsweill as I: therefore at last
　　Do go with mine, with mind inwart,[7]
And bide with her thou lovis best.

---

[1] because.　　[2] haste.　　[3] beleaguered·　　[4] entirely.
[5] worthy.　　[6] remainder.　　[7] sincere.

Return thee, Heart

RETURN thee, heart, hameward again,
  And bide where thou was wont to be;
Thou art ane fool to suffer pain
  For love of her that loves not thee.
  My heart, lat be sic fantasy;
Love nane but as they mak thee cause;
  And lat her seek ane heart for thee,
For fiend a crumb of thee sho faws.[1]

To what effect sould thou be thrall
  But[2] thank, sen thou has thy free will?
My heart, be not sa bestial,
  But knaw who does thee good or ill;
  Remain with me and tarry still,
And see wha playis best their pawis,[3]
  And lat fillok[4] ga fling her fill,
For fiend a crumb of thee sho faws.

Though sho be fair I will not fenyie[5];
  Sho is the kind of others ma;[6]
For why there is a fellone menye,[7]
  That semis good, and are not sa.
  My heart, tak neither pain nor wa,[8]
For Meg, for Marjory, or yet Mause,
  But be thou glad and lat her ga,
For fiend a crumb of thee sho faws.

Because I find sho took in ill,[9]
  At her departing thou mak na care;
But all beguiled, go where sho will,
  Beshrew the heart that mane[10] maks mair.

---

[1] possesses.   [2] without.   [3] part.   [4] the filly.
[5] feign fondness.   [6] she is more like others.   [7] a great
number.   [8] woe.   [9] took it amiss.   [10] moan.

My heart, be merry late and air,
This is the final end and clause,
   And lat her follow ane filly fair,[1]
For feind a crumb of thee sho faws.

Lament of the Master of Erskine

DEPART, depart, depart,
Alas! I must depart
From her that has my heart,
   With heart full sore,
Aganis my will indeed,
And can find no remeid:
I wait[2] the pains of deid
   Can do no more.

Now must I go, alas!
From sight of her sweet face,
The ground of all my grace,
   And sovereign;
What chance that may fall me,
Sall I never merry be,
Unto the time I see
   My sweet again.

I go, and wait not where,
I wander here and there,
I weep and sighs richt sair
   With painis smart;
Now must I pass away, away,
In wilderness and wilsome[3] way,
Alas! this woeful day
   We suld depart.

[1] foppish youth.   [2] know.   [3] dreary.

My spreit does quake for dread,
My thirlit[1] heart does bleed,
My painis does exceed—
    What suld I say?
I, woeful wicht, alone,
Makand ane piteous moan,
Alas! my heart is gone
    For ever and aye.

Through languor of my sweet
So thirlit is my spreit,
My days are most complete[2]
    Through her absence:
Christ sen[3] sho knew my smart,
Ingravit in my heart,
Because I must depart
    From her presence.

Adieu, my ain sweet thing,
My joy and comforting,
My mirth and solacing
    Of erdly gloir:
Fair weel, my lady bricht,
And my remembrance richt;
Fare weel and have gude nicht:
    I say no more.

To Love Unloved

To love unloved is ane pain;
For sho that is my sovereign,
   Some wanton man so he has set her,
That I can get no love again,
   But breks my heart, and not the better.

[1] pierced.   [2] ended.   [3] send.

When that I went with that sweet may,[1]
To dance, to sing, to sport and play,
   And oft times in my armis plet[2] her;
I do now mourn both nicht and day,
   And breks my heart, and not the better.

Where I was wont to see her go
Richt trimly passand to and fro,
   With comely smiles when that I met her;
And now I live in pain and woe,
   And breks my heart, and not the better.

Whattan ane glaikit[3] fool am I
To slay myself with melancholy,
   Sen weel I ken I may not get her!
Or what suld be the cause, and why,
   To brek my heart, and not the better?

My heart, sen thou may not her please,
Adieu, as good love comes as gaes,
   Go choose ane other and forget her;
God give him dolour and disease,
   That breks their heart, and not the better.

ALEXANDER MONTGOMERIE
1540?–1610?

The Nicht is Neir Gone

Hey! now the day dawis;
The jolly cock crawis;
Now shroudis[4] the shawis[5]
   Thro' Nature anon.

---

[1] maid.   [2] embrace.   [3] silly.   [4] dress themselves.
[5] woods.

The thissel-cock cryis
On lovers wha lyis:
Now skaillis[1] the skyis;
   The nicht is neir gone.

The fieldis ouerflowis
With gowans[2] that growis,
Quhair lilies like low[3] is
   As red as the rone.[4]
The turtle that true is,
With notes that renewis,
Her pairty[5] pursuis:
   The nicht is neir gone.

Now hairtis with hindis
Conform to their kindis,
Hie tursis[6] their tyndis[7]
   On ground quhair they grone.[8]
Now hurchonis,[9] with hairis,
Aye passis in pairis;
Quhilk duly declaris
   The nicht is neir gone.

The season excellis
Through sweetness that smellis;
Now Cupid compellis
   Our hairtis echone
On Venus wha waikis,
To muse on our maikis,[10]
Syne sing for their saikis—
   'The nicht is neir gone!'

---

[1] clears.   [2] daisies.   [3] flame.   [4] rowan.
[5] partner, mate.   [6] carry.   [7] antlers.   [8] groan, bell.   [9] hedgehogs, 'urchins'.   [10] mates.

All courageous knichtis
Aganis the day dichtis
The breist-plate that bright is
  To fight with their fone.[1]
The stonèd steed[2] stampis
Through courage, and crampis,[3]
Syne on the land lampis[4]:
  The nicht is neir gone.

The freikis[5] on feildis
That wight wapins[6] weildis
With shyning bright shieldis
  At Titan in trone;[7]
Stiff speiris in reistis
Ouer corseris crestis
Are broke on their breistis:
  The nicht is neir gone.

So hard are their hittis,
Some sweyis, some sittis,
And some perforce flittis[8]
  On ground quhile they grone.
Syne groomis that gay is
On blonkis[9] that brayis
With swordis assayis:—
  The nicht is neir gone.

An Admonition to Young Lassies

A BONNIE 'No' with smiling looks again
  I wald ye learned, sen they so comely are.
As touching 'Yes', if ye suld speak so plain,
  I might reprove you to have said so far.

---

[1] foes.   [2] stallion.   [3] prances.   [4] gallops.
[5] men, warriors.   [6] stout weapons.   [7] over against Titan
(the sun), or read 'as'.   [8] are cast.   [9] white palfreys.

Nocht that your grant, in ony ways, micht
 gar[1]
Me loathe the fruit that courage ocht to
 choose;
 But I wald only have you seem to skar,[2]
And let me tak it, feigning to refuse;

And warsle, as it war against your will,
 Appearing angry, though ye have no ire:
For have, ye hear, is halden half a fill.[3]
 I speak not this, as trowing for to tire:
 But as the forger when he feeds his fire
With sparks of water maks it burn more bauld;
 So, sweet denial doubles but desire,
And quickens courage fra becoming cauld.

Wald ye be made of, ye maun mak it nice;
 For dainties here are delicate and dear,
But plenty things are prized to little price;[4]
 Then though ye hearken, let no wit ye
 hear,
 But look away, and len them aye your ear:
For, follow love, they say, and it will flee.
 Wald ye be loved, this lesson maun ye leir[5]:
Flee whilom love, and it will follow thee.

Sweetheart, Rejoice in Mind

SWEETHEART, rejoice in mind,
 With comfort day and nicht,
Ye have ane love as kind
 As ever loved wicht;

---

[1] make. [2] discourage. [3] possession, you hear, is
held to halve desire. [4] things that are plentiful are
little valued. [5] must you learn.

Though I be out of sicht,
   Lat nocht your courage fall,
My joyful heart and licht,
   Ye have and ever sall.

My bonnie burd,[1] be blithe,
   And ye sall find me so
Imprent to you, I kyith,[2]
   To lat you nocht be woe;
Wherever I ride or go,
   Ye sall nocht sorry be,
My leal love, heart, and jo,[3]
   Nane has my heart but thee.

And ye, my true love sweet,
   This do ye nocht gang stand,[4]
My blitheness for to beit,[5]
   As I serve at your hand;
To think me nocht constand,
   My bonnie burd, lat be:
My constant heart sall stand
   To you till that I die.

I bid[6] no mair of you,
   But God grant you his bliss:
God be as blithe of you
   As I wald be of this,
Your lily lips to kiss,
   Thinkand that mind of yours,
My ain true love she is,
   That loves her paramours.[7]

---

[1] maid.   [2] constant to you, I declare.   [3] sweetheart.
[4] gainsay.   [5] kindle.   [6] pray.   [7] *par amour.*

MARK ALEXANDER BOYD
1563–1601

Sonnet

FRA bank to bank, fra wood to wood I rin,
  Ourhailit[1] with my feeble fantasie;
  Like til a leaf that fallis from a tree,
Or til a reed ourblawin with the win.

Twa gods guides me: the ane of tham is blin,
  Yea and a bairn brocht up in vanitie;
  The next a wife ingenrit of the sea,
And lichter nor a dauphin with her fin.

Unhappy is the man for evermair
  That tills the sand and sawis in the air;
  But twice unhappier is he, I lairn,
That feidis in his hairt a mad desire,
And follows on a woman throw the fire,
  Led by a blind and teachit by a bairn.

ANON.

Go, heart, unto the lamp of licht

Go, heart, unto the lamp of licht,
  Go, heart, do service and honour,
Go, heart, and serve him day and nicht,
  Go, heart, unto thy Saviour.

Go, heart, to thy only remeid[2]
  Descending from the heavenly tour:
Thee to deliver from pyne and deide,[3]
  Go, heart, unto thy Saviour.

---

[1] overwhelmed.   [2] remedy.   [3] pain and death.

Go, heart, but[1] dissimulatioun,
    To Christ, that took our vile nature,
For thee to suffer passioun,
    Go, heart, unto thy Saviour.

Go, heart, richt humill and meek,
    Go, heart, as leal and true servitour,
To him that heill[2] is for all seek,[3]
    Go, heart, unto thy Saviour.

Go, heart, with true and haill intent,
    To Christ thy help and haill succour,
Thee to redeem he was all rent,
    Go, heart, unto thy Saviour.

To Christ, that raise from death to live,[4]
    Go, heart, unto thy latter hour,
Whais great mercy can nane discrive,[5]
    Go, heart, unto thy Saviour.

          (From *The Gude and Godlie Ballatis*, 1567.)

Ane Sang of the Birth of Christ, with the Tune of Baw Lula Low

My saul and life stand up and see
Wha lyis in ane crib of tree.
What Babe is that, sa gude and fair?
It is Christ, Goddis son and heir.

Welcome now, gracious God of micht,
To sinners vile, puir, and unricht.
Thou come to save us from distress;
How can we thank thy gentleness?

---

[1] without.   [2] health.   [3] sick.   [4] life.   [5] describe.

O God that made all creature,
How art thou now becumit sa puir,
That on the hay and stray will lie,
Amang the asses, oxen, and kye!

And war the warld ten times sa wide,
Cled owre with gold and stanes of pride,
Unworthy it war, yet to thee,
Under thy feet ane stool to be.

The silk and sandell[1] thee to ease,
Are hay, and simple sweilling[2] claes,
Wherein thou glories, greatest King,
As thou in heaven war in thy Ring.[3]

Thou took sic painis temporal,
To make me rich perpetual,
For all this warldis wealth and gude
Can nathing rich thy celsitude.

O my dear heart, young Jesus sweet,
Prepare thy cradle for my spreit,
And I sall rock thee in my heart,
And never mair fra thee depart.

But I sall praise thee evermore
With sangis sweet unto thy gloir;
The knees of my heart sall I bow,
And sing this richt Balulalow.

Gloir be to God eternallie,
Whilk gave his only Son for me:
The angellis joyis for to hear
The gracious gift of this New Year.

(From *The Gude and Godlie Ballatis*, 1567—a translation of
Luther's hymn for Christmas Eve 'Vom himel hoch da
kom ich her'.   The first six stanzas are omitted.)

[1] sendal, rich silk.   [2] swaddling.   [3] kingdom.

Welcome, Fortune

WELCOME, Fortune, welcome again,
The day and hour I may weel bliss,[1]
Thou has exilit all my pain,
Whilk to my heart great pleasure is.

For I may say, that few men may,
Seeing of pain I am drest,[2]
I have obtainit all my pay,—
The love of her that I love best.

I knaw nane sic as sho is one,
Sa true, sa kind, sa lovandly,
What suld I do, an sho war gone?
Alas! yet had I lever[3] die.

To me sho is baith true and kind,
Worthy it war sho had the praise,
For na disdain in her I find,
I pray to God I may her please.

When that I hear her name exprest,
My heart for joy does loup[4] therefor.
Above all other I love her best,
Until I die, what wald sho more?

(From *The Gude and Godlie Ballatis*, 1567.)

SIR RICHARD MAITLAND
1496–1586

Against the Thieves of Liddesdale

OF Liddesdale the common thieves
Sa pertly steals now and reives

---

[1] bless.   [2] redressed.   [3] rather.   [4] leap.

That nane can keep,
Horse, nowt,[1] or sheep,
Nor yet daur sleep,
For their mischieves.

They plainly through the country rides;
I trow the meikle deil them guides.
Where they on set
Aye in they get,
There is na yett[2]
Nor door them bides.

They leave richt nocht where'er they gae;
There can nathing be hid them frae,
For gif men wald
Their houses hald,
Then wax they bauld
To burn and slay.

They have nearhand harriet hale
Ettrick Forest and Lauderdale;
Now are they gane
In Lothiane,
And sparis nane
That they will wale.

Thai landis is with stouthe[3] sa socht
To extreme poverty are brocht,
Thai wicked shrewis
Has laid the plewis
That nane or few is
That are left ocht.

By common taking of blackmail
They that had flesh, gude bread and ale

---

[1] cattle.   [2] barred gate.   [3] stealing.

Now are sa wrackit,
Made puir and naked,
Fain to be stakit[1]
With water kale.

Thai theves that steals and turses[2] hame
Ilkane[3] of them has ane to-name[4];
Will of the Laws,
Hob of the Shaws,
To make bare wa's
They think na shame.

They spuilye puir men of their packs;
They leave them nocht on bed nor backs;
Baith hen and cock,
With reel and rock,[5]
The Lairdis Jock,
All with him taks.

They leave not spindle, spoon, nor speit,[6]
Bed, bouster, blanket, sark, nor sheet;
John of the Park
Ripes kist and ark,[7]
For all sic wark
He is richt meet.

He is weel kenned John of the Side,
A greater thief did never ride;
He never tires
For to brek byres—
Owre muir and mires
Owre guid a guide.

There is ane callit Clement's Hob
Fra ilk puir wife reivis their wob[8];

---

[1] supplied.   [2] carry.   [3] each.   [4] nickname.
[5] distaff.   [6] spit.   [7] chest.   [8] web.

And all the lave,
Whatever they have
The deil receive
Therefore his gob.[1]

To see sa grit stouthe wha wald trow it
Unless some grit man it allowit,
Richt sair I rue
Though it be true,
There is sa few
That dare avow it.

Of some grit men they have sic gait[2]
That ready are them to debate,[3]
And will upweir[4]
Their stollen gear
That nane daur steer
Them air or late.

What causes thevis us owregang[5]
But want of justice us amang;
Nane takis care,
Though all forfare,[6]
Na man will spare
Now to do wrang.

Of stouthe now though they come guid speed
That nowder of God nor man has dreid,
Yet or I dee
Some sall them see
Hing on a tree
Till they be deid.

---

[1] mouth.   [2] influence.   [3] champion.   [4] defend.
[5] oppress.   [6] perish.

ALEXANDER HUME
1557?–1609

Of the Day Estivall[1]

O PERFECT Light, whilk shed away,
    The darkness from the light,
And set a ruler o'er the day,
    Ane other o'er the night.

Thy glory when the day forth flies,
    Mair vively[2] does appear,
Nor[3] at midday unto our eyes,
    The shining sun is clear.

The shadow of the earth anon,
    Removes and drawes by,
Syne in the east, when it is gone,
    Appears a clearer sky.

Whilk sun perceives the little larks,[4]
    The lapwing and the snipe,
And tunes their sangs like Nature's clerks,
    O'er meadow, muir, and stryp.[5]

But every bais'd[6] nocturnal beast,
    Na langer may abide,
They hie away baith maist and least
    Themselves in howes[7] to hide.

They dread the day fra they it see,
    And from the sight of men,
To saits and covers[8] fast they flee,
    As lions to their den.

---

[1] summer.   [2] vividly.   [3] than.   [4] which sun the little larks, &c. perceive.   [5] rill.   [6] abased.   [7] hollows. [8] retreats and coverts.

Our hemisphere is polished clear,
   And lightened more and more,
While every thing be clearly seen,
   Whilk seemed dim before.

Except the glistering astres bright,
   Which all the night were clear,
Offusked[1] with a greater light,
   Na langer does appear.

For joy the birds with boulden[2] throats,
   Agains his visage sheen,
Takes up their kindly[3] music notes,
   In woods and gardens green.

Up braids[4] the careful husbandman,
   His corns and vines to see,
And every timeous[5] artizan
   In booth work busily.

The pastor quits the slothful sleep,
   And passes forth with speed,
His little camow[6]-nosed sheep,
   And routing[7] kye to feed.

The passenger from perils sure,
   Gangs gladly forth the way:
Brief, every living creature,
   Takes comfort of the day.

The subtle mottie rayons[8] light,
   At rifts they are in wonne,[9]
The glancing thains,[10] and vitre[11] bright,
   Resplends against the sun.

---

[1] obscured.   [2] swollen.   [3] natural.   [4] hastens.
[5] early rising.   [6] crooked.   [7] lowing.   [8] rays full
of motes.   [9] have entered.   [10] vanes.   [11] glass.

The dew upon the tender crops,
    Like pearles white and round,
Or like to melted silver drops,
    Refreshes all the ground.

The misty rock,[1] the clouds of rain,
    From tops of mountains skails,[2]
Clear are the highest hills and plain,
    The vapour takes the vales.

Begaried[3] is the sapphire pend,[4]
    With spraigns[5] of scarlet hue,
And preciously from end to end,
    Damasked white and blue.

The ample heaven of fabric sure
    In cleanness doth surpass,
The crystal and the silver pure,
    Or clearest poleist glass.

The time sa tranquil is and still,
    That na where sall ye find,
Save on ane high and barren hill,
    Ane air of peeping[6] wind.

All trees and simples[7] great and small,
    That balmy leaf do bear,
Nor they were painted in a wall,
    Na mair they move or steer.

Calm is the deep and purpour sea,
    Yea, smoother nor the sand,
The waves that woltring wont to be,
    Are stable like the land.

---

[1] vapour.   [2] melts.   [3] variegated.   [4] vault (of
the sky).   [5] streaks.   [6] whispering.   [7] herbs.

So silent is the cessile[1] air,
   That every cry and call,
The hills, and dales, and forest fair,
   Again repeats them all.

The rivers fresh, the caller[2] streams,
   O'er rocks can softly rin;
The water clear like crystal seems,
   And makes a pleasant din.

The fields, and earthly superfice,[3]
   With verdure green is spread,
And naturally, but[4] artifice,
   In party colours cled.

The flourishes[5] and fragrant flowers,
   Through Phoebus' fost'ring heat
Refreshed with dew and silver showers,
   Casts up ane odour sweet.

The clogged busy humming bees,
   That never thinks to drown,
On flowers and flourishes of trees
   Collects their liquor brown.

The sun maist like a speedy post,
   With ardent course ascends;
The beauty of the heavenly host
   Up to the zenith tends.

Nocht guided by na Phaeton,
   Nor trained in a chyre,[6]
But by the high and haly One,
   Whilk does all where empire.

---

[1] yielding.   [2] cool.   [3] surface of the earth.
[4] without.   [5] blossom on trees or shrubs.   [6] drawn in a chariot.

The burning beams down from his face
    Sa fervently can beat,
That man and beast now seeks a place
    To save them fra the heat.

The breathless flocks draws to the shade,
    And fraicheur of their fauld;
The startling nolt[1] as they were mad
    Runs to the rivers cauld.

The herds beneath some leafy tree
    Amids the flowers they lie;
The stable ships upon the sea
    Tends up their sails to dry.

The hart, the hind, and fallow deer,
    Are tapisht[2] at their rest;
The fowls and birds that made the beir[3]
    Prepares their pretty nest.

The rayons dour[4] descending down
    All kindles in a gleid[5];
In city nor in boroughstown[6]
    May nane set forth their heid.

Back from the blue paymented whun,[7]
    And from ilk plaister wall,
The hot reflexing of the sun
    Inflames the air and all.

The labourers that timely raise,[8]
    All weary, faint, and weak,
For heat down to their houses gais,
    Noon-meat and sleep to take.

---

[1] cattle.   [2] crouching.   [3] sound.   [4] keen.
[5] flame.   [6] burgh.   [7] whinstone used for a pavement.   [8] rose early.

The caller wine in cave[1] is sought,
　　Men's brothing[2] breasts to cool;
The water cauld and clear is brought,
　　And sallets[3] steept in ule.[4]

Some plucks the honey plum and pear,
　　The cherry and the pêche;
Some likes the reamand[5] London beer,
　　The body to refresh.

Forth of their skeps[6] some raging bees
　　Lies out and will not cast[7];
Some other swarms hives on the trees
　　In knots togidder fast.

The corbies[8] and the keckling kais[9]
　　May scarce the heat abide;
Hawks prunyeis[10] on the sunny braes,
　　And wedders, back and side.

With gilted eyes and open wings,
　　The cock his courage shaws;
With claps of joy his breast he dings,[11]
　　And twenty times he craws.

The doo[12] with whistling wings sa blue,
　　The winds can fast collect,
Her purpour pens[13] turns mony hue
　　Against the sun direct.

Now noon is went; gane is midday;
　　The heat does slake at last;
The sun descends down west away,
　　Fra three o'clock be past.

---

[1] cellar.　　[2] steaming.　　[3] salads.　　[4] oil.
[5] foaming.　　[6] hives.　　[7] swarm.　　[8] crows.　　[9] jackdaws.　　[10] preen themselves.　　[11] strikes.　　[12] dove.
[13] wings.

A little cool of braithing wind
   Now softly can arise;
The warks through heat that lay behind
   Now men may enterprise.

Furth fares the flocks to seek their food
   On every hill and plain;
Ilk[1] labourer as he thinks good
   Steps to his turn again.

The rayons of the sun we see
   Diminish in their strength;
The shade of every tower and tree
   Extended is in length.

Great is the calm, for everywhere
   The wind is sitten down;
The reek[2] thraws[3] right up in the air
   From every tower and town.

Their firdoning[4] the bonnie birds
   In banks they do begin;
With pipes of reeds the jolly herds
   Halds up the merry din.

The mavis and the philomene,[5]
   The starling whistles loud;
The cushats[6] on the branches green
   Full quietly they crowd.[7]

The gloaming comes; the day is spent;
   The sun goes out of sight;
And painted is the occident
   With purpour sanguine bright.

---

[1] each.   [2] smoke.   [3] rises in a spiral.   [4] piping.
[5] nightingale.   [6] wood pigeons.   [7] coo.

The scarlet nor the golden thread,
  Who would their beauty try,
Are nothing like the colour red
  And beauty of the sky.

Our west horizon circular,
  Fra time the sun be set,
Is all with rubies, as it were,
  Or roses red o'erfret.

What pleasure were to walk and see,
  Endlang a river clear,
The perfect form of every tree
  Within the deep appear.

The salmon out of cruives and creels[1]
  Up hailed into skowts[2];
The bells, and circles on the weills,[3]
  Through louping[4] of the trouts.

O then it were a seemly thing,
  While all is still and calm,
The praise of God to play and sing,
  With cornet and with shalm.

But now the herds with mony shout
  Calls other by their name;
'Ga, Billie, turn our good about.
  Now time is to go hame.'

With belly fu' the beasts belyve[5]
  Are turned fra the corn,
Whilk soberly they hameward drive,
  With pipe and lilting horn.

---

[1] osier-traps for fish.   [2] boats.   [3] pools.   [4] leaping.
[5] straightway.

Through all the land great is the gild[1]
    Of rustic folks that cry,
Of bleating sheep fra they be filled,
    Of calves and routing kye.

All labourers draws hame at even,
    And can till other say,
Thanks to the gracious God of heaven
    Whilk sent this summer day.

ANONYMOUS

Sir Patrick Spens

THE King sits in Dunfermline town,
    Drinking the blude-red wine;
'O whare will I get a skeely skipper,
    To sail this new ship of mine?'—

O up and spake an eldern knight,
    Sat at the King's right knee,—
'Sir Patrick Spens is the best sailor,
    That ever sailed the sea.'--

Our King has written a braid letter,
    And seal'd it with his hand,
And sent it to Sir Patrick Spens,
    Was walking on the strand.

'To Noroway, to Noroway,
    To Noroway o'er the faem;
The King's daughter of Noroway,
    'Tis thou maun bring her hame.'

[1] noise.

The first word that Sir Patrick read,
  Sae loud loud laughed he;
The neist word that Sir Patrick read,
  The tear blinded his ee.

'O wha is this has done this deed,
  And tauld the King o' me,
To send us out, at this time of the year,
  To sail upon the sea?

'Be it wind, be it weet, be it hail, be it sleet,
  Our ship must sail the faem;
The King's daughter of Noroway,
  'Tis we must fetch her hame.'—

They hoysed their sails on Monenday morn,
  Wi' a' the speed they may;
They hae landed in Noroway,
  Upon a Wodensday.

They hadna been a week, a week,
  In Noroway, but twae,
When that the lords o' Noroway
  Began aloud to say,—

'Ye Scottishmen spend a' our King's gowd,
  And a' our Queenis fee.'—
'Ye lie, ye lie, ye liars loud!
  Fu' loud I hear ye lie;

'For I brought as much white monie,
  As gane my men and me,
And I brought a half-fou[1] of gude red gowd,
  Out o'er the sea wi' me.

'Make ready, make ready, my merrymen a'!
  Our gude ship sails the morn.'—
'Now, ever alake, my master dear,
  I fear a deadly storm!

[1] eighth of a peck.

'I saw the new moon, late yestreen,
  Wi' the auld moon in her arm;
And, if we gang to sea, master,
  I fear we'll come to harm.'

They hadna sail'd a league, a league,
  A league but barely three,
When the lift grew dark, and the wind blew loud,
  And gurly[1] grew the sea.

The ankers brak, and the topmasts lap,
  It was sic a deadly storm;
And the waves cam o'er the broken ship,
  Till a' her sides were torn.

'O where will I get a gude sailor,
  To take my helm in hand,
Till I get up to the tall top-mast,
  To see if I can spy land?'—

'O here am I, a sailor gude,
  To take the helm in hand,
Till you go up to the tall top-mast;
  But I fear you'll ne'er spy land.'—

He hadna gane a step, a step,
  A step but barely ane,
When a bout[2] flew out of our goodly ship,
  And the salt sea it came in.

'Gae, fetch a web o' the silken claith,
  Another o' the twine,
And wap[3] them into our ship's side,
  And let nae the sea come in.'—

They fetch'd a web o' the silken claith,
  Another o' the twine,

---

[1] boisterous.   [2] bolt.   [3] wrap.

And they wapp'd them round that gude ship's
    side,
  But still the sea cam in.

O laith, laith, were our gude Scots lords
  To weet their cork-heel'd shoon!
But lang or a' the play was play'd,
  They wat their hats aboon.

And mony was the feather bed,
  That flatter'd on the faem;
And mony was the gude lord's son,
  That never mair cam hame.

The ladyes wrang their fingers white,
  The maidens tore their hair,
A' for the sake of their true loves;
  For them they'll see nae mair.

O lang, lang, may the ladyes sit,
  Wi' their fans into their hand,
Before they see Sir Patrick Spens
  Come sailing to the strand!

And lang, lang, may the maidens sit,
  With their gowd kaims in their hair,
A' waiting for their ain dear loves!
  For them they'll see nae mair.

Half-owre, half-owre to Aberdour,
  'Tis fifty fathoms deep,
And there lies gude Sir Patrick Spens,
  Wi' the Scots lords at his feet.

The Battle of Otterbourne

It fell about the Lammas tide,
  When the muir-men win their hay,
The doughty Douglas bound him to ride
  Into England, to drive a prey.

He chose the Gordons and the Græmes,
    With them the Lindesays, light and gay
But the Jardines wald not with him ride,
    And they rue it to this day.

And he has burn'd the dales of Tyne,
    And part of Bambrough shire;
And three good towers on Reidswire fells,
    He left them all on fire.

And he march'd up to Newcastle,
    And rode it round about;
'O wha's the lord of this castle,
    Or wha's the lady o't?'—

But up spake proud Lord Percy, then,
    And O but he spake hie!
'I am the lord of this castle,
    My wife's the lady gay.'

'If thou'rt the lord of this castle,
    Sae weel it pleases me!
For, ere I cross the Border fells,
    The tane of us shall die.'—

He took a lang spear in his hand,
    Shod with the metal free,
And for to meet the Douglas there,
    He rode right furiouslie.

But O how pale his lady look'd,
    Frae aff the castle wa',
When down before the Scottish spear
    She saw proud Percy fa'.

'Had we twa been upon the green,
    And never an eye to see,
I wad hae had you, flesh and fell;
    But your sword sall gae wi' me.'—

'But gae ye up to Otterbourne,
  And wait there dayis three;
And, if I come not ere three dayis end,
  A fause knight ca' ye me.'—

'The Otterbourne 's a bonnie burn;
  'Tis pleasant there to be;
But there is nought at Otterbourne,
  To feed my men and me.

'The deer rins wild on hill and dale,
  The birds fly wild from tree to tree;
But there is neither bread nor kale,
  To fend my men and me.

'Yet I will stay at Otterbourne,
  Where you shall welcome be;
And, if ye come not at three dayis end,
  A fause lord I'll ca' thee.'—

'Thither will I come,' proud Percy said,
  'By the might of Our Ladye!'—
'There will I bide thee,' said the Douglas,
  'My troth I plight to thee.'

They lighted high on Otterbourne,
  Upon the bent sae brown;
They lighted high on Otterbourne,
  And threw their pallions down.

And he that had a bonnie boy,
  Sent out his horse to grass;
And he that had not a bonnie boy,
  His ain servant he was.

But up then spake a little page,
  Before the peep of dawn—
'O waken ye, waken ye, my good lord,
  For Percy 's hard at hand.'—

'Ye lie, ye lie, ye liar loud!
  Sae loud I hear ye lie:
For Percy had not men yestreen
  To dight my men and me.

'But I have dream'd a dreary dream,
  Beyond the Isle of Skye;
I saw a dead man win a fight,
  And I think that man was I.'

He belted on his guid braid sword,
  And to the field he ran;
But he forgot the helmet good,
  That should have kept his brain.

When Percy wi' the Douglas met,
  I wat he was fu' fain!
They swakked their swords, till sair they swat,
  And the blood ran down like rain.

But Percy with his good broad sword,
  That could so sharply wound,
Has wounded Douglas on the brow,
  Till he fell to the ground.

Then he call'd on his little foot-page,
  And said—'Run speedilie,
And fetch my ain dear sister's son,
  Sir Hugh Montgomery.

'My nephew good,' the Douglas said,
  'What recks the death of ane!
Last night I dream'd a dreary dream,
  And I ken the day's thy ain.

'My wound is deep; I fain would sleep;
  Take thou the vanguard of the three,
And hide me by the braken bush,
  That grows on yonder lilye lee.

'O bury me by the braken bush,
  Beneath the blooming brier,
Let never living mortal ken,
  That ere a kindly Scot lies here.'

He lifted up that noble lord,
  Wi' the saut tear in his ee;
He hid him in the braken bush,
  That his merrie-men might not see.

The moon was clear, the day drew near,
  The spears in flinders flew,
But mony a gallant Englishman
  Ere day the Scotsmen slew.

The Gordons good, in English blood,
  They steep'd their hose and shoon;
The Lindsays flew like fire about,
  Till all the fray was done.

The Percy and Montgomery met,
  That either of other were fain;
They swapped swords, and they twa swat,
  And aye the blood ran down between.

'Now yield thee, yield thee, Percy,' he said,
  'Or else I vow I'll lay thee low!'—
'To whom must I yield,' quoth Earl Percy,
  'Now that I see it must be so?'—

'Thou shalt not yield to lord nor loun,
  Nor yet shalt thou yield to me;
But yield thee to the braken bush,
  That grows upon yon lilye lee!'—

'I will not yield to a braken bush,
  Nor yet will I yield to a brier;
But I would yield to Earl Douglas,
  Or Sir Hugh the Montgomery, if he were here.'

As soon as he knew it was Montgomery,
  He struck his sword's point in the gronde;
The Montgomery was a courteous knight,
  And quickly took him by the honde.

This deed was done at the Otterbourne
  About the breaking of the day;
Earl Douglas was buried at the braken bush,
  And the Percy led captive away.

The Border Widow's Lament

I

My love he built me a bonny bower,
  And cled it a' wi' lilye flour;
A brawer bower ye ne'er did see,
  Than my true love he built to me.

II

There came a man by middle day,
  He spied his sport, and went away;
And brought the King that very night,
  Who brak my bower, and slew my knight.

III

He slew my knight, to me sae dear;
  He slew my knight, and poin'd[1] his gear;
My servants all for life did flee,
  And left me in extremitie.

IV

I sew'd his sheet, making my mane;
  I watch'd the corpse, myself alane;
I watch'd his body, night and day;
  No living creature came that way.

[1] made forfeit.

V

I took his body on my back,
And whiles I gaed, and whiles I sat;
I digg'd a grave, and laid him in,
And happ'd him with the sod sae green.

VI

But think na ye my heart was sair,
When I laid the mool on his yellow hair;
O think na ye my heart was wae,
When I turn'd about away to gae?

VII

Nae living man I'll love again,
Since that my lovely knight is slain;
Wi' ae lock of his yellow hair
I'll chain my heart for evermair.

Kinmont Willie

I

O HAVE ye na heard o' the fause Sakelde?
    O have ye na heard o' the keen Lord Scroope?
How they hae ta'en bauld Kinmont Willie,
    On Haribee to hang him up?

II

Had Willie had but twenty men,
    But twenty men as stout as he,
Fause Sakelde had never the Kinmont ta'en,
    Wi' eight score in his companie.

III

They band his legs beneath the steed,
    They tied his hands behind his back;
They guarded him, fivesome on each side,
    And they brought him ower the Liddel-rack.[1]

IV

They led him thro' the Lidde.-rack,
    And also thro' the Carlisle sands;
They brought him in to Carlisle castell,
    To be at my Lord Scroope's commands.

V

'My hands are tied, but my tongue is free,
    And whae will dare this deed avow?
Or answer by the Border law?
    Or answer to the bauld Buccleuch?'—

VI

'Now haud thy tongue, thou rank reiver!
    There's never a Scot shall set thee free:
Before ye cross my castle yate,
    I trow ye shall take farewell o' me.'

VII

'Fear na ye that, my lord,' quo' Willie:
    'By the faith o' my body, Lord Scroope,' he said,
'I never yet lodged in a hostelrie
    But I paid my lawing[2] before I gaed.'

VIII

Now word is gane to the bauld Keeper,
    In Branksome Ha', where that he lay,
That Lord Scroope has ta'en the Kinmont Willie,
    Between the hours of night and day.

---

[1] a ford on the Liddel.   [2] reckoning.

IX

He has ta'en the table wi' his hand,
   He garr'd the red wine spring on hie—
'Now Christ's curse on my head,' he said,
   'But avengèd of Lord Scroope I'll be!

X

'O is my basnet a widow's curch?[1]
   Or my lance a wand of the willow-tree?
Or my arm a ladye's lilye hand,
   That an English lord should lightly[2] me!

XI

'And have they ta'en him, Kinmont Willie,
   Against the truce of Border tide?
And forgotten that the bauld Buccleuch
   Is Keeper here on the Scottish side?

XII

'And have they e'en ta'en him, Kinmont Willie,
   Withouten either dread or fear?
And forgotten that the bauld Buccleuch
   Can back a steed, or shake a spear?

XIII

'O were there war between the lands,
   As well I wot that there is nane,
I would slight Carlisle castell high,
   Though it were builded of marble stane.

XIV

'I would set that castell in a low,[3]
   And sloken it with English blood!
There 's never a man in Cumberland
   Should ken where Carlisle castell stood.

---

[1] kerchief, coif.   [2] treat disrespectfully.   [3] flame.

XV

'But since nae war 's between the lands,
   And there is peace, and peace should be;
I'll neither harm English lad or lass,
   And yet the Kinmont freed shall be!'

XVI

He has call'd him forty Marchmen bauld,
   I trow they were of his ain name,
Except Sir Gilbert Elliot, call'd
   The Laird of Stobs, I mean the same.

XVII

He has call'd him forty Marchmen bauld,
   Were kinsmen to the bauld Buccleuch;
With spur on heel, and splent[1] on spauld,[2]
   And gleuves of green, and feathers blue.

XVIII

There were five and five before them a',
   Wi' hunting-horns and bugles bright:
And five and five came wi' Buccleuch,
   Like Warden's men, array'd for fight.

XIX

And five and five, like a mason-gang,
   That carried the ladders lang and hie;
And five and five, like broken men;
   And so they reach'd the Woodhouselee.

XX

And as we cross'd the Bateable Land,[3]
   When to the English side we held,
The first o' men that we met wi',
   Whae sould it be but fause Sakelde?

---

[1] split, or overlapping armour.   [2] shoulder, épaule.
[3] debatable land; a stretch of frontier between the Solway
Firth and Scots Dyke, claimed by both nations.

XXI

'Where be ye gaun, ye hunters keen?'
  Quo' fause Sakelde; 'come tell to me!'—
'We go to hunt an English stag,
  Has trespass'd on the Scots countrie.'

XXII

'Where be ye gaun, ye marshal men?'
  Quo' fause Sakelde; 'come tell me true!'—
'We go to catch a rank reiver,
  Has broken faith wi' the bauld Buccleuch.'

XXIII

'Where be ye gaun, ye mason lads,
  Wi' a' your ladders, lang and hie?'—
'We gang to herry a corbie's nest,
  That wons not far frae Woodhouselee.'—

XXIV

'Where be ye gaun, ye broken men?'
  Quo' fause Sakelde; 'come tell to me!'—
Now Dickie of Dryhope led that band,
  And the never a word of lear[1] had he.

XXV

'Why trespass ye on the English side?
  Row-footed[2] outlaws, stand!' quo' he;
The never a word had Dickie to say,
  Sae he thrust the lance through his fause bodie.

XXVI

Then on we held for Carlisle toun,
  And at Staneshaw-bank the Eden we cross'd;
The water was great and meikle of spate,
  But the never a horse nor man we lost

---

[1] lore.   [2] rough-footed.

XXVII

And when we reach'd the Staneshaw-bank,
  The wind was rising loud and hie;
And there the Laird gar'd leave our steeds,
  For fear that they should stamp and neigh.

XXVIII

And when we left the Staneshaw-bank,
  The wind began fu' loud to blaw;
But 'twas wind and weet, and fire and sleet,
  When we came beneath the castle wa'.

XXIX

We crept on knees, and held our breath,
  Till we placed the ladders against the wa';
And sae ready was Buccleuch himsell
  To mount the first before us a'.

XXX

He has ta'en the watchman by the throat,
  He flung him down upon the lead—
'Had there not been peace between our lands,
  Upon the other side thou hadst gaed!—

XXXI

'Now sound out, trumpets!' quo' Buccleuch;
  'Let 's waken Lord Scroope right merrilie!'
Then loud the Warden's trumpet blew—
  O wha dare meddle wi' me?

XXXII

Then speedilie to wark we gaed,
  And raised the slogan ane and a',
And cut a hole through a sheet of lead,
  And so we wan to the castle ha'.

XXXIII

They thought King James and a' his men
  Had won the house wi' bow and spear;
It was but twenty Scots and ten,
  That put a thousand in sic a stear![1]

XXXIV

Wi' coulters, and wi' forehammers,[2]
  We gar'd the bars bang merrilie,
Until we came to the inner prison,
  Where Willie o' Kinmont he did lie.

XXXV

And when we cam to the lower prison,
  Where Willie o' Kinmont he did lie—
'O sleep ye, wake ye, Kinmont Willie,
  Upon the morn that thou's to die?'—

XXXVI

'O I sleep saft, and I wake aft;
  It's lang since sleeping was fley'd[3] frae me!
Gie my service back to my wife and bairns,
  And a' gude fellows that spier[4] for me.'

XXXVII

The Red Rowan has hente him up,
  The starkest man in Teviotdale—
'Abide, abide now, Red Rowan,
  Till of my Lord Scroope I take farewell.

XXXVIII

'Farewell, farewell, my gude Lord Scroope!
  My gude Lord Scroope, farewell!' he cried;
'I'll pay you for my lodging mail,[5]
  When first we meet on the Border side.'—

---

  [1] stir, commotion.   [2] sledge-hammers.   [3] scared.
[4] inquire.   [5] rent.

XXXIX

Then shoulder high, with shout and cry,
  We bore him down the ladder lang;
At every stride Red Rowan made,
  I wot the Kinmont's airns play'd clang!

XL

'O mony a time,' quo' Kinmont Willie,
  'I have ridden horse baith wild and wood[1];
But a rougher beast than Red Rowan
  I ween my legs have ne'er bestrode.

XLI

And mony a time,' quo' Kinmont Willie,
  'I've prick'd a horse out oure the furs[2];
But since the day I back'd a steed,
  I never wore sic cumbrous spurs!'

XLII

We scarce had won the Staneshaw-bank
  When a' the Carlisle bells were rung,
And a thousand men on horse and foot
  Cam wi' the keen Lord Scroope along.

XLIII

Buccleuch has turn'd to Eden Water,
  Even where it flow'd frae bank to brim,
And he has plunged in wi' a' his band,
  And safely swam them through the stream.

XLIV

He turn'd him on the other side,
  And at Lord Scroope his glove flung he;
'If ye like na my visit in merry England,
  In fair Scotland come visit me!'

                    [1] mad.   [2] furrows.

XLV

All sore astonish'd stood Lord Scroope,
  He stood as still as rock of stane;
He scarcely dared to trew[1] his eyes,
  When through the water they had gane.

XLVI

'He is either himsell a devil frae hell,
  Or else his mother a witch maun be;
I wadna have ridden that wan water
  For a' the gowd in Christentie.'

Jamie Telfer in the Fair Dodhead

I

It fell about the Martinmas tyde,
  When our Border steeds get corn and hay,
The Captain of Bewcastle bound him to ryde,
  And he's ower to Tividale to drive a prey.

II

The first ae guide that they met wi',
  It was high up in Hardhaughswire;
The second guide that they met wi',
  It was laigh[2] down in Borthwick water.

III

'What tidings, what tidings, my trusty guide?'—
  'Nae tidings, nae tidings, I hae to thee;
But gin ye'll gae to the fair Dodhead,
  Mony a cow's cauf I'll let thee see.'

IV

And when they cam to the fair Dodhead,
  Right hastily they clam the peel[3];
They loosed the kye out, ane and a',
  And ranshackled the house right weel.

    [1] trust.   [2] low.   [3] stockade or wall.

V

Now Jamie Telfer's heart was sair,
    The tear aye rowing[1] in his ee;
He pled wi' the Captain to hae his gear,
    Or else revengèd he wad be.

VI

The Captain turned him round and leugh;
    Said—'Man, there's naething in thy house,
But ae auld sword without a sheath,
    That hardly now would fell a mouse.'

VII

The sun wasna up, but the moon was down,
    It was the gryming[2] of a new-fa'n snaw,
Jamie Telfer has run ten myles a-foot,
    Between the Dodhead and the Stobs's Ha'.

VIII

And when he cam to the fair tower-yate,
    He shouted loud, and cried weel hie,
Till out bespak auld Gibby Elliot—
    'Whae's this that brings the fraye[3] to me?'—

IX

'It's I, Jamie Telfer in the fair Dodhead,
    And a harried man I think I be!
There's naething left at the fair Dodhead,
    But a waefu' wife and bairnies three.'

X

'Gae seek your succour at Branksome Ha',
    For succour ye'se get nane frae me!
Gae seek your succour where ye paid black-mail,
    For, man, ye ne'er paid money to me.'—

    [1] rolling.   [2] sprinkling.   [3] fright, alarm.

XI

Jamie has turned him round about,
  I wat the tear blinded his ee—
'I'll ne'er pay mail to Elliot again,
  And the fair Dodhead I'll never see.

XII

'My hounds may a' rin masterless,
  My hawks may fly frae tree to tree,
My lord may grip my vassal lands,
  For there again maun I never be!'—

XIII

He has turn'd him to the Tiviot-side,
  E'en as fast as he could drie,
Till he cam to the Coultart Cleugh,
  And there he shouted baith loud and hie.

XIV

Then up bespak him auld Jock Grieve,
  'Whae's this that brings the fraye to me?'—
'It's I, Jamie Telfer in the fair Dodhead,
  A harried man I trow I be.

XV

'There's naething left in the fair Dodhead.
  But a greeting wife and bairnies three,
And sax poor ca's[1] stand in the sta',
  A' routing loud for their minnie.'[2]—

XVI

'Alack a wae!' quo' auld Jock Grieve,
  'Alack! my heart is sair for thee!
For I was married on the elder sister,
  And you on the youngest of a' the three.'

[1] calves. [2] mother.

XVII

Then he has ta'en out a bonny black,
  Was right weel fed with corn and hay,
And he's set Jamie Telfer on his back,
  To the Catslockhill to tak the fraye.

XVIII

And whan he cam to the Catslockhill,
  He shouted loud, and cried weel hie,
Till out and spak him William's Wat,
  'O whae's this brings the fraye to me?'—

XIX

'It's I, Jamie Telfer in the fair Dodhead,
  A harried man I think I be!
The Captain of Bewcastle has driven my gear;
  For God's sake rise, and succour me!'—

XX

'Alas for wae!' quoth William's Wat,
  'Alack, for thee my heart is sair!
I never cam by the fair Dodhead,
  That ever I fand thy basket bare.'

XXI

He's set his twa sons on coal-black steeds,
  Himsell upon a freckled gray,
And they are on wi' Jamie Telfer,
  To Branksome Ha' to tak the fraye.

XXII

And when they cam to Branksome Ha',
  They shouted a' baith loud and hie,
Till up and spak him auld Buccleuch,
  Said, 'Whae's this brings the fraye to me?'—

XXIII

'It's I, Jamie Telfer in the fair Dodhead,
　And a harried man I think I be!
There's nought left in the fair Dodhead,
　But a greeting wife and bairnies three.'—

XXIV

'Alack for wae!' quoth the gude auld lord,
　'And ever my heart is wae for thee!
But fye gar cry on Willie, my son,
　And see that he come to me speedilie!

XXV

'Gar warn the water,[1] braid and wide,
　Gar warn it sune and hastilie!
They that winna ride for Telfer's kye,
　Let them never look in the face o' me!

XXVI

'Warn Wat o' Harden, and his sons,
　Wi' them will Borthwick Water ride;
Warn Gaudilands, and Allanhaugh,
　And Gilmanscleugh, and Commonside.

XXVII

'Ride by the gate at Priesthaughswire,
　And warn the Currors o' the Lee;
As ye cum down the Hermitage Slack,
　Warn doughty Willie o' Gorrinberry.'

XXVIII

The Scotts they rade, the Scotts they ran,
　Sae starkly and sae steadilie!
And aye the ower-word o' the thrang
　Was—'Rise for Branksome readilie!'

---

[1] raise the cry along the waterside.

XXIX

The gear was driven the Frostylee up,
　　Frae the Frostylee unto the plain,
Whan Willie has look'd his men before,
　　And saw the kye right fast drivand.

XXX

'Whae drives thir kye?' 'gan Willie say,
　　'To make an outspeckle[1] o' me?'—
'It's I, the Captain o' Bewcastle, Willie;
　　I winna layne[2] my name for thee.'—

XXXI

'O will ye let Telfer's kye gae back?
　　Or will ye do aught for regard o' me?
Or, by the faith of my body,' quo' Willie Scott,
　　'I'se ware[3] my dame's cauf skin on thee!'—

XXXII

'I winna let the kye gae back,
　　Neither for thy love, nor yet thy fear;
But I will drive Jamie Telfer's kye,
　　In spite of every Scott that's here.'—

XXXIII

'Set on them, lads!' quo' Willie than;
　　'Fye, lads, set on them cruellie!
For ere they win to the Ritterford,
　　Mony a toom[4] saddle there sall be!'

XXXIV

Then till't[5] they gaed wi' heart and hand,
　　The blows fell thick as bickering hail;
And mony a horse ran masterless,
　　And mony a comely cheek was pale.

---

[1] laughing-stock.　　[2] lie, falsen.　　[3] spend, use my
mother's calf-skin whip.　　[4] empty.　　[5] to it.

XXXV

But Willie was stricken ower the head,
    And thro' the knapscap[1] the sword has gane;
And Harden grat[2] for very rage,
    Whan Willie on the grund lay slane.

XXXVI

But he's ta'en aff his gude steel cap,
    And thrice he's waved it in the air—
The Dinlay snaw was ne'er mair white
    Nor the lyart[3] locks of Harden's hair.

XXXVII

'Revenge! revenge!' auld Wat 'gan cry;
    'Fye, lads, lay on them cruellie!
We'll ne'er see Tiviot-side again,
    Or Willie's death revenged sall be.'

XXXVIII

O mony a horse ran masterless,
    The splinter'd lances flew on hie;
But or they wan to the Kershope ford,
    The Scotts had gotten the victory.

XXXIX

John o' Brigham there was slane,
    And John o' Barlow, as I heard say;
And thirty mae o' the Captain's men
    Lay bleeding on the grund that day.

XL

The Captain was run through the thick of the
        thigh,
    And broken was his right leg-bane;
If he had lived this hundred years,
    He had never been loved by woman again.

---

[1] headpiece.　　[2] wept.　　[3] grizzled.

XLI

'Hae back the kye!' the Captain said;
  'Dear kye, I trow, to some they be!
For gin I suld live a hundred years,
  There will ne'er fair lady smile on me.'

XLII

Then word is gane to the Captain's bride,
  Even in the bower where that she lay,
That her lord was prisoner in enemy's land,
  Since into Tividale he had led the way.

XLIII

'I wad lourd[1] have had a winding-sheet,
  And helped to put it ower his head,
Ere he had been disgraced by the Border Scot,
  Whan he ower Liddel his men did lead!'

XLIV

There was a wild gallant amang us a',
  His name was Watty wi' the Wudspurs,[2]
Cried—'On for his house in Stanegirthside,
  If ony man will ride with us!'

XLV

When they cam to the Stanegirthside,
  They dang wi' trees, and burst the door;
They loosed out a' the Captain's kye,
  And set them forth our lads before.

XLVI

There was an auld wyfe ayont the fire,
  A wee bit o' the Captain's kin—
'Whae dar loose out the Captain's kye,
  Or answer to him and his men?'—

[1] liefer, rather.   [2] hotspur, or madspur.

XLVII

'It's I, Watty Wudspurs, loose the kye,
  I winna layne my name frae thee!
And I will loose out the Captain's kye,
  In scorn of a' his men and he.'

XLVIII

Whan they cam to the fair Dodhead,
  They were a wellcum sight to see!
For instead of his ain ten milk kye,
  Jamie Telfer has gotten thirty and three.

XLIX

And he has paid the rescue shot,
  Baith wi' gowd and white monie;
And at the burial o' Willie Scott,
  I wat was mony a weeping e'e.

Bonny George Campbell

I

HIE upon Hielands,
    And laigh[1] upon Tay,
Bonny George Campbell
    Rade out on a day:
Saddled and bridled,
    Sae gallant to see,
Hame cam' his gude horse,
    But never cam' he.

II

Down ran his auld mither,
    Greetin'[2] fu' sair;
Out ran his bonny bride,
    Reaving[3] her hair;

---

[1] low.   [2] crying, lamenting.   [3] tearing.

'My meadow lies green,
  And my corn is unshorn,
My barn is to bigg,[1]
  And my babe is unborn.'

III

Saddled and bridled
  And booted rade he;
A plume in his helmet,
  A sword at his knee;
But toom[2] cam' his saddle
  A' bluidy to see,
O hame cam' his gude horse,
  But never cam' he!

Edom o' Gordon

I

It fell about the Martinmas,
  When the wind blew shrill and cauld,
Said Edom o' Gordon to his men,
  'We maun draw to a hauld.[3]

II

'And what a hauld sall we draw to,
  My merry men and me?
We will gae to the house o' the Rodes,
  To see that fair ladye.'

III

The lady stood on her castle wa',
  Beheld baith dale and down;
There she was 'ware of a host of men
  Cam' riding towards the town.[4]

---

[1] build.　　[2] empty.　　[3] place of shelter.　　[4] stead.

IV

'O see ye not, my merry men a',
  O see ye not what I see?
Methinks I see a host of men;
  I marvel wha they be.'

V

She ween'd it had been her lovely lord,
  As he cam riding hame;
It was the traitor, Edom o' Gordon,
  Wha reck'd nae sin nor shame.

VI

She had nae sooner buskit[1] hersell,
  And putten on her gown,
But Edom o' Gordon an' his men
  Were round about the town.

VII

They had nae sooner supper set,
  Nae sooner said the grace,
But Edom o' Gordon an' his men
  Were lighted about the place.

VIII

The lady ran up to her tower-head,
  Sae fast as she could hie,
To see if by her fair speeches
  She could wi' him agree.

IX

'Come doun to me, ye lady gay,
  Come doun, come doun to me;
This night sall ye lig within mine arms,
  To-morrow my bride sall be.'—

---

[1] attired.

X

'I winna come down, ye fals Gordon,
    I winna come down to thee;
I winna forsake my ain dear lord,
    That is sae far frae me.'—

XI

'Gie owre your house, ye lady fair,
    Gie owre your house to me;
Or I sall brenn yoursel therein,
    But and your babies three.'—

XII

'I winna gie owre, ye fals Gordon,
    To nae sic traitor as yee;
And if ye brenn my ain dear babes,
    My lord shall mak ye dree.[1]

XIII

'Now reach my pistol, Glaud, my man,
    And charge ye weel my gun;
For, but an I pierce that bluidy butcher,
    My babes, we been undone!'

XIV

She stood upon her castle wa',
    And let twa bullets flee:
She miss'd that bluidy butcher's heart,
    And only razed his knee.

XV

'Set fire to the house!' quo' fals Gordon,
    All wud[2] wi' dule and ire:
'Fals lady, ye sall rue this deid
    As ye brenn in the fire!'—

---

[1] suffer.   [2] mad.

XVI

'Wae worth, wae worth ye, Jock, my man!
  I paid ye weel your fee;
Why pu' ye out the grund-wa' stane,[1]
  Lets in the reek to me?

XVII

'And e'en wae worth ye, Jock, my man!
  I paid ye weel your hire;
Why pu' ye out the grund-wa' stane,
  To me lets in the fire?'—

XVIII

'Ye paid me weel my hire, ladye,
  Ye paid me weel my fee:
But now I'm Edom o' Gordon's man,
  Maun either do or dee.'

XIX

O then bespake her little son,
  Sat on the nurse's knee:
Says, 'Mither dear, gie owre this house,
  For the reek it smithers me.'—

XX

'I wad gie a' my gowd, my bairn,
  Sae wad I a' my fee,
For ae blast o' the western wind,
  To blaw the reek frae thee.'

XXI

O then bespake her dochter dear—
  She was baith jimp[2] and sma':
'O row me in a pair o' sheets,
  And tow me owre the wa'!'

---

[1] stone closing a garderobe flue.   [2] slender, trim.

XXII

They row'd[1] her in a pair o' sheets,
  And tow'd her owre the wa';
But on the point o' Gordon's spear
  She gat a deadly fa'.

XXIII

O bonnie, bonnie was her mouth,
  And cherry were her cheiks,
And clear, clear was her yellow hair,
  Whereon the red blood dreips.

XXIV

Then wi' his spear he turn'd her owre;
  O gin her face was wane!
He said, 'Ye are the first that e'er
  I wish'd alive again.'

XXV

He turn'd her owre and owre again;
  O gin her skin was white!
'I might hae spared that bonnie face
  To hae been some man's delight.

XXVI

'Busk and boun,[2] my merry men a',
  For ill dooms I do guess;
I canna look in that bonnie face
  As it lies on the grass.'—

XXVII

'Wha looks to freits,[3] my master dear,
  It's freits will follow them;
Let it ne'er be said that Edom o' Gordon
  Was daunted by a dame.'

[1] wrapped. [2] trim up and prepare to go. [3] ill omens.

XXVIII

But when the lady saw the fire
  Come flaming owre her head,
She wept, and kiss'd her children twain,
  Says, 'Bairns, we been but dead.'

XXIX

The Gordon then his bugle blew,
  And said, 'Awa', awa'!
This house o' the Rodes is a' in a flame;
  I hauld it time to ga'.'

XXX

And this way lookit her ain dear lord,
  As he cam owre the lea;
He saw his castle a' in a lowe,[1]
  As far as he could see.

XXXI

Then sair, O sair, his mind misgave,
  And all his heart was wae:
'Put on, put on, my wighty[2] men,
  Sae fast as ye can gae.

XXXII

'Put on, put on, my wighty men,
  Sae fast as ye can drie!
For he that's hindmost o' the thrang
  Sall ne'er get good o' me.'

XXXIII

Then some they rade, and some they ran,
  Out-owre the grass and bent;
But ere the foremost could win up,
  Baith lady and babes were brent.

---

[1] flame.   [2] sturdy, active.

XXXIV

And after the Gordon he is gane,
    Sae fast as he might drie;
And soon i' the Gordon's foul heart's blude
    He's wroken[1] his dear ladye.

The Bonny Earl o' Moray

I

YE Highlands and ye Lawlands,
    O where hae ye been?
They hae slain the Earl o' Moray,
    And hae laid him on the green.

II

Now wae be to thee, Huntley!
    And whairfore did ye sae!
I bade you bring him wi' you,
    But forbade you him to slay.

III

He was a braw gallant,
    And he rid at the ring;
And the bonny Earl o' Moray,
    O he might hae been a king!

IV

He was a braw gallant,
    And he play'd at the ba';
And the bonny Earl o' Moray
    Was the flower amang them a'!

V

He was a braw gallant,
    And he play'd at the gluve;
And the bonny Earl o' Moray,
    O he was the Queen's luve!

[1] avenged.

VI

O lang will his Lady
    Look owre the Castle Downe,
Ere she see the Earl o' Moray
    Come sounding through the town!

The Twa Corbies[1]

I

As I was walking all alane,
I heard twa corbies making a mane:
The tane unto the tither did say,
'Whar sall we gang and dine the day?'

II

'—In behint yon auld fail[2] dyke
I wot there lies a new-slain knight;
And naebody kens that he lies there
But his hawk, his hound, and his lady fair.

III

'His hound is to the hunting gane,
His hawk to fetch the wild-fowl hame,
His lady's ta'en anither mate,
So we may mak' our dinner sweet.

IV

'Ye'll sit on his white hause[3]-bane,
And I'll pike out his bonny blue e'en:
Wi' ae lock o' his gowden hair
We'll theek[4] our nest when it grows bare.

V

'Mony a one for him maks mane,
But nane sall ken whar he is gane:
O'er his white banes, when they are bare,
The wind sall blaw for evermair.'

    [1] ravens.   [2] turf.   [3] neck.   [4] thatch.

Lord Randal

'O WHERE ha ye been, Lord Randal, my son?
And where ha ye been, my handsome young
    man?'
'I ha been at the greenwood; mother, mak my
    bed soon,
For I'm wearied wi' hunting, and fain wad lie
    down.'

'And wha met ye there, Lord Randal, my son?
And wha met you there, my handsome young
    man?'
'O I met wi' my true-love; mother, mak my bed
    soon,
For I'm wearied wi' hunting, an fain wad lie
    down.'

'And what did she give you, Lord Randal, my
    son?
And what did she give you, my handsome young
    man?'
'Eels fried in a pan; mother, mak my bed soon,
For I'm wearied wi' hunting, and fain wad lie
    down.'

'And wha gat your leavins, Lord Randal, my
    son?
And wha gat your leavins, my handsome young
    man?'
'My hawks and my hounds; mother, mak my bed
    soon,
For I'm wearied wi' hunting, and fain wad lie
    down.'

'And what becam of them, Lord Randal, my
    son?
And what becam of them, my handsome young
    man?'
'They stretched their legs out and died; mother,
    mak my bed soon,
For I'm wearied wi' hunting, and fain wad lie
    down.'

'O I fear you are poisoned, Lord Randal, my
    son!
I fear you are poisoned, my handsome young
    man!'
'O yes, I am poisoned; mother, mak my bed
    soon,
For I'm sick at the heart, and I fain wad lie
    down.'

'What d'ye leave to your mother, Lord Randal,
    my son?
What d'ye leave to your mother, my handsome
    young man?'
'Four and twenty milk kye; mother, mak my bed
    soon,
For I'm sick at the heart, and I fain wad lie
    down.'

'What d'ye leave to your sister, Lord Randal, my
    son?
What d'ye leave to your sister, my handsome
    young man?'
'My gold and my silver; mother, mak my bed
    soon,
For I'm sick at the heart, and I fain wad lie
    down.'

'What d'ye leave to your brother, Lord Randal,
    my son?
What d'ye leave to your brother, my handsome
    young man?'
'My houses and my lands; mother, mak my bed
    soon,
For I'm sick at the heart, and I fain wad lie
    down.'

'What d'ye leave to your true-love, Lord Randal,
    my son?
What d'ye leave to your true-love, my handsome
    young man?'
'I leave her hell and fire; mother, mak my bed
    soon,
For I'm sick at the heart, and I fain wad lie
    down.'

Edward

I

'WHY does your brand sae drop wi' blude,
      Edward, Edward?
Why does your brand sae drop wi' blude,
      And why sae sad gang ye, O?'—
'O I hae kill'd my hawk sae gude,
      Mither, mither;
O I hae kill'd my hawk sae gude,
      And I had nae mair but he, O.'

II

'Your hawk's blude was never sae red,
      Edward, Edward;
Your hawk's blude was never sae red,
      My dear son, I tell thee, O.'—

'O I hae kill'd my red-roan steed,
   Mither, mither;
O I hae kill'd my red-roan steed,
  That erst was sae fair and free, O.'

III

'Your steed was auld, and ye hae got mair,
   Edward, Edward;
Your steed was auld, and ye hae got mair;
  Some other dule ye dree,[1] O.'—
'O I hae kill'd my father dear,
   Mither, mither;
O I hae kill'd my father dear,
  Alas, and wae is me, O!'

IV

'And whatten penance will ye dree for that,
   Edward, Edward?
Whatten penance will ye dree for that?
  My dear son, now tell me, O.'—
'I'll set my feet in yonder boat,
   Mither, mither;
I'll set my feet in yonder boat,
  And I'll fare over the sea, O.'

V

'And what will ye do wi' your tow'rs and your ha',
   Edward Edward?
And what will ye do wi' your tow'rs and your ha',
  That were sae fair to see, O?'—
'I'll let them stand till they doun fa',
   Mither, mither;
I'll let them stand till they doun fa',
  For here never mair maun I be, O.'

[1] grief you suffer.

VI

'And what will ye leave to your bairns and your
      wife,
        Edward, Edward?
And what will ye leave to your bairns and your
      wife,
        When ye gang owre the sea, O?'—
'The warld's room: let them beg through life,
        Mither, mither;
The warld's room: let them beg through life;
        For them never mair will I see, O.'

VII

'And what will ye leave to your ain mither dear,
        Edward, Edward?
And what will ye leave to your ain mither dear,
        My dear son, now tell me, O?'—
'The curse of hell frae me sall ye bear,
        Mither, mither;
The curse of hell frae me sall ye bear:
        Sic counsels ye gave to me, O!'

The Dowie Houms o' Yarrow

I

LATE at een, drinkin' the wine,
    And ere they paid the lawin',[1]
They set a combat them between,
    To fight it in the dawin'.

II

'O stay at hame, my noble lord!
    O stay at hame, my marrow![2]
My cruel brother will you betray,
    On the dowie[3] houms o' Yarrow.'—

    [1] reckoning.   [2] married mate.   [3] doleful.

III

'O fare ye weel, my lady gay!
  O fare ye weel, my Sarah!
For I maun gae, tho' I ne'er return
  Frae the dowie banks o' Yarrow.'

IV

She kiss'd his cheek, she kamed his hair,
  As she had done before, O;
She belted on his noble brand,
  An' he's awa to Yarrow.

V

O he's gane up yon high, high hill—
  I wat he gaed wi' sorrow—
An' in a den spied nine arm'd men,
  I' the dowie houms¹ o' Yarrow.

VI

'O are ye come to drink the wine,
  As ye hae doon before, O?
Or are ye come to wield the brand,
  On the dowie houms o' Yarrow?'—

VII

'I am no come to drink the wine,
  As I hae done before, O,
But I am come to wield the brand,
  On the dowie houms o' Yarrow.'

VIII

Four he hurt an' five he slew,
  On the dowie houms o' Yarrow,
Till that stubborn knight came him behind,
  An' ran his body thorrow.

¹ water-meads.

IX

'Gae hame, gae hame, good brother John,
    An' tell your sister Sarah
To come an' lift her noble lord,
    Who's sleepin' sound on Yarrow.'

X

'Yestreen I dream'd a dolefu' dream;
    I ken'd there wad be sorrow;
I dream'd I pu'd the heather green,
    On the dowie banks o' Yarrow.'

XI

She gaed up yon high, high hill—
    I wat she gaed wi' sorrow—
An' in a den spied nine dead men,
    On the dowie houms o' Yarrow.

XII

She kiss'd his cheek, she kamed his hair,
    As oft she did before, O;
She drank the red blood frae him ran,
    On the dowie houms o' Yarrow.

XIII

'O haud your tongue, my douchter dear,
    For what needs a' this sorrow?
I'll wed you on a better lord
    Than him you lost on Yarrow.'—

XIV

'O haud your tongue, my father dear,
    An' dinna grieve your Sarah;
A better lord was never born
    Than him I lost on Yarrow.

XV

'Tak hame your ousen,[1] tak hame your kye,
   For they hae bred our sorrow;
I wiss that they had a' gane mad
   Whan they cam' first to Yarrow.'

Rare Willy drowned in Yarrow

I

'WILLY's rare, and Willy's fair,
   And Willy's wondrous bonny;
And Willy heght[6] to marry me,
   Gin e'er he marryd ony.

II

'Yestreen I made my bed fu' braid,
   The night I'll make it narrow,
For a' the live-long winter's night
   I lie twin'd[3] of my marrow.[4]

III

'O came you by yon water-side?
   Pu'd you the rose or lily?
Or came you by yon meadow green?
   Or saw you my sweet Willy?'

IV

She sought him east, she sought him west,
   She sought him braid and narrow;
Sine, in the clifting[5] of a craig,
   She found him drown'd in Yarrow.

---

[1] oxen.   [2] promised.   [3] deprived.   [4] mate.
[5] cleft.

Clyde's Water

'YE gie corn unto my horse,
    An' meat unto my man;
For I will gae to my true love's gates
    This night, that I can win.'

O stay at hame this ae night, Willy,
    This ae bare night wi' me;
The best bed in a' my house
    Shall be well made to thee.'

'I carena for your beds, mither,
    I carena a pin;
For I'll gae to my love's gates
    This night, gin I can win.'

'Oh stay, my son Willy, this night,
    This ae night wi' me;
The best hen in a' my roost
    Shall be well made ready for thee.'

'I carena for your hens, mither,
    I carena a pin;
I shall gae to my love's gates
    This night, gin I can win.'

'Gin ye winna stay, my son Willy,
    This ae bare night wi' me,
Gin Clyde's waters be deep and fu' o' flood,
    My malison drown thee!'

He rade up yon high hill,
    And down yon dowie den,
The roaring of Clyde's water
    Wad hae fleyed ten thousand men.

'O spare me, Clyde's water,
  O spare me as I gae!
Mak' me your wrack as I come back,
  But spare me as I gae!'

He rade in, and farther in,
  Till he came to the chin;
And he rade in, and farther in,
  Till he came to dry land.

And when he came to his love's gates,
  He tirled at the pin.
'Open your gates, Meggie,
  Open your gates to me;
For my boots are fu' o' Clyde's water
  And the rain rains ower my chin.'

'I hae nae lovers thereout,' she says,
  'I hae nae love within;
My true-love is in my arms twa,
  An' nane will I let in.'

'Open your gates, Meggie, this ae night,
  Open your gates to me;
For Clyde's water is fu' o' flood,
  And my mother's malison 'll drown me.'

'Ane o' my chambers is fu' o' corn,
  An' ane is fu' o' hay;
Another is fu' o' gentlemen;—
  An' they winna move till day.'

Out waked her may Meggie,
  Out of her drowsy dream.
'I dreamed a dream sin the yestreen,
  God read a' dreams to guid,
That my true love Willy,
  Was staring at my bed-feet.'

'Lay still, lay still, my ae dochter,
  An' keep my back frae the call,[1]
For it's na the space o' half an hour,
  Sen he gaed frae your hall.'

An' hey Willy, an' hoa, Willy,
  Winna ye turn agen;
But aye the louder that she cried,
  He rade against the win'.

He rade up yon high hill,
  And doun yon dowie den;
The roaring that was in Clyde's water
  Wad ha fleyed ten thousand men.

He rade in, an' farther in,
  Till he came to the chin;
An' he rade in, an' farther in,
  But never mair was seen.

.   .   .   .   .

There was na mair seen o' that guid lord,
  But his hat frae his head;
There was na mair seen o' that lady,
  But her comb and her snood.

There waders went up and doun,
  Saying 'Clyde's water
  Hath done us wrang.'

Helen of Kirkconnell

I

I WISH I were where Helen lies,
Night and day on me she cries;
O that I were where Helen lies,
  On fair Kirkconnell lea!

    [1] cold.

II

Curst be the heart that thought the thought,
And curst the hand that fired the shot,
When in my arms burd Helen dropt,
   And died to succour me!

III

O think na ye my heart was sair,
When my Love dropp'd and spak nae mair!
There did she swoon wi' meikle care,
   On fair Kirkconnell lea.

IV

As I went down the water side,
None but my foe to be my guide,
None but my foe to be my guide,
   On fair Kirkconnell lea;

V

I lighted down my sword to draw,
I hackèd him in pieces sma',
I hackèd him in pieces sma',
   For her sake that died for me.

VI

O Helen fair, beyond compare!
I'll mak a garland o' thy hair,
Shall bind my heart for evermair,
   Until the day I dee!

VII

O that I were where Helen lies!
Night and day on me she cries;
Out of my bed she bids me rise,
   Says, 'Haste, and come to me!'

VIII

O Helen fair! O Helen chaste!
If I were with thee, I'd be blest,
Where thou lies low an' taks thy rest,
    On fair Kirkconnell lea.

IX

I wish my grave were growing green,
A winding-sheet drawn owre my een,
And I in Helen's arms lying,
    On fair Kirkconnell lea.

X

I wish I were where Helen lies!
Night and day on me she cries;
And I am weary of the skies,
    For her sake that died for me.

Bessie Bell and Mary Gray

I

O BESSIE BELL and Mary Gray,
    They war twa bonnie lasses;
They biggit[1] a bower on yon burn-brae,
    And theekit[2] it o'er wi' rashes.

II

They theekit it o'er wi' rashes green,
    They theekit it o'er wi' heather;
But the pest cam frae the burrows-town,
    And slew them baith thegither.

III

They thought to lye in Methven kirkyard,
    Amang their noble kin;
But they maun lye in Stronach haugh,[3]
    To biek[4] forenent the sin.[5]

[1] built.   [2] thatched.   [3] water-mead.   [4] bask.   [5] sun

IV

And Bessie Bell and Mary Gray,
   They war twa bonnie lasses;
They biggit a bower on yon burn-brae,
   And theekit it o'er wi' rashes.

The Lowlands o' Holland

I

'My love has built a bonny ship, and set her on
   the sea,
With seven score good mariners to bear her
   companie;
There's three score is sunk, and three score dead
   at sea,
And the Lowlands o' Holland has twin'd[1] my
   love and me.

II

'My love he built another ship, and set her on
   the main,
And nane but twenty mariners for to bring her
   hame;
But the weary wind began to rise, and the sea
   began to rout,
My love then and his bonny ship turn'd wither-
   shins[2] about.

III

'Then shall neither coif come on my head nor
   comb come in my hair;
Then shall neither coal nor candle-light shine in
   my bower mair;
Nor will I love another one until the day I die,
Sin' the Lowlands o' Holland has twin'd my love
   and me.'—

      [1] parted.   [2] around against the sun.

IV

'O haud your tongue, my daughter dear, be still
    and be content;
There are mair lads in Galloway, ye need nae
    sair lament.'—
'O there is none in Galloway, there's none at
    a' for me,
For I never loved a love but one, and he's
    drown'd in the sea.'

Marie Hamilton

I

MARIE HAMILTON'S to the kirk gane,
    Wi' ribbons in her hair;
The King thought mair o' Marie Hamilton
    Than ony that were there.

II

Marie Hamilton's to the kirk gane
    Wi' ribbons on her breast;
The King thought mair o' Marie Hamilton
    Than he listen'd to the priest.

III

Marie Hamilton's to the kirk gane,
    Wi' gloves upon her hands;
The King thought mair o' Marie Hamilton
    Than the Queen and a' her lands.

IV

She hadna been about the King's court
    A month, but barely ane,
Till she was beloved by a' the King's court,
    And the King the only man.

V

She hadna been about the King's court
  A month, but barely three,
Till frae the King's court Marie Hamilton,
  Marie Hamilton durstna be.

VI

The King is to the Abbey gane,
  To pu' the Abbey tree,
To scale[1] the babe frae Marie's heart;
  But the thing it wadna be.

VII

O she has row'd[2] it in her apron,
  And set it on the sea—
'Gae sink ye or swim ye, bonny babe,
  Ye'se get nae mair o' me.'

VIII

Word is to the kitchen gane,
  And word is to the ha',
And word is to the noble room
  Amang the ladies a',
That Marie Hamilton's brought to bed,
  And the bonny babe's miss'd and awa'.

IX

Scarcely had she lain down again,
  And scarcely fa'en asleep,
When up and started our gude Queen
  Just at her bed-feet;
Saying—'Marie Hamilton, where's your babe?
  For I am sure I heard it greet.'[3]—

---

[1] drive away, get rid of.   [2] wrapped.   [3] wail, cry.

X

'O no, O no, my noble Queen!
  Think no sic thing to be;
'Twas but a stitch into my side,
  And sair it troubles me!'—

XI

'Get up, get up, Marie Hamilton:
  Get up and follow me;
For I am going to Edinburgh town,
  A rich wedding for to see.'

XII

O slowly, slowly rase she up,
  And slowly put she on;
And slowly rade she out the way
  Wi' mony a weary groan.

XIII

The Queen was clad in scarlet,
  Her merry maids all in green;
And every town that they cam to,
  They took Marie for the Queen.

XIV

'Ride hooly,¹ hooly, gentlemen,
  Ride hooly now wi' me!
For never, I am sure, a wearier burd
  Rade in your companie.'

XV

But little wist Marie Hamilton,
  When she rade on the brown,
That she was gaen to Edinburgh town,
  And a' to be put down.

¹ gently.

XVI

'Why weep ye sae, ye burgess wives,
 Why look ye sae on me?
O I am going to Edinburgh town,
 A rich wedding for to see.'

XVII

When she gaed up the tolbooth stairs,
 The corks frae her heels did flee;
And lang or e'er she cam down again,
 She was condemn'd to die.

XVIII

When she cam to the Netherbow port,
 She laugh'd loud laughters three;
But when she came to the gallows foot
 The tears blinded her e'e.

XIX

'Yestreen the Queen had four Maries,
 The night she'll hae but three;
There was Marie Seaton, and Marie Beaton,
 And Marie Carmichael, and me.

XX

'O often have I dress'd my Queen,
 And put gowd upon her hair;
But now I've gotten for my reward
 The gallows to be my share.

XXI

'Often have I dress'd my Queen
 And often made her bed;
But now I've gotten for my reward
 The gallows tree to tread.

XXII

'I charge ye all, ye mariners,
    When ye sail owre the faem,
Let neither my father nor mother get wit
    But that I'm coming hame.

XXIII

'I charge ye all, ye mariners,
    That sail upon the sea,
That neither my father nor mother get wit
    The dog's death I'm to die.

XXIV

'For if my father and mother got wit,
    And my bold brethren three,
O mickle wad be the gude red blude
    This day wad be spilt for me!

XXV

'O little did my mother ken,
    The day she cradled me,
The lands I was to travel in
    Or the death I was to die!'

The Gipsy Laddie

THE gipsies came to our good lord's gate,
    And wow but they sang sweetly!
They sang sae sweet and sae very complete
    That down came the fair lady.

And she came tripping down the stair,
    And a' her maids before her;
As soon as they saw her weel-faured[1] face,
    They coost the glamour o'er her.

---

[1] well-favoured.

'Gae tak frae me this gay mantile,
  And bring to me a plaidie;
For if kith and kin and a' had sworn,
  I'll follow the gipsy laddie.

'Yestreen I lay in a well-made bed,
  And my good lord beside me;
This night I'll lie in a tenant's barn,
  Whatever shall betide me.'

'Come to your bed,' says Johnnie Faa,
  'Oh come to your bed, my dearie;
For I vow and I swear, by the hilt of my sword,
  That your lord shall nae mair come near ye.

'I'll go to bed to my Johnnie Faa,
  I'll go to bed to my dearie;
For I vow and I swear, by what passed yestreen,
  That my lord shall nae mair come near me.

'I'll mak a hap to my Johnnie Faa,
  And I'll mak a hap to my dearie;
And he's get a' the coat gaes round,
  And my lord shall nae mair come near me.'

And when our lord came hame at een,
  And speired for his fair lady,
The tane she cried, and the other replied,
  'She's away with the gipsy laddie.'

'Gae saddle to me the black, black steed,
  Gae saddle and make him ready;
Before that I either eat or sleep,
  I'll gae seek my fair lady.'

And we were fifteen well-made men,
  Although we were nae bonnie;
And we were a' put down for ane,
  A fair young wanton lady.

Barbara Allen

I

In Scarlet town, where I was born,
    There was a fair maid dwellin',
Made every youth cry *Well-a-way!*
    Her name was Barbara Allen.

II

All in the merry month of May,
    When green buds they were swellin',
Young Jemmy Grove on his death-bed lay,
    For love of Barbara Allen.

III

He sent his man in to her then,
    To the town where she was dwellin';
'O haste and come to my master dear,
    If your name be Barbara Allen.'

IV

So slowly, slowly rase she up,
    And slowly she came nigh him,
And when she drew the curtain by—
    'Young man, I think you're dyin'.'

V

'O it's I am sick and very sick,
    And it's all for Barbara Allen.'—
'O the better for me ye'se never be,
    Tho' your heart's blood were a-spillin'!

VI

'O dinna ye mind, young man,' says she,
    'When the red wine ye were fillin',
That ye made the healths go round and round,
    And slighted Barbara Allen?'

VII

He turn'd his face unto the wall,
  And death was with him dealin':
'Adieu, adieu, my dear friends all,
  And be kind to Barbara Allen!'

VIII

As she was walking o'er the fields,
  She heard the dead-bell knellin';
And every jow[1] the dead-bell gave
  Cried 'Woe to Barbara Allen'.

IX

'O mother, mother, make my bed,
  O make it saft and narrow:
My love has died for me to-day,
  I'll die for him to-morrow.

X

'Farewell,' she said, 'ye virgins all,
  And shun the fault I fell in:
Henceforth take warning by the fall
  Of cruel Barbara Allen'.

Thomas the Rhymer

I

TRUE Thomas lay on Huntlie bank;
  A ferlie[2] he spied wi' his e'e;
And there he saw a ladye bright
  Come riding down by the Eildon Tree.

II

Her skirt was o' the grass-green silk,
  Her mantle o' the velvet fyne;
At ilka tett[3] o' horse's mane
  Hung fifty siller bells and nine.

---

[1] beat, toll.   [2] marvel.   [3] tuft.

III

True Thomas he pu'd aff his cap,
  And louted low down on his knee:
'Hail to thee, Mary, Queen of Heaven!
  For thy peer on earth could never be.'

IV

'O no, O no, Thomas,' she said,
  'That name does not belang to me;
I'm but the Queen o' fair Elfland,
  That am hither come to visit thee.

V

'Harp and carp,[1] Thomas,' she said;
  'Harp and carp along wi' me;
And if ye dare to kiss my lips,
  Sure of your bodie I will be.'

VI

'Betide me weal, betide me woe,
  That weird[2] shall never daunten me.'
Syne he has kiss'd her rosy lips,
  All underneath the Eildon Tree.

VII

'Now ye maun go wi' me,' she said,
  'True Thomas, ye maun go wi' me;
And ye maun serve me seven years,
  Thro' weal or woe as may chance to be.'

VIII

She's mounted on her milk-white steed,
  She's ta'en true Thomas up behind;
And aye, whene'er her bridle rang,
  The steed gaed swifter than the wind.

        [1] play and recite (as a minstrel).   [2] doom.

IX

O they rade on, and farther on,
 The steed gaed swifter than the wind;
Until they reach'd a desert wide,
 And living land was left behind.

X

'Light down, light down now, true Thomas,
 And lean your head upon my knee;
Abide ye there a little space,
 And I will show you ferlies three.

XI

'O see ye not yon narrow road,
 So thick beset wi' thorns and briers?
That is the Path of Righteousness,
 Though after it but few inquires.

XII

'And see ye not yon braid, braid road,
 That lies across the lily leven?[1]
That is the Path of Wickedness,
 Though some call it the Road to Heaven.

XIII

'And see ye not yon bonny road
 That winds about the fernie brae?
That is the Road to fair Elfland,
 Where thou and I this night maun gae.

XIV

'But, Thomas, ye sall haud your tongue,
 Whatever ye may hear or see;
For speak ye word in Elfyn-land,
 Ye'll ne'er win back to your ain countrie.'

[1] lawn.

XV

O they rade on, and farther on,
   And they waded rivers abune the knee;
And they saw neither sun nor moon,
   But they heard the roaring of the sea.

XVI

It was mirk, mirk night, there was nae starlight,
   They waded thro' red blude to the knee;
For a' the blude that's shed on the earth
   Rins through the springs o' that countrie.

XVII

Syne they came to a garden green,
   And she pu'd an apple frae a tree:
'Take this for thy wages, true Thomas;
   It will give thee the tongue that can never lee.'

XVIII

'My tongue is my ain,' true Thomas he said;
   'A gudely gift ye wad gie to me!
I neither dought[1] to buy or sell
   At fair or tryst where I might be.

XIX

'I dought neither speak to prince or peer,
   Nor ask of grace from fair ladye!'—
'Now haud thy peace, Thomas,' she said,
   'For as I say, so must it be.'

XX

He has gotten a coat of the even cloth,[2]
   And a pair o' shoon of the velvet green;
And till seven years were gane and past,
   True Thomas on earth was never seen.

      [1] could.   [2] smooth cloth.

Binnorie

I

THERE were twa sisters sat in a bour;
  Binnorie, O Binnorie!
There cam a knight to be their wooer,
  By the bonnie milldams o' Binnorie.

II

He courted the eldest with glove and ring,
But he lo'ed the youngest abune a' thing.

III

The eldest she was vexèd sair,
And sair envied her sister fair.

IV

Upon a morning fair and clear,
She cried upon her sister dear:

V

'O sister, sister, tak my hand,
And we'll see our father's ships to land.'

VI

She's ta'en her by the lily hand,
And led her down to the river-strand.

VII

The youngest stood upon a stane,
The eldest cam and push'd her in.

VIII

'O sister, sister, reach your hand!
And ye sall be heir o' half my land:

IX

'O sister, reach me but your glove!
And sweet William sall be your love.'—

X

'Foul fa' the hand that I should take;
It twin'd[1] me o' my warldis make.[2]

XI

'Your cherry cheeks and your yellow hair
Gar'd me gang maiden evermair.'

XII

Sometimes she sank, sometimes she swam,
Until she cam to the miller's dam.

XIII

Out then cam the miller's son,
And saw the fair maid soummin'[3] in.

XIV

'O father, father, draw your dam!
There's either a mermaid or a milk-white swan.'

XV

The miller hasted and drew his dam,
And there he found a drown'd womàn.

XVI

You couldna see her middle sma',
Her gowden girdle was sae braw.

XVII

You couldna see her lily feet,
Her gowden fringes were sae deep.

XVIII

You couldna see her yellow hair
For the strings o' pearls was twisted there.

---

[1] robbed, deprived.   [2] my one mate in the world.
[3] swimming.

XIX

You couldna see her fingers sma',
Wi' diamond rings they were cover'd a'.

XX

And by there cam a harper fine,
That harpit to the king at dine.

XXI

And when he look'd that lady on,
He sigh'd and made a heavy moan.

XXII

He's made a harp of her breast-bane,
Whose sound wad melt a heart of stane.

XXIII

He's ta'en three locks o' her yellow hair,
And wi' them strung his harp sae rare.

XXIV

He went into her father's hall,
And there was the court assembled all.

XXV

He laid his harp upon a stane,
And straight it began to play by lane.[1]

XXVI

'O yonder sits my father, the King,
And yonder sits my mother, the Queen;

XXVII

'And yonder stands my brother Hugh,
And by him my William, sweet and true.'

[1] alone, of itself.

XXVIII

But the last tune that the harp play'd then—
    Binnorie, O Binnorie!
Was, 'Woe to my sister, false Helèn!'
    By the bonnie milldams o' Binnorie.

The Wife of Usher's Well

I

THERE lived a wife at Usher's well,
    And a wealthy wife was she;
She had three stout and stalwart sons,
    And sent them o'er the sea.

II

They hadna been a week from her,
    A week but barely ane,
When word came to the carline[1] wife
    That her three sons were gane.

III

They hadna been a week from her,
    A week but barely three,
When word came to the carline wife
    That her sons she'd never see.

IV

'I wish the wind may never cease,
    Nor fashes[2] in the flood,
Till my three sons come hame to me
    In earthly flesh and blood!'

    [1] old woman.   [2] troubles.

V

It fell about the Martinmas,
  When nights are lang and mirk,
The carline wife's three sons came hame,
  And their hats were o' the birk.

VI

It neither grew in syke[1] nor ditch,
  Nor yet in ony sheugh[2];
But at the gates o' Paradise
  That birk grew fair eneugh.

VII

'Blow up the fire, my maidens!
  Bring water from the well!
For a' my house shall feast this night,
  Since my three sons are well.'

VIII

And she has made to them a bed,
  She's made it large and wide;
And she's ta'en her mantle her about,
  Sat down at the bedside.

IX

Up then crew the red, red cock,
  And up and crew the gray;
The eldest to the youngest said,
  ''Tis time we were away.'

X

The cock he hadna craw'd but once,
  And clapp'd his wings at a',
When the youngest to the eldest said,
  'Brother, we must awa'.

[1] marsh.   [2] trench.

XI

'The cock doth craw, the day doth daw,
　　The channerin'[1] worm doth chide;
Gin we be miss'd out o' our place,
　　A sair pain we maun bide.'—

XII

'Lie still, lie still but a little wee while,
　　Lie still but if we may;
Gin my mother should miss us when she wakes,
　　She'll go mad ere it be day.'—

XIII

'Fare ye weel, my mother dear!
　　Fareweel to barn and byre!
And fare ye weel, the bonny lass
　　That kindles my mother's fire!'

Tam Lin

I

'O I FORBID you, maidens a',
　　That wear gowd on your hair,
To come or gae by Carterhaugh,
　　For young Tam Lin is there.

II

'For even about that knight's middle
　　O' siller bells are nine;
And nae maid comes to Carterhaugh
　　And a maid returns again.'

---

[1] fretting.

III

Fair Janet sat in her bonny bower,
　Sewing her silken seam,
And wish'd to be in Carterhaugh
　Amang the leaves sae green.

IV

She's lat her seam fa' to her feet,
　The needle to her tae,[1]
And she's awa' to Carterhaugh
　As fast as she could gae.

V

And she has kilted her green kirtle
　A little abune her knee;
And she has braided her yellow hair
　A little abune her bree[2];
And she has gaen for Carterhaugh
　As fast as she can hie.

VI

She hadna pu'd a rose, a rose,
　A rose but barely ane,
When up and started young Tam Lin;
　Says, 'Ladye, let alane.

VII

'What gars ye pu' the rose, Janet?
　What gars ye break the tree?
What gars ye come to Carterhaugh
　Without the leave o' me?'

VIII

'Weel may I pu' the rose,' she says,
　'And ask no leave at thee;
For Carterhaugh it is my ain,
　My daddy gave it me.'

---

[1] toe.　　[2] eye-brow.

IX

He's ta'en her by the milk-white hand,
   And by the grass-green sleeve,
He's led her to the fairy ground
   At her he ask'd nae leave.

X

Janet has kilted her green kirtle
   A little abune her knee,
And she has snooded her yellow hair
   A little abune her bree,
And she is to her father's ha'
   As fast as she can hie.

XI

But when she came to her father's ha',
   She look'd sae wan and pale,
They thought the lady had gotten a fright,
   Or with sickness she did ail.

XII

Four and twenty ladies fair
   Were playing at the ba',
And out then came fair Janet
   Ance the flower amang them a'.

XIII

Four and twenty ladies fair
   Where playing at the chess,
And out then came fair Janet
   As green as onie glass.

XIV

Out then spak' an auld grey knight
   'Lay owre the Castle wa',
And says, 'Alas, fair Janet!
   For thee we'll be blamèd a'.'

XV

'Hauld your tongue, ye auld-faced knight,
    Some ill death may ye die!
Father my bairn on whom I will,
    I'll father nane on thee.

XVI

'O if my love were an earthly knight,
    As he is an elfin gay,
I wadna gie my ain true-love
    For nae laird that ye hae.

XVII

'The steed that my true-love rides on
    Is fleeter nor the wind;
Wi' siller he is shod before,
    Wi' burning gold behind.'

XVIII

Out then spak' her brither dear—
    He meant to do her harm:
'There grows an herb in Carterhaugh
    Will twine[1] you an' the bairn.'

XIX

Janet has kilted her green kirtle
    A little abune her knee,
And she has snooded her yellow hair
    A little abune her bree,
And she's awa' to Carterhaugh
    As fast as she can hie.

XX

She hadna pu'd a leaf, a leaf,
    A leaf but only twae,
When up and started young Tam Lin,
    Says, 'Ladye, thou's pu' nae mae.

[1] part, sunder.

XXI

'How dar' ye pu' a leaf?' he says,
  'How dar' ye break the tree?
How dar' ye scathe[1] my babe,' he says,
  'That's between you and me?'

XXII

'O tell me, tell me, Tam,' she says,
  'For His sake that died on tree,
If ye were ever in holy chapel
  Or sain'd[2] in Christentie?'

XXIII

'The truth I'll tell to thee, Janet,
  Ae word I winna lee;
A knight me got, and a lady me bore,
  As well as they did thee.

XXIV

'Roxburgh he was my grandfather,
  Took me with him to bide;
And ance it fell upon a day,
  As hunting I did ride,

XXV

'There came a wind out o' the north,
  A sharp wind an' a snell,[3]
A dead sleep it came over me
  And frae my horse I fell;
And the Queen o' Fairies she took me
  In yon green hill to dwell.

XXVI

'And pleasant is the fairy land
  For those that in it dwell,

---

[1] harm.   [2] blessed, baptized.   [3] keen, cold.

But ay at end of seven years
    They pay a teind[1] to hell;
I am sae fair and fu' o' flesh
    I'm fear'd 'twill be mysell.

XXVII

'But the night is Hallowe'en, Janet,
    The morn is Hallowday;
Then win me, win me, an ye will,
    For weel I wat ye may.

XXVIII

'The night it is gude Hallowe'en,
    The fairy folk to ride,
And they that wad their true-love win,
    At Miles Cross they maun bide.'—

XXIX

'But how should I you ken, Tam Lin,
    How should I borrow[2] you,
Amang a pack of uncouth[3] knights
    The like I never saw?'—

XXX

'You'll do you down to Miles Cross
    Between twel' hours and ane,
And fill your hands o' the holy water
    And cast your compass roun'.

XXXI

'The first company that passes by,
    Say na, and let them gae;
The neist company that passes by,
    Say na, and do right sae;
The third company that passes by,
    Then I'll be ane o' thae.

[1] tithe.   [2] ransom.   [3] unknown.

XXXII

'O first let pass the black, ladye,
  And syne let pass the brown;
But quickly run to the milk-white steed,
  Pu' ye his rider down.

XXXIII

'For some ride on the black, ladye,
  And some ride on the brown;
But I ride on a milk-white steed,
  A gowd star on my crown:
Because I was an earthly knight
  They gie me that renown.

XXXIV

'My right hand will be gloved, ladye,
  My left hand will be bare,
And thae's the tokens I gie thee:
  Nae doubt I will be there.

XXXV

'Ye'll tak' my horse then by the head
  And let the bridle fa';
The Queen o' Elfin she'll cry out
  "True Tam Lin he 's awa'!"

XXXVI

'They'll turn me in your arms, ladye,
  An aske[1] but and a snake;
But hauld me fast, let me na gae,
  To be your warldis make.[2]

XXXVII

'They'll turn me in your arms, ladye,
  But and a deer so wild;
But hauld me fast, let me na gae,
  The father o' your child.

----

[1] newt, lizard.   [2] mate, husband.

XXXVIII

'They'll shape me in your arms, ladye,
  A hot iron at the fire;
But hauld me fast, let me na go,
  To be your heart's desire.

XXXIX

'They'll shape me last in your arms, Janet,
  A mother-naked man;
Cast your green mantle over me,
  And sae will I be won.'

XL

Janet has kilted her green kirtle
  A little abune the knee;
And she has snooded her yellow hair
  A little abune her bree,
And she is on to Miles Cross
  As fast as she can hie.

XLI

About the dead hour o' the night
  She heard the bridles ring;
And Janet was as glad at that
  As any earthly thing.

XLII

And first gaed by the black, black steed,
  And syne gaed by the brown;
But fast she gript the milk-white steed
  And pu'd the rider down.

XLIII

She's pu'd him frae the milk-white steed,
  An' loot[1] the bridle fa',
And up there rase an eldritch[2] cry,
  'True Tam Lin he's awa'!'

          [1] let.   [2] unearthly.

XLIV

They shaped him in her arms twa
    An aske but and a snake;
But aye she grips and hau'ds him fast
    To be her warldis make.

XLV

They shaped him in her arms twa
    But and a deer sae wild;
But aye she grips and hau'ds him fast,
    The father o' her child.

XLVI

They shaped him in her arms twa
    A hot iron at the fire;
But aye she grips and hau'ds him fast
    To be her heart's desire.

XLVII

They shaped him in her arms at last
    A mother-naked man;
She cast her mantle over him,
    And sae her love she wan.

XLVIII

Up then spak' the Queen o' Fairies,
    Out o' a bush o' broom,
'She that has borrow'd young Tam Lin
    Has gotten a stately groom.'

XLIX

Out then spak' the Queen o' Fairies,
    And an angry woman was she,
'She's ta'en awa' the bonniest knight
    In a' my companie!

L

'But what I ken this night, Tam Lin,
  Gin I had kent yestreen,
I wad ta'en out thy heart o' flesh,
  And put in a heart o' stane.

LI

'And adieu, Tam Lin! But gin I had kent
  A ladye wad borrow'd thee,
I wad ta'en out thy twa grey e'en,
  Put in twa e'en o' tree.[1]

LII

'And had I the wit yestreen, yestreen,
  That I have coft[2] this day,
I'd paid my teind seven times to hell
  Ere you had been won away!'

Fair Annie

I

It's narrow, narrow, mak your bed,
  And learn to lie your lane;
For I'm gaun owre the sea, Fair Annie,
  A braw bride to bring hame.
Wi' her I will get gowd and gear,
  Wi' you I ne'er gat nane.

II

'But wha will bake my bridal bread,
  Or brew my bridal ale?
And wha will welcome my bright bride,
  That I bring owre the dale?'—

---

[1] wood.　　[2] bought.

III

'It's I will bake your bridal bread,
    And brew your bridal ale;
And I will welcome your bright bride,
    That you bring owre the dale.'—

IV

'But she that welcomes my bright bride
    Maun gang like maiden fair;
She maun lace on her robe sae jimp,[1]
    And comely braid her hair.

V

'Bind up, bind up your yellow hair,
    And tie it on your neck;
And see you look as maiden-like
    As the day that first we met.'—

VI

'O how can I gang maiden-like,
    When maiden I am nane?
Have I not borne six sons to thee,
    And am wi' child again?'—

VII

'I'll put cooks into my kitchen,
    And stewards in my hall,
And I'll have bakers for my bread,
    And brewers for my ale;
But you're to welcome my bright bride,
    That I bring owre the dale.'

VIII

Three months and a day were gane and past,
    Fair Annie she gat word
That her love's ship was come at last,
    Wi' his bright young bride aboard.

[1] slender, trim.

IX

She 's ta'en her young son in her arms,
  Anither in her hand;
And she's gane up to the highest tower,
  Looks over sea and land.

X

'Come doun, come doun, my mother dear,
  Come aff the castle wa'!
I fear if langer ye stand there,
  Ye'll let yoursell doun fa'.'

XI

She's ta'en a cake o' the best bread,
  A stoup o' the best wine,
And a' the keys upon her arm,
  And to the yett[1] is gane.

XII

'O ye're welcome hame, my ain gude lord,
  To your castles and your towers;
Ye're welcome hame, my ain gude lord,
  To your ha's, but and your bowers.
And welcome to your hame, fair lady!
  For a' that's here is yours.'

XIII

'O whatna lady's that, my lord,
  That welcomes you and me?
Gin I be lang about this place,
  Her friend I mean to be.'

XIV

Fair Annie served the lang tables
  Wi' the white bread and the wine;
But ay she drank the wan water
  To keep her colour fine.

---

[1] gate.

XV

And aye she served the lang tables
    Wi' the white bread and the brown,
And aye she turn'd her round about,
    Sae fast the tears fell doun.

XVI

She took a napkin lang and white,
    And hung it on a pin;
It was to wipe away the tears,
    As she gaed out and in.

XVII

When bells were rung and mass was sung,
    And a' men bound for bed,
The bridegroom and the bonny bride
    In ae chamber were laid.

XVIII

Fair Annie 's ta'en a harp in her hand,
    To harp thir twa asleep;
But ay, as she harpit and she sang,
    Fu' sairly did she weep.

XIX

'O gin my sons were seven rats,
    Rinnin' on the castle wa',
And I mysell a great grey cat,
    I soon wad worry them a'!

XX

'O gin my sons were seven hares,
    Rinnin' owre yon lily lea,
And I mysell a good greyhound,
    Soon worried they a' should be!'

XXI

Then out and spak the bonny young bride,
  In bride-bed where she lay:
'That's like my sister Annie,' she says;
  'Wha is it doth sing and play?

XXII

'I'll put on my gown,' said the new-come bride,
  'And my shoes upon my feet;
I will see wha doth sae sadly sing,
  And what is it gars her greet.

XXIII

'What ails you, what ails you, my housekeeper,
  That ye mak sic a mane?
Has ony wine-barrel cast its girds,
  Or is a' your white bread gane?'—

XXIV

'It isna because my wine is spilt,
  Or that my white bread's gane;
But because I've lost my true love's love,
  And he's wed to anither ane.'—

XXV

'Noo tell me wha was your father?' she says,
  'Noo tell me wha was your mither?
And had ye ony sister?' she says,
  'And had ye ever a brither?'—

XXVI

'The Earl of Wemyss was my father,
  The Countess of Wemyss my mither,
Young Elinor she was my sister dear,
  And Lord John he was my brither.'—

XXVII

'If the Earl of Wemyss was your father,
    I wot sae was he mine;
And it's O my sister Annie!
    Your love ye sallna tyne.[1]

XXVIII

'Tak your husband, my sister dear;
    You ne'er were wrang'd for me,
Beyond a kiss o' his merry mouth
    As we cam owre the sea.

XXIX

'Seven ships, loaded weel,
    Cam owre the sea wi' me;
Ane o' them will tak me hame,
    And six I'll gie to thee.'

Get up and Bar the Door

I

It fell about the Martinmas time,
    And a gay time it was then,
When our goodwife got puddings to make,
    And she's boil'd them in the pan.

II

The wind sae cauld blew south and north,
    And blew into the floor;
Quoth our goodman to our goodwife,
    'Gae out and bar the door.'—

III

'My hand is in my hussyfskap,[2]
    Goodman, as ye may see;
An' it shou'dna be barr'd this hundred year,
    It's no be barr'd for me.'

   [1] lose.   [2] I am busy with my housewifery.

IV

They made a paction 'tween them twa,
    They made it firm and sure,
That the first word whae'er shou'd speak,
    Shou'd rise and bar the door.

V

Then by there came two gentlemen,
    At twelve o'clock at night,
And they could neither see house nor hall,
    Nor coal nor candle-light.

VI

'Now whether is this a rich man's house,
    Or whether is it a poor?'
But ne'er a word wad ane o' them speak,
    For barring of the door.

VII

And first they ate the white puddings,
    And then they ate the black.
Tho' muckle thought the goodwife to hersel'
    Yet ne'er a word she spake.

VIII

Then said the one unto the other,
    'Here, man, tak ye my knife;
Do ye tak aff the auld man's beard,
    And I'll kiss the goodwife.'—

IX

'But there's nae water in the house,
    And what shall we do than?'—
'What ails ye at the pudding-broo,
    That boils into the pan?'

X

O up then started our goodman,
    An angry man was he:
'Will ye kiss my wife before my een,
    And sca'd me wi' pudding-bree?'

XI

Then up and started our goodwife,
    Gied three skips on the floor:
'Goodman, you've spoken the foremost word!
    Get up and bar the door.'

WILLIAM DRUMMOND OF HAWTHORNDEN
1585–1649

I know that all beneath the moon decays

I KNOW that all beneath the moon decays,
And what by mortals in this world is brought,
In Time's great periods shall return to nought;
That fairest states have fatal nights and days;
I know how all the Muse's heavenly lays,
With toil of spright which are so dearly bought,
As idle sounds, of few or none are sought,
And that nought lighter is than airy praise;
I know frail beauty like the purple flower,
To which one morn oft birth and death
    affords;
That love a jarring is of minds' accords,
Where sense and will invassal reason's power:
    Know what I list, this all can not me move,
    But that, O me! I both must write and love.

Sleep, Silence' child, sweet father of soft rest

SLEEP, Silence' child, sweet father of soft rest,
Prince, whose approach peace to all mortals
    brings,
Indifferent host to shepherds and to kings,
Sole comforter of minds with grief opprest;
Lo, by thy charming rod all breathing things
Lie slumb'ring, with forgetfulness possest,
And yet o'er me to spread thy drowsy wings
Thou spares, alas! who cannot be thy guest.
Since I am thine, O come, but with that face
To inward light which thou art wont to show,
With feigned solace ease a true-felt woe;
Or if, deaf god, thou do deny that grace,
    Come as thou wilt, and what thou wilt be-
      queath,
    I long to kiss the image of my death.

Fair Moon, who with thy cold and silver shine

FAIR Moon, who with thy cold and silver shine
Makes sweet the horror of the dreadful night,
Delighting the weak eye with smiles divine,
Which Phœbus dazzles with his too much light;
Bright Queen of the first Heaven, if in thy shrine,
By turning oft, and Heaven's eternal might,
Thou hast not yet that once sweet fire of thine,
Endymion, forgot, and lover's plight;
If cause like thine may pity breed in thee,
And pity somewhat else to it obtain,
Since thou hast power of dreams, as well as he
Who paints strange figures in the slumb'ring
    brain,
    Now while she sleeps, in doleful guise her show
    These tears, and the black map of all my woe.

Fair is my yoke, though grievous be my pains

FAIR is my yoke, though grievous be my pains,
Sweet are my wounds, although they deeply
    smart,
My bit is gold, though shortened be the reins,
My bondage brave, though I may not depart:
Although I burn, the fire which doth impart
Those flames, so sweet reviving force contains,
That, like Arabia's bird, my wasted heart,
Made quick by death, more lively still remains.
I joy, though oft my waking eyes spend tears,
I never want delight, even when I groan,
Best companied when most I am alone;
A heaven of hopes I have midst hells of fears.
    Thus every way contentment strange I find,
    But most in her rare beauty, my rare mind.

Like the Idalian queen

LIKE the Idalian queen,
Her hair about her eyne,
With neck and breast's ripe apples to be seen,
At first glance of the morn,
In Cyprus' gardens gathering those fair flow'rs
Which of her blood were born,
I saw, but fainting saw, my paramours.
The Graces naked danc'd about the place,
The winds and trees amaz'd
With silence on her gaz'd;
The flow'rs did smile, like those upon her face,
And as their aspen stalks those fingers band,
That she might read my case,
A hyacinth I wish'd me in her hand.

Phœbus, arise

PHŒBUS, arise,
And paint the sable skies
With azure, white, and red;
Rouse Memnon's mother from her Tithon's
    bed,
That she thy career may with roses spread;
The nightingales thy coming each where
    sing;
Make an eternal spring,
Give life to this dark world which lieth dead;
Spread forth thy golden hair
In larger locks than thou wast wont before,
And, emperor-like, decore
With diadem of pearl thy temples fair:
Chase hence the ugly night,
Which serves but to make dear thy glorious
    light.
This is that happy morn,
That day, long-wished day,
Of all my life so dark
(If cruel stars have not my ruin sworn,
And fates not hope betray),
Which, only white, deserves
A diamond for ever should it mark:
This is the morn should bring unto this
    grove
My love, to hear and recompense my love.
Fair king, who all preserves,
But show thy blushing beams,
And thou two sweeter eyes
Shalt see, than those which by Peneus' streams
Did once thy heart surprise;
Nay, suns, which shine as clear

As thou when two thou did to Rome appear.
Now, Flora, deck thyself in fairest guise;
If that ye, winds, would hear
A voice surpassing far Amphion's lyre,
Your stormy chiding stay;
Let zephyr only breathe,
And with her tresses play,
Kissing sometimes those purple ports of death.
The winds all silent are,
And Phœbus in his chair,
Ensaffroning sea and air,
Makes vanish every star:
Night like a drunkard reels
Beyond the hills to shun his flaming wheels;
The fields with flow'rs are deck'd in every hue,
The clouds bespangle with bright gold their
    blue:
Here is the pleasant place,
And ev'ry thing, save her, who all should grace.

My thoughts hold mortal strife

My thoughts hold mortal strife;
I do detest my life,
And with lamenting cries,
Peace to my soul to bring,
Oft call that prince which here doth monarchise;
But he, grim-grinning king,
Who caitives scorns, and doth the blest sur-
    prise,
    Late having deckt with beauty's rose his tomb,
    Disdains to crop a weed, and will not come.

As, in a dusky and tempestuous night

As, in a dusky and tempestuous night,
A star is wont to spread her locks of gold,
And while her pleasant rays abroad are roll'd,
Some spiteful cloud doth rob us of her sight;
Fair soul, in this black age so shin'd thou bright,
And made all eyes with wonder thee behold,
Till ugly Death, depriving us of light,
In his grim misty arms thee did enfold.
Who more shall vaunt true beauty here to see?
What hope doth more in any heart remain,
That such perfections shall his reason rein,
If beauty, with thee born, too died with thee?
  World, plain no more of Love, nor count his
    harms;
  With his pale trophies Death hath hung his
    arms.

How many times night's silent queen her face

How many times night's silent queen her face
Hath hid, how oft with stars in silver mask
In Heaven's great hall she hath begun her task,
And cheer'd the waking eye in lower place!
How oft the sun hath made by Heaven's swift
    race
The happy lover to forsake the breast
Of this dear lady, wishing in the west
His golden coach to run had larger space!
I ever count, and number, since, alas!
I bade farewell to my heart's dearest guest;
The miles I compass, and in mind I chase
The floods and mountains hold me from my rest:
  But, woe is me! long count and count may I,
  Ere I see her whose absence makes me die.

My lute, be as thou wast when thou didst grow

My lute, be as thou wast when thou didst grow
With thy green mother in some shady grove,
When immelodious winds but made thee move,
And birds on thee their ramage[1] did bestow.
Sith that dear voice which did thy sounds ap-
    prove,
Which us'd in such harmonious strains to flow,
Is reft from earth to tune those spheres above,
What art thou but a harbinger of woe?
Thy pleasing notes be pleasing notes no more,
But orphan wailings to the fainting ear,
Each stop a sigh, each sound draws forth a
    tear:
Be therefore silent as in woods before,
  Or if that any hand to touch thee deign,
    Like widow'd turtle, still her loss complain.

This life, which seems so fair

This life, which seems so fair,
Is like a bubble blown up in the air
By sporting children's breath,
Who chase it everywhere,
And strive who can most motion it bequeath:
And though it sometime seem of its own might,
Like to an eye of gold, to be fix'd there,
And firm to hover in that empty height,
That only is because it is so light.
But in that pomp it doth not long appear;
  For even when most admir'd, it in a thought,
    As swell'd from nothing, doth dissolve in
    nought.

---

[1] songs.

The Permanency of Life

LIFE a right shadow is,
For if it long appear,
Then is it spent, and death's long night draws
    near:
Shadows are moving, light,
And is there aught so moving as is this?
When it is most in sight,
It steals away, and none can tell how, where,
So near our cradles to our coffins are.

The World a Game

THIS world a hunting is,
The prey poor man, the Nimrod fierce is Death;
His speedy greyhounds are
Lust, sickness, envy, care,
Strife that ne'er falls amiss,
With all those ills which haunt us while we
    breathe.
Now, if by chance we fly
Of these the eager chase,
Old age with stealing pace
Casts up his nets, and there we panting die.

If crost with all mishaps be my poor life

IF crost with all mishaps be my poor life,
If one short day I never spent in mirth,
If my spright with itself holds lasting strife,
If sorrow's death is but new sorrow's birth;
If this vain world be but a sable stage
Where slave-born man plays to the scoffing stars,
If youth be toss'd with love, with weakness age,
If knowledge serve to hold our thoughts in wars;
If time can close the hundred mouths of fame,
And make, what long since past, like that to be,
If virtue only be an idle name,
If I, when I was born, was born to die;
   Why seek I to prolong these loathsome days?
   The fairest rose in shortest time decays.

Doth then the world go thus, doth all thus move?

DOTH then the world go thus, doth all thus move?
Is this the justice which on earth we find?
Is this that firm decree which all doth bind?
Are these your influences, Powers above?
Those souls which vice's moody mists most blind,
Blind Fortune blindly most their friend doth prove;
And they who thee, poor idol, Virtue, love,
Ply like a feather toss'd by storm and wind.
Ah! if a Providence doth sway this all,
Why should best minds groan under most distress,
Or why should pride humility make thrall,
And injuries the innocent oppress?
   Heavens, hinder, stop this fate, or grant a time
   When good may have, as well as bad, their
    prime.

No Trust in Time

Look how the flower which ling'ringly doth fade,
The morning's darling late, the summer's queen,
Spoil'd of that juice which kept it fresh and green,
As high as it did raise, bows low the head:
Right so my life, contentments being dead,
Or in their contraries but only seen,
With swifter speed declines than erst it spread,
And, blasted, scarce now shows what it hath
    been.
As doth the pilgrim therefore, whom the night
By darkness would imprison on his way,
Think on thy home, my soul, and think aright
Of what yet rests thee of life's wasting day:
Thy sun posts westward, passed is thy morn,
And twice it is not given thee to be born.

Change should breed Change

New doth the sun appear,
The mountains' snows decay,
Crown'd with frail flowers forth comes the baby
    year.
My soul, time posts away,
And thou yet in that frost
Which flower and fruit hath lost,
As if all here immortal were, dost stay:
For shame! thy powers awake,
Look to that heaven which never night makes
    black,
And there, at that immortal sun's bright rays,
Deck thee with flowers which fear not rage of
    days.

The Book of the World

OF this fair volume which we world do name,
If we the sheets and leaves could turn with care,
Of him who it corrects, and did it frame,
We clear might read the art and wisdom rare;
Find out his power which wildest pow'rs doth
    tame,
His providence extending everywhere,
His justice which proud rebels doth not spare,
In every page, no, period of the same:
But silly we, like foolish children, rest
Well pleas'd with colour'd vellum, leaves of gold,
Fair dangling ribbons, leaving what is best,
On the great writer's sense ne'er taking hold;
    Or if by chance our minds do muse on aught,
    It is some picture on the margin wrought.

For the Baptist

THE last and greatest herald of heaven's King,
Girt with rough skins, hies to the deserts wild,
Among that savage brood the woods forth bring,
Which he than man more harmless found and
    mild:
His food was locusts, and what young doth spring,
With honey that from virgin hives distill'd;
Parch'd body, hollow eyes, some uncouth thing
Made him appear, long since from earth exil'd.
There burst he forth: 'All ye, whose hopes rely
On God, with me amidst these deserts mourn;
Repent, repent, and from old errors turn.'
Who listen'd to his voice, obey'd his cry?
    Only the echoes, which he made relent,
    Rung from their marble caves, 'Repent,
    repent!'

SIR ROBERT AYTON

1570–1638

Inconstancy Reproved

I DO confess thou'rt smooth and fair,
  And I might have gone near to love thee,
Had I not found the slightest prayer
  That lips could speak, had power to move
    thee;
But I can let thee now alone
As worthy to be loved by none.

I do confess thou'rt sweet; yet find
  Thee such an unthrift of thy sweets,
Thy favours are but like the wind
  That kisseth everything it meets:
And since thou canst with more than one,
Thou'rt worthy to be kiss'd by none.

The morning rose that untouch'd stands
  Arm'd with her briers, how sweet she
    smells!
But pluck'd and strain'd through ruder hands,
  Her sweets no longer with her dwells:
But scent and beauty both are gone,
And leaves fall from her, one by one.

Such fate ere long will thee betide
  When thou hast handled been awhile,
Like fair flowers to be thrown aside;
  And thou shalt sigh, when I shall smile,
To see thy love to every one
Hath brought thee to be loved by none.

To an Inconstant Mistress

I LOVED thee once; I'll love no more—
　Thine be the grief as is the blame;
Thou art not what thou wast before,
　What reason I should be the same?
　　He that can love unloved again,
　　Hath better store of love than brain:
　God send me love my debts to pay,
　While unthrifts fool their love away!

Nothing could have my love o'erthrown
　If thou hadst still continued mine;
Yea, if thou hadst remain'd thine own,
　I might perchance have yet been thine.
　　But thou thy freedom didst recall
　　That it thou might elsewhere enthral:
　And then how could I but disdain
　A captive's captive to remain?

When new desires had conquer'd thee
　And changed the object of thy will,
It had been lethargy in me,
　Not constancy, to love thee still.
　　Yea, it had been a sin to go
　　And prostitute affection so:
　Since we are taught no prayers to say
　To such as must to others pray.

Yet do thou glory in thy choice—
　Thy choice of his good fortune boast;
I'll neither grieve nor yet rejoice
　To see him gain what I have lost:
　　The height of my disdain shall be
　　To laugh at him, to blush for thee;
　To love thee still, but go no more
　A-begging at a beggar's door.

JAMES GRAHAM, MARQUIS OF MONTROSE
1612–50

My dear and only Love

My dear and only Love, I pray
  That little world of thee
Be govern'd by no other sway
  Than purest monarchy;
For if confusion have a part
  (Which virtuous souls abhor),
And hold a synod in thine heart,
  I'll never love thee more.

Like Alexander I will reign,
  And I will reign alone;
My thoughts did evermore disdain
  A rival on my throne.
He either fears his fate too much,
  Or his deserts are small,
That dares not put it to the touch,
  To gain or lose it all.

And in the empire of thine heart,
  Where I should solely be,
If others do pretend a part
  Or dare to vie with me,
Or if *Committees* thou erect,
  And go on such a score,
I'll laugh and sing at thy neglect,
  And never love thee more.

But if thou wilt prove faithful then,
  And constant of thy word,
I'll make thee glorious by my pen
  And famous by my sword;

I'll serve thee in such noble ways
    Was never heard before;
I'll crown and deck thee all with bays,
    And love thee more and more.

ANON.

Epitaphs

i

MAN, tak heed to me,
How thou shalt be,
    Whan thou art dead;
Dry as a tree,
Worms sall eat thee,
Thy great beauty
    Sall be like lead.

The time hath been,
In my youth green,
That I was clean
    Of body as ye are;
But for my een
Now two holes been;
Of me is seen
    But banes bare.

ii

THIS earthly tomb so low, and heaven so hie
Keeps in divided pairts my dear from me;
The heavens her soul, earth corpse, so must ensue
That this division rendered both their due;
But while that each has repossessed his pairt,
I want the whole, and with the whole, my hairt.

(From Tombstones in the Howff Cemetery, Dundee.)

The Gaberlunzie[1] Man

THE pawky auld carle cam ower the lea
Wi' mony good-e'ens and days to me,
Saying, 'Gudewife, for your courtesie,
 Will you lodge a silly poor man?'
The night was cauld, the carle was wat,
And down ayont the ingle he sat;
My dochter's shoulders he 'gan to clap,
 And cadgily[2] ranted and sang.

'O wow!' quo' he, 'were I as free
As first when I saw this countrie,
How blyth and merry wad I be!
 And I wad nevir think lang.'
He grew canty,[3] and she grew fain,
But little did her auld minny ken
What thir twa togither were say'n
 When wooing they were sa thrang.

'An' O!' quo' he, 'an' ye were as black
As e'er the crown of your daddy's hat,
'Tis I wad lay thee by my back,
 And awa' wi' me thou sould gang.'
'An' O!' quo' she, 'an' I were as white
As e'er the snaw lay on the dike,
I'd clead me braw and lady-like,
 And awa' wi' thee I would gang.'

Between the twa was made a plot;
They raise a wee before the cock,
And wilily they shot the lock,
 And fast to the bent are gane.
Up in the morn the auld wife raise,
And at her leisure put on her claiths,
Syne to the servant's bed she gaes,
 To speir for the silly poor man.

[1] strolling beggar. [2] merrily. [3] cheerful.

She gaed to the bed where the beggar lay,
The strae was cauld, he was away;
She clapt her hand, cried 'Waladay!
   For some of our gear will be gane.'
Some ran to coffers and some to kist,
But nought was stown, that could be mist;
She danced her lane, cried 'Praise be blest,
   I have lodg'd a leal poor man.

'Since naething's awa' as we can learn,
The kirn's to kirn and milk to earn;
Gae but the house, lass, and waken my bairn,
   And bid her come quickly ben.'
The servant gaed where the dochter lay,
The sheets were cauld, she was away,
And fast to her goodwife did say,
   'She's aff with the gaberlunzie man.'

'O fy gar ride and fy gar rin,
And haste ye find these traitors again;
For she's be burnt, and he's be slain,
   The wearifu' gaberlunzie man.'
Some rade upo' horse, some ran afit,
The wife was wud, and out of her wit:
She could na gang, nor yet could she sit,
   But ay she curs'd and she bann'd.

Meantime far 'hind out o'er the lea,
Fu' snug in a glen, where nane could see,
The twa, with kindly sport and glee,
   Cut frae a new cheese a whang[1]:
The priving[2] was gude, it pleas'd them baith,
To lo'e her for ay, he ga'e her his aith.
Quo' she, 'To leave thee I will be laith,
   My winsome gaberlunzie man.

---

     [1] thick slice.   [2] tasting.

'O kend my minny¹ I were wi' you,
Ill-fardly wad she crook her mou';
Sic a poor man she'd never trow,
   After the gaberlunzie man.'
'My dear,' quo' he, 'ye're yet ower young,
And hae na learn'd the beggar's tongue,
To follow me frae toun to toun,
   And carry the gaberlunzie on.

'Wi' cauk and keel² I'll win your bread,
And spindles and whorles for them wha need,
Whilk is a gentle trade indeed,
   The gaberlunzie to carry, O.
I'll bow my leg, and crook my knee,
And draw a black clout ower my e'e;
A cripple or blind they will ca' me,
   While we sall sing and be merry, O.'

LADY GRISELL BAILLIE
1665–1746

There ance was a may

THERE ance was a may, and she loo'd na
    men;
She biggit her bonnie bower doun in yon glen;
But now she cries, Dool! and well-a-day!
Come doun the green gait³ and come here away!

When bonnie young Johnnie cam' ower the sea,
He said he saw naething sae lovely as me;
He hecht⁴ me baith rings and mony braw
    things,—
And werena my heart licht I wad dee.

---

¹ mother.   ² chalk and ruddle.   ³ way.   ⁴ promised.

He had a wee titty[1] that loo'd na me,
Because I was twice as bonnie as she;
She raised such a pother 'twixt him and his
   mother
That werena my heart licht I wad dee.

The day it was set, and the bridal to be:
The wife took a dwam,[2] and lay doun to dee;
She maned and she graned out o' dolour and
   pain,
Till he vow'd he never wad see me again.

His kin was for ane of a higher degree,
Said, What had he to do wi' the like of me?
Albeit I was bonnie, I wasna for Johnnie,—
And werena my heart licht I wad dee.

They said I had neither cow nor calf,
Nor dribbles o' drink rins through the draff,
Nor pickles o' meal rins through the mill-e'e;
And werena my heart licht I wad dee.

His titty she was baith wylie and slee:
She spied me as I cam' ower the lea;
And then she ran in and made a loud din,—
Believe your ain een an' ye trow na me.

His bonnet stood aye fu' round on his brow,—
His auld ane look'd aye as weel as some 's new;
But now he lets 't wear ony gait it will hing,
And casts himself dowie upon the corn-bing.[3]

And now he gaes daund'ring about the dykes,
And a' he dow do is to hund the tykes:
The live-lang nicht he ne'er steeks his e'e;
And werena my heart licht I wad dee.

   [1] sister.   [2] swoon.   [3] heap of corn.

Were I but young for thee, as I hae been,
We should hae been gallopin' doun on yon green,
And linkin' it on the lily-white lea,—
And wow! gin I were but young for thee!

ANON.

Waly, Waly

O WALY, waly, up the bank,
    And waly, waly, doun the brae,
And waly, waly, yon burn-side,
    Where I and my Love wont to gae!
I lean'd my back unto an aik,
    I thocht it was a trustie tree;
But first it bow'd and syne it brak—
    Sae my true love did lichtlie me.

O waly, waly, gin love be bonnie
    A little time while it is new!
But when 'tis auld it waxeth cauld,
    And fades awa' like morning dew.
O wherefore should I busk my heid,
    Or wherefore should I kame my hair?
For my true Love has me forsook,
    And says he'll never lo'e me mair.

Now Arthur's Seat sall be my bed,
    The sheets sall ne'er be 'filed by me;
Saint Anton's well sall be my drink;
    Since my true Love has forsaken me.
Marti'mas wind, when wilt thou blaw,
    And shake the green leaves aff the tree?
O gentle Death, when wilt thou come?
    For of my life I am wearìe.

'Tis not the frost, that freezes fell,
  Nor blawing snaw's inclemencie,
'Tis not sic cauld that makes me cry;
  But my Love's heart grown cauld to me.
When we cam in by Glasgow toun,
  We were a comely sicht to see;
My Love was clad in the black velvèt,
  And I mysel in cramasie.[1]

But had I wist, before I kist,
  That love had been sae ill to win,
I had lock'd my heart in a case o' gowd,
  And pinn'd it wi' a siller pin.
And O! if my young babe were born,
  And set upon the nurse's knee;
And I mysel were dead and gane,
  And the green grass growing over me!

ALLAN RAMSAY
1686–1758

The Lass of Patie's Mill

THE lass of Patie's mill,
  So bonny, blythe, and gay,
In spite of all my skill,
  Hath stole my heart away.
When tedding[2] of the hay,
  Bare-headed on the green,
Love 'midst her locks did play,
  And wanton'd in her een.

---

[1] crimson.   [2] spreading.

Her arms, white, round, and smooth,
  Breasts rising in their dawn,
To age it would give youth,
  To press them with his hand.
Thro' all my spirits ran
  An extasy of bliss,
When I such sweetness fan'd
  Wrapt in a balmy kiss.

Without the help of art,
  Like flowers which grace the wild,
She did her sweets impart,
  Whene'er she spoke or smil'd.
Her looks they were so mild,
  Free from affected pride,
She me to love beguil'd;
  I wish'd her for my bride.

O had I all the wealth
  Hopetoun's high mountains fill,
Insur'd lang life and health,
  And pleasure at my will;
I'd promise and fulfil,
  That none but bonny she,
The lass of Patie's mill,
  Shou'd share the same with me.

My Peggy

My Peggy is a young thing
  Just enter'd in her teens,
Fair as the day, and sweet as May,
Fair as the day, and always gay.
  My Peggy is a young thing.
  And I'm na very auld,
Yet weel I like to meet her at
  The wauking[1] o' the fauld.

  [1] watching.

My Peggy speaks sae sweetly,
　　Whene'er we meet alane,
I wish nae mair to lay my care,
I wish nae mair o' a' that 's rare.
My Peggy speaks sae sweetly,
　　To a' the lave I'm cauld,
But she gars a' my spirits glow
　　At wauking o' the fauld.

My Peggy smiles sae kindly
　　Whene'er I whisper love,
That I look doun on a' the toun,
That I look doun upon a croun.
My Peggy smiles sae kindly,
　　It maks me blythe and bauld,
An' naething gies me sic delight
　　As wauking o' the fauld.

My Peggy sings sae saftly
　　When on my pipe I play,
By a' the rest it is confest,
By a' the rest that she sings best.
My Peggy sings sae saftly,
　　And in her sangs are tauld
Wi' innocence, the wale[1] o' sense,
　　At wauking o' the fauld.

Look up to Pentland's tow'ring tap

Look up to Pentland's tow'ring tap,
　　Buried beneath big wreaths o' snaw,
O'er ilka cleugh,[2] ilk scar[3] an' slap,[4]
　　As high as ony Roman wa'.

---

[1] choice.　　　[2] hollow.　　　[3] cliff.　　　[4] pass.

Driving their ba's frae whins or tee,
    There 's no ae gowfer to be seen;
Nor douser[1] fouk, wysing a-jee[2]
    The byas bouls[3] on Tamson's green.

Then fling on coals, an' ripe[4] the ribs,
    An' beek[5] the house baith butt an' ben[6];
That mutchkin[7]-stoup it hauds but dribs,[8]
    Then let 's get in the tappit hen.[9]

Guid claret best keeps out the cauld,
    An' drives awa the winter soon;
It maks a man baith gash[10] an' bauld,
    An' heaves his saul ayont the moon.

Leave to the gods your ilka[11] care;
    If that they think us worth their while,
They can a rowth[12] o' blessings spare,
    Which will our fashious[13] fears beguile.

For what they hae a mind to do,
    That will they do, shou'd we gang wud;
If they command the storms to blaw,
    Then upo' sight the hailstanes thud.

But soon as e'er they cry, Be quiet,
    The blatt'ring winds daur nae mair move,
But cour into their caves, an' wait
    The high command o' supreme Jove.

Let neist day come as it thinks fit,
    The present minute 's only ours;
On pleasure let 's employ our wit,
    An' laugh at fortune's feckless[14] pow'rs.

---

[1] quieter.   [2] gently pushing off the straight.   [3] biased bowls.   [4] poke.   [5] heat.   [6] in both its rooms. [7] pint.   [8] drops.   [9] Scots quart measure.   [10] talkative. [11] every.   [12] abundance.   [13] vexing.   [14] weak and foolish.

Be sure ye dinna quat the grip
　　O' ilka joy whan ye are young,
Before auld age your vitals nip,
　　An' lay ye twafald o'er a rung.[1]

Sweet youth 's a blythe an' heartsome time;
　　Then, lads an' lasses, while it 's May,
Gae pu' the gowan[2] in its prime,
　　Before it wither an' decay.

Watch the saft minutes o' delight,
　　Whan Jenny speaks beneath her breath,
An' kisses, laying a' the wyte[3]
　　On you, if she kepp ony skaith.[4]

Haith[5] ye're ill-bred, she'll smiling say,
　　Ye'll worry me, ye greedy rook;
Syne frae your arms she'll rin away,
　　An' hide hersell in some dark nook;

Her laugh will lead you to the place
　　Whare lies the happiness you want,
An' plainly tells you to your face,
　　Nineteen nay-says[6] are hauf a grant.

Now to her heaving bosom cling,
　　An' sweetly toolie[7] for a kiss,
Frae her fair finger whup a ring,
　　As taiken o' a future bliss.

These bennisons, I'm very sure,
　　Are o' the gods' indulgent grant;
Then, surly carles, whisht, forbear
　　To plague us wi' your whining cant.

　　　　　　　　(*Imitations of Horace: Car. I, 9.*)

---

[1] doubled over a staff.　　[2] daisy.　　[3] blame.　　[4] catch
any harm.　　[5] faith.　　[6] denials.　　[7] struggle.

Up in the Air

Now the sun 's gane out o' sight,
Beet the ingle,[1] an' snuff the light;
In glens the fairies skip an' dance,
An' witches wallop o'er to France.
     Up in the air
     On my bonny grey mare;
An' I see her yet, an' I see her yet.
     Up in, etc.

The wind 's drifting hail an' snaw
O'er frozen hags[2] like a foot ba';
Nae starns keek[3] thro' the azure slit,
It 's cauld an' mirk as ony pit.
     The man i' the moon
     Is carousing aboon,
D'ye see, d'ye see, d'ye see him yet.
     The man, etc.

Tak your glass to clear your een,
It 's the elixir hales[4] the spleen,
Baith wit and mirth it will inspire,
An' gently puffs the lover's fire.
     Up i' the air,
     It drives away care;
Hae wi' ye, hae wi' ye, an' hae wi' ye, lads, yet.
     Up in, etc.

Steek the doors, keep out the frost;
Come, Willy, gie's about your toast;
Till't lads, an' lilt it out,
An' let us hae a blythesome bout.

---

[1] stir up the fire.   [2] marshes.   [3] stars peep.
[4] heals.

Up wi't there, there,
Dinna cheat, but drink fair,
Huzza, huzza, an' huzza, lads, yet.
Up wi't, etc.

JAMES THOMSON
1700–48

Winter

Now, when the cheerless empire of the sky
To Capricorn the Centaur-Archer yields,
And fierce Aquarius stains the inverted year—
Hung o'er the farthest verge of heaven, the sun
Scarce spreads o'er ether the dejected day.
Faint are his gleams, and ineffectual shoot
His struggling rays in horizontal lines
Through the thick air; as clothed in cloudy
        storm,
Weak, wan, and broad, he skirts the southern
        sky;
And, soon descending, to the long dark night,
Wide-shading all, the prostrate world resigns.
Nor is the night unwished; while vital heat,
Light, life, and joy the dubious day forsake.
Meantime, in sable cincture, shadows vast,
Deep-tinged and damp, and congregated clouds,
And all the vapoury turbulence of heaven
Involve the face of things. Thus Winter falls,
A heavy gloom oppressive o'er the world,
Through Nature shedding influence malign,
And rouses up the seeds of dark disease.
The soul of man dies in him, loathing life,
And black with more than melancholy views.
The cattle droop; and o'er the furrowed land,

Fresh from the plough, the dun discoloured flocks,
Untended spreading, crop the wholesome root.
Along the woods, along the moorish fens,
Sighs the sad genius of the coming storm;
And up among the loose disjointed cliffs
And fractured mountains wild, the brawling
brook
And cave, presageful, send a hollow moan,
Resounding long in listening fancy's ear.
  Then comes the father of the tempest forth,
Wrapt in black glooms. First, joyless rains
obscure
Drive through the mingling skies with vapour
foul,
Dash on the mountain's brow, and shake the
woods
That grumbling wave below. The unsightly
plain
Lies a brown deluge; as the low-bent clouds
Pour flood on flood, yet unexhausted still
Combine, and, deepening into night, shut up
The day's fair face. The wanderers of heaven,
Each to his home, retire; save those that love
To take their pastime in the troubled air,
Or skimming flutter round the dimply pool.
The cattle from the untasted fields return
And ask, with meaning low, their wonted stalls,
Or ruminate in the contiguous shade.
Thither the household feathery people crowd,
The crested cock, with all his female train,
Pensive and dripping; while the cottage-hind
Hangs o'er the enlivening blaze, and taleful there
Recounts his simple frolic: much he talks,
And much he laughs, nor recks the storm that
blows

Without, and rattles on his humble roof.
   Wide o'er the brim, with many a torrent
      swelled,
And the mixed ruin of its banks o'erspread,
At last the roused-up river pours along:
Resistless, roaring, dreadful, down it comes,
From the rude mountain and the mossy wild,
Tumbling through rocks abrupt, and sounding
      far;
Then o'er the sanded valley floating spreads,
Calm, sluggish, silent; till again, constrained
Between two meeting hills, it bursts a way
Where rocks and woods o'erhang the turbid
      stream;
There, gathering triple force, rapid and deep,
It boils, and wheels, and foams, and thunders
      through.

   Nature! great parent! whose unceasing hand
Rolls round the Seasons of the changeful year,
How mighty, how majestic are thy works!
With what a pleasing dread they swell the soul,
That sees astonished, and astonished sings!
Ye too, ye winds! that now begin to blow
With boisterous sweep, I raise my voice to you.
Where are your stores, ye powerful beings! say,
Where your aerial magazines reserved
To swell the brooding terrors of the storm?
In what far-distant region of the sky,
Hushed in deep silence, sleep you when 'tis calm?

   When from the pallid sky the Sun descends,
With many a spot, that o'er his glaring orb
Uncertain wanders, stained; red fiery streaks
Begin to flush around. The reeling clouds

Stagger with dizzy poise, as doubting yet
Which master to obey; while, rising slow,
Blank in the leaden-coloured east, the moon
Wears a wan circle round her blunted horns.
Seen through the turbid, fluctuating air,
The stars obtuse emit a shivering ray;
Or frequent seem to shoot athwart the gloom,
And long behind them trail the whitening blaze.
Snatched in short eddies, plays the withered leaf;
And on the flood the dancing feather floats.
With broadened nostrils to the sky upturned,
The conscious heifer snuffs the stormy gale.
Even, as the matron, at her nightly task,
With pensive labour draws the flaxen thread,
The wasted taper and the crackling flame
Foretell the blast. But chief the plumy race,
The tenants of the sky, its changes speak.
Retiring from the downs, where all day long
They picked their scanty fare, a blackening train
Of clamorous rooks thick-urge their weary flight,
And seek the closing shelter of the grove.
Assiduous, in his bower, the wailing owl
Plies his sad song. The cormorant on high
Wheels from the deep, and screams along the
    land.
Loud shrieks the soaring hern; and with wild
    wing
The circling sea-fowl cleave the flaky clouds.
Ocean, unequal pressed, with broken tide
And blind commotion heaves; while from the
    shore,
Eat into caverns by the restless wave,
And forest-rustling mountain comes a voice
That, solemn-sounding, bids the world prepare.
Then issues forth the storm with sudden burst,

And hurls the whole precipitated air
Down in a torrent. On the passive main
Descends the ethereal force, and with strong gust
Turns from its bottom the discoloured deep.
Through the black night that sits immense
          around,
Lashed into foam, the fierce-conflicting brine
Seems o'er a thousand raging waves to burn.
Meantime the mountain-billows, to the clouds
In dreadful tumult swelled, surge above surge,
Burst into chaos with tremendous roar,
And anchored navies from their stations drive
Wild as the winds, across the howling waste
Of mighty waters: now the inflated wave
Straining they scale, and now impetuous shoot
Into the secret chambers of the deep,
The wintry Baltic thundering o'er their head.
Emerging thence again, before the breath
Of full-exerted heaven they wing their course,
And dart on distant coasts—if some sharp rock
Or shoal insidious break not their career,
And in loose fragments fling them floating round.
    Nor less at land the loosened tempest reigns.
The mountain thunders, and its sturdy sons
Stoop to the bottom of the rocks they shade.
Lone on the midnight steep, and all aghast,
The dark wayfaring stranger breathless toils,
And, often falling, climbs against the blast.
Low waves the rooted forest, vexed, and sheds
What of its tarnished honours yet remain—
Dashed down and scattered, by the tearing wind's
Assiduous fury, its gigantic limbs.
Thus struggling through the dissipated grove,
The whirling tempest raves along the plain;
And, on the cottage thatched or lordly roof

Keen-fastening, shakes them to the solid base.
Sleep frighted flies; and round the rocking dome,
For entrance eager, howls the savage blast.
Then too, they say, through all the burdened air
Long groans are heard, shrill sounds, and distant
    sighs,
That, uttered by the demon of the night,
Warn the devoted wretch of woe and death.
    Huge uproar lords it wide. The clouds, com-
    mixed
With stars swift-gliding, sweep along the sky.
All Nature reels: till Nature's King, who oft
Amid tempestuous darkness dwells alone,
And on the wings of the careering wind
Walks dreadfully serene, commands a calm;
Then straight air, sea, and earth are hushed at
    once.
    As yet 'tis midnight deep. The weary clouds,
Slow-meeting, mingle into solid gloom.
Now, while the drowsy world lies lost in sleep,
Let me associate with the serious Night,
And Contemplation, her sedate compeer;
Let me shake off the intrusive cares of day,
And lay the meddling senses all aside.
    Where now, ye lying vanities of life!
Ye ever-tempting, ever-cheating train!
Where are you now? and what is your amount?
Vexation, disappointment, and remorse.
Sad, sickening thought! and yet deluded man,
A scene of crude disjointed visions past,
And broken slumbers, rises still resolved,
With new-flushed hopes, to run the giddy round.
    Father of light and life! thou Good Supreme!
O teach me what is good! teach me Thyself!
Save me from folly, vanity, and vice,

From every low pursuit; and feed my soul
With knowledge, conscious peace, and virtue
    pure—
Sacred, substantial, never-fading bliss!

The keener tempests come: and, fuming dun
From all the livid east or piercing north,
Thick clouds ascend, in whose capacious womb
A vapoury deluge lies, to snow congealed.
Heavy they roll their fleecy world along,
And the sky saddens with the gathered storm.
Through the hushed air the whitening shower
    descends,
At first thin-wavering; till at last the flakes
Fall broad and wide and fast, dimming the day
With a continual flow. The cherished fields
Put on their winter-robe of purest white.
'Tis brightness all; save where the new snow
    melts
Along the mazy current. Low the woods
Bow their hoar head; and, ere the languid sun
Faint from the west emits his evening ray,
Earth's universal face, deep-hid and chill,
Is one wild dazzling waste, that buries wide
The works of man. Drooping, the labourer-ox
Stands covered o'er with snow, and then demands
The fruit of all his toil. The fowls of heaven,
Tamed by the cruel season, crowd around
The winnowing tree, and claim the little boon
Which Providence assigns them. One alone,
The redbreast, sacred to the household gods,
Wisely regardful of the embroiling sky,
In joyless fields and thorny thickets leaves
His shivering mates, and pays to trusted man
His annual visit. Half afraid, he first
Against the window beats; then brisk alights

On the warm hearth; then, hopping o'er the
 floor,
Eyes all the smiling family askance,
And pecks, and starts, and wonders where he is—
Till, more familiar grown, the table-crumbs
Attract his slender feet. The foodless wilds
Pour forth their brown inhabitants. The hare,
Though timorous of heart, and hard beset
By death in various forms, dark snares, and dogs,
And more unpitying men, the garden seeks,
Urged on by fearless want. The bleating kind
Eye the bleak heaven, and next the glistening
 earth,
With looks of dumb despair; then, sad-dispersed,
Dig for the withered herb through heaps of snow.
 Now, shepherds, to your helpless charge be
 kind:
Baffle the raging year, and fill their pens
With food at will; lodge them below the storm,
And watch them strict: for, from the bellowing
 east,
In this dire season, oft the whirlwind's wing
Sweeps up the burden of whole wintry plains
In one wide waft, and o'er the hapless flocks,
Hid in the hollow of two neighbouring hills,
The billowy tempest whelms; till, upward urged,
The valley to a shining mountain swells,
Tipt with a wreath high-curling in the sky.
 As thus the snows arise, and, foul and fierce,
All Winter drives along the darkened air,
In his own loose-revolving fields the swain
Disastered stands; sees other hills ascend,
Of unknown joyless brow; and other scenes,
Of horrid prospect, shag the trackless plain;
Nor finds the river nor the forest, hid

Beneath the formless wild; but wanders on
From hill to dale, still more and more astray—
Impatient flouncing through the drifted heaps,
Stung with the thoughts of home: the thoughts of
    home
Rush on his nerves and call their vigour forth
In many a vain attempt. How sinks his soul!
What black despair, what horror fills his heart,
When, for the dusky spot which fancy feigned
His tufted cottage rising through the snow,
He meets the roughness of the middle waste,
Far from the track and blest abode of man;
While round him night resistless closes fast,
And every tempest, howling o'er his head,
Renders the savage wilderness more wild.
Then throng the busy shapes into his mind
Of covered pits, unfathomably deep,
A dire descent! beyond the power of frost;
Of faithless bogs; of precipices huge,
Smoothed up with snow; and (what is land
    unknown,
What water) of the still unfrozen spring,
In the loose marsh or solitary lake,
Where the fresh fountain from the bottom boils.
These check his fearful steps; and down he sinks
Beneath the shelter of the shapeless drift,
Thinking o'er all the bitterness of death,
Mixed with the tender anguish nature shoots
Through the wrung bosom of the dying man—
His wife, his children, and his friends unseen.
In vain for him the officious wife prepares
The fire fair-blazing and the vestment warm;
In vain his little children, peeping out
Into the mingling storm, demand their sire
With tears of artless innocence. Alas!

Nor wife nor children more shall he behold,
Nor friends, nor sacred home. On every nerve
The deadly Winter seizes, shuts up sense,
And, o'er his inmost vitals creeping cold,
Lays him along the snows a stiffened corse,
Stretched out, and bleaching in the northern
    blast.

(The Seasons, Winter, ll. 41–321.)

To Amanda

COME, dear Amanda, quit the town,
  And to the rural hamlets fly;
Behold! the wintry storms are gone,
  A gentle radiance glads the sky;

The birds awake, the flowers appear,
  Earth spreads a verdant couch for thee;
'Tis joy and music all we hear,
  'Tis love and beauty all we see.

Come, let us mark the gradual spring,
  How peeps the bud, the blossom blows;
Till Philomel begins to sing,
  And perfect May to swell the rose.

Even so thy rising charms improve,
  As life's warm season grows more bright;
And, opening to the sighs of love,
  Thy beauties glow with full delight.

To Fortune

FOR ever, Fortune, wilt thou prove
An unrelenting foe to love,
And, when we meet a mutual heart,
Come in between and bid us part;

Bid us sigh on from day to day,
And wish, and wish the soul away;
Till youth and genial years are flown,
And all the life of life is gone?

But busy, busy still art thou,
To bind the loveless joyless vow,
The heart from pleasure to delude,
And join the gentle to the rude.

For once, O Fortune! hear my prayer,
And I absolve thy future care—
All other blessings I resign;
Make but the dear Amanda mine!

Enchanted Ground

In lowly dale, fast by a river's side,
With woody hill o'er hill encompassed round,
A most enchanting wizard did abide,
Than whom a fiend more fell is nowhere
    found.
It was, I ween, a lovely spot of ground;
And there a season atween June and May,
Half prankt with spring, with summer half
    imbrowned,
A listless climate made, where, sooth to say,
No living wight could work, ne carèd even for
    play.

Was nought around but images of rest:
Sleep-soothing   groves,   and   quiet   lawns
    between;
And flowery beds that slumbrous influence kest,
From poppies breathed; and beds of pleasant
    green,

Where never yet was creeping creature seen.
Meantime unnumbered glittering streamlets
    played,
And hurlèd everywhere their waters sheen;
That, as they bickered through the sunny
    glade,
Though restless still themselves, a lulling murmur
    made.

Joined to the prattle of the purling rills,
Were heard the lowing herds along the vale,
And flocks loud-bleating from the distant
    hills,
And vacant shepherds piping in the dale:
And now and then sweet Philomel would
    wail,
Or stock-doves plain amid the forest deep,
That drowsy rustled to the sighing gale;
And still a coil the grasshopper did keep:
Yet all these sounds yblent inclinèd all to
    sleep.

Full in the passage of the vale, above,
A sable, silent, solemn forest stood;
Where nought but shadowy forms were seen to
    move,
As Idless fancied in her dreaming mood.
And up the hills, on either side, a wood
Of blackening pines, ay waving to and fro,
Sent forth a sleepy horror through the
    blood;
And where this valley winded out, below,
The murmuring main was heard, and scarcely
    heard, to flow.

A pleasing land of drowsyhed it was:
Of dreams that wave before the half-shut eye;
And of gay castles in the clouds that pass,
For ever flushing round a summer sky:
There eke the soft delights, that witchingly
Instil a wanton sweetness through the breast,
And the calm pleasures always hovered nigh;
But whate'er smacked of noyance, or unrest,
Was far far off expelled from this delicious nest.

(*The Castle of Indolence*, stanzas II–VI.)

Finis

As those we love decay, we die in part,
String after string is severed from the heart;
Till loosened life, at last but breathing clay,
Without one pang is glad to fall away.
Unhappy he who latest feels the blow,
Whose eyes have wept o'er every friend laid low,
Dragged lingering on from partial death to
    death,
Till, dying, all he can resign is breath.

(*On the death of Mr. William Aikman the Painter*, ll. 35–42.)

ANON.

Low doun in the Broom

My daddie is a cankert carle,[1]
    He'll no twine[2] wi' his gear;
My minnie she's a scauldin' wife,[3]
    Hauds a' the house asteer.[4]

---

[1] crusty old man.   [2] part.   [3] My mother she's a scolding
woman.   [4] keeps all the house in a turmoil.

But let them say, or let them do,
    It 's a' ane to me,
For he 's low doun, he 's in the broom,
    That 's waitin' on me:
Waitin' on me, my love,
    He 's waitin' on me:
For he 's low doun, he 's in the broom,
    That 's waitin' on me.

My auntie Kate sits at her wheel,
   And sair she lightlies me;
But weel I ken it 's a' envy,
   For ne'er a joe[1] has she.

My cousin Kate was sair beguiled
   Wi' Johnnie o' the Glen;
And aye sinsyne she cries, Beware
   O' fause deluding men.

Gleed[2] Sandy he cam west yestreen,
   And speired[3] when I saw Pate;
And aye sinsyne the neebors round
   They jeer me air and late.
    But let them say, or let them do,
        It 's a' ane to me,
    For he 's low doun, he 's in the broom,
        That 's waitin' on me:
    Waitin' on me, my love,
        He 's waitin' on me:
    For he 's low doun, he 's in the broom,
        That 's waitin' on me.

    [1] sweetheart.   [2] squinting.   [3] asked.

Aye Waukin' O!

O SPRING 's a pleasant time,
  Flowers o' every colour—
The sweet bird builds her nest,
  And I long for my lover.
    Aye waukin' O,
      Waukin' aye, and weary,
    Sleep can I get nane,
      For thinkin' o' my dearie.

O I'm wat, wat,
  O I'm wat and weary;
Yet fain I'd rise and run
  If I thought to meet my dearie.

When I sleep I dream,
  When I wauk I'm eerie;
Sleep can I get nane,
  For thinkin' o' my dearie.

Lanely night comes on;
  A' the lave are sleeping;
I think on my love,
  And blear my een wi' greeting.

Feather-beds are soft,
  Painted rooms are bonnie;
But a kiss o' my dear love
  Is better far than ony.

O for Friday's night,
  Friday at the gloaming!
O for Friday's night!
  Friday 's lang o' coming.
    Aye waukin' O,
      Waukin' aye, and weary,
    Sleep can I get nane,
      For thinkin' o' my dearie.

DAVID MALLET

1700?–65

William and Margaret

'Twas at the silent, solemn hour
  When night and morning meet;
In glided Margaret's grimly ghost,
  And stood at William's feet.

Her face was like an April morn
  Clad in a wintry cloud;
And clay-cold was her lily hand,
  That held her sable shroud.

So shall the fairest face appear
  When youth and years are flown:
Such is the robe that kings must wear,
  When death has reft their crown.

Her bloom was like the springing flower,
  That sips the silver dew;
The rose was budded in her cheek—
  Just opening to the view.

But love had, like the canker-worm,
  Consumed her early prime:
The rose grew pale, and left her cheek—
  She died before her time.

'Awake!' she cried, 'thy true love calls—
  Come from her midnight grave:
Now let thy pity hear the maid
  Thy love refused to save.

'This is the dumb and dreary hour
  When injured ghosts complain;—
When yawning graves give up their dead
  To haunt the faithless swain.

'Bethink thee, William, of thy fault,
　Thy pledge and broken oath!
And give me back my maiden-vow,
　And give me back my troth.

'Why did you promise love to me,
　And not that promise keep?
Why did you swear my eyes were bright—
　Yet leave those eyes to weep?

'How could you say my face was fair,
　And yet that face forsake?
How could you win my virgin heart,
　Yet leave that heart to break?

'Why did you say my lip was sweet,
　And made the scarlet pale?
And why did I, young witless maid!
　Believe the flattering tale?

'That face, alas! no more is fair,
　Those lips no longer red:
Dark are my eyes, now closed in death,
　And every charm is fled.

'The hungry worm my sister is;
　This winding-sheet I wear:
And cold and weary lasts our night,
　Till that last morn appear.

'But hark! the cock has warn'd me hence—
　A long and last adieu!
Come see, false man, how low she lies,
　Who died for love of you.'

The lark sang loud; the morning smiled,
　With beams of rosy red:
Pale William quaked in every limb,
　And raving left his bed.

He hied him to the fatal place
    Where Margaret's body lay;
And stretch'd him on the green-grass turf
    That wrapt her breathless clay.

And thrice he call'd on Margaret's name,
    And thrice he wept full sore;
Then laid his cheek to her cold grave,
    And word spake never more!

ALISON RUTHERFORD
(MRS. COCKBURN)
1712–94

The Flowers of the Forest

I'VE seen the smiling of Fortune beguiling,
    I've tasted her favours, and felt her decay:
Sweet is her blessing, and kind her caressing;
    But soon it is fled—it is fled far away.

I've seen the Forest adornéd the foremost
    With flowers of the fairest—most pleasant and
        gay:
Full sweet was their blooming—their scent the
    air perfuming;
    But now they are wither'd and a' wede away.

I've seen the morning with gold the hills adorning,
    And the red tempest storming before parting
        day:
I've seen Tweed's silver streams, glittering in the
    sunny beams,
    Grow drumly[1] and dark as they roll'd on their
    way.

[1] muddy.

O fickle Fortune! why this cruel sporting?
  Why thus perplex us poor sons of a day?
Thy frowns cannot fear me, thy smiles cannot
    cheer me—
  Since the Flowers of the Forest are a' wede
    away.

JANE ELLIOT

1727–1805

The Flowers of the Forest

I'VE heard them lilting at our yowe-milking—
  Lasses a-lilting before dawn of day;
But now they are moaning on ilka green loan-
    ing—
  The Flowers of the Forest are a' wede away.

At buchts,[1] in the morning, nae blythe lads are
    scorning;
  Lasses are lonely and dowie and wae;—
Nae daffin', nae gabbin'—but sighing and sab-
    bing
  Ilk ane lifts her leglin[2] and hies her away.

In hairst, at the shearing, nae youths now are
    jeering—
  Bandsters[3] are runkled[4] and lyart[5] or grey:
At fair or at preaching, nae wooing, nae fleech-
    ing[6]—
  The Flowers of the Forest are a' wede away.

---

  [1] sheep-folds.   [2] milk-pail.   [3] binders.   [4] wrinkled.
[5] grizzled.   [6] flattering.

At e'en, in the gloaming, nae swankies[1] are roam-
  ing,
  'Bout stacks with the lasses at bogle to play;
But ilk maid sits drearie, lamenting her dearie—
  The Flowers of the Forest are a' wede away.

Dool and wae for the order sent our lads to the
  Border!
  The English, for ance, by guile wan the day;—
The Flowers of the Forest, that foucht aye the
  foremost—
  The prime of our land—are cauld in the clay.

We'll hear nae mair lilting at the yowe-milking;
  Women and bairns are heartless and wae,
Sighing and moaning on ilka green loaning—
  The Flowers of the Forest are a' wede away.

JOHN SKINNER

1721–1807

Tullochgorum

Come, gie's a sang, Montgomery cry'd,
And lay your disputes a' aside;
What signifies't for folks to chide
  For what was done before them?
Let Whig and Tory a' agree,
  Whig and Tory, Whig and Tory,
  Whig and Tory a' agree
    To drop their whigmigmorum;
Let Whig and Tory a' agree
To spend this night wi' mirth and glee,
And cheerfu' sing, alang wi' me,
  The Reel o' Tullochgorum.

[1] smart young fellows.

O Tullochgorum's my delight,
It gars us a' in ane unite,
And ony sumph[1] that keeps up spite,
   In conscience I abhor him.
Blithe and merry we'll be a',
   Blithe and merry, blithe and merry,
   Blithe and merry we'll be a'
      And mak a cheerfu' quorum.
For blithe and merry we'll be a'
As lang as we hae breath to draw,
And dance, till we be like to fa',
    The Reel o' Tullochgorum.

What needs there be sae great a fraise[2]
Wi' dringing[3] dull Italian lays,
I wadna gie our ain strathspeys
   For half a hunder score o' them:
They're dowf and dowie[4] at the best,
   Dowf and dowie, dowf and dowie,
   Dowf and dowie at the best,
      Wi' a' their variorum;
They're dowf and dowie at the best,
Their allegros and a' the rest;
They canna please a Scottish taste
    Compared wi' Tullochgorum.

Let warldly worms their minds oppress
Wi' fears o' want and double cess,[5]
And sullen sots themselves distress
   Wi' keeping up decorum.
Shall we sae sour and sulky sit,
   Sour and sulky, sour and sulky,
   Sour and sulky shall we sit
      Like auld philosophorum?

---

[1] blockhead.   [2] fuss.   [3] droning.   [4] dull **and heavy.**
[5] tax.

Shall we sae sour and sulky sit,
Wi' neither sense, nor mirth, nor wit,
Nor ever rise to shake a fit
    To the Reel o' Tullochgorum?

May choicest blessings aye attend
Each honest, open-hearted friend,
And calm and quiet be his end,
    And a' that's good watch o'er him;
May peace and plenty be his lot,
  Peace and plenty, peace and plenty,
  Peace and plenty be his lot,
    And dainties a great store o' them;
May peace and plenty be his lot,
Unstained by any vicious spot,
And may he never want a groat,
    That's fond o' Tullochgorum!

But for the sullen, frumpish fool,
Who wants to be oppression's tool,
May envy gnaw his rotten soul,
    And discontent devour him;
May dule and sorrow be his chance,
  Dule and sorrow, dule and sorrow,
  Dule and sorrow be his chance,
    And nane say, Wae's me for him!
May dule and sorrow be his chance,
And a' the ills that come frae France,
Whae'er he be that winna dance
    The Reel o' Tullochgorum.

WILLIAM JULIUS MICKLE
1734–88
The Sailor's Wife

AND are ye sure the news is true?
  And are ye sure he's weel?
Is this a time to think o' wark?
  Ye jauds, fling bye your wheel!
Is this the time to spin a thread,
  When Colin's at the door?
Rax[1] down my cloak—I'll to the quay,
  And see him come ashore.
    For there's nae luck aboot the house,
      There's nae luck ava;
    Three's little pleasure in the house
      When our gudeman's awa'.

And gie to me my bigonet,[2]
  My bishop's satin gown;
For I maun tell the bailie's wife
  That Colin's in the town.
My Turkey slippers maun gae on,
  My hose o' pearly blue,—
It's a' to pleasure our gudeman,
  For he's baith leal and true.

Rise up and mak' a clean fireside,
  Put on the muckle pot;
Gie little Kate her button gown,
  And Jock his Sunday coat;
And mak' their shoon as black as slaes,
  Their stockin's white as snaw,—
It's a' to please my ain gudeman—
  He likes to see them braw.

  [1] reach.   [2] linen cap.

There's twa fat hens upon the bauk,[1]
   Hae fed this month and mair;
Mak' haste and thraw[2] their necks about,
   That Colin weel may fare;
And spread the table neat and clean—
   Gar ilka thing look braw;
For wha can tell how Colin fared
   When he was far awa'?

Sae true his heart, sae smooth his speech,
   His breath like caller air;
His very foot has music in't
   As he comes up the stair.
And will I see his face again?
   And will I hear him speak?
I'm downright dizzy wi' the thought,—
   In troth I'm like to greet!

If Colin 's weel, and weel content,
   I hae nae mair to crave;
And gin I live to keep him sae,
   I'm blest aboon the lave.
And will I see his face again,
   And will I hear him speak?—
I'm downright dizzy wi' the thought,—
   In troth I'm like to greet!
     For there 's nae luck aboot the house,
      There 's nae luck ava;
     There 's little pleasure in the house
      When our gudeman 's awa'.

---

[1] cross-beam.   [2] wring.

ROBERT CUNNINGHAME-GRAHAM OF GARTMORE

1735–97

If Doughty Deeds

IF doughty deeds my lady please,
 Right soon I'll mount my steed;
And strong his arm and fast his seat,
 That bears frae me the meed.
I'll wear thy colours in my cap,
 Thy picture in my heart;
And he that bends not to thine eye
 Shall rue it to his smart!
   Then tell me how to woo thee, Love;
    O tell me how to woo thee!
   For thy dear sake nae care I'll take,
    Tho' ne'er another trow me.

If gay attire delight thine eye
 I'll dight me in array;
I'll tend thy chamber door all night,
 And squire thee all the day.
If sweetest sounds can win thine ear,
 These sounds I'll strive to catch;
Thy voice I'll steal to woo thysel',
 That voice that nane can match.
   Then tell me how to woo thee, Love . . .

But if fond love thy heart can gain,
 I never broke a vow;
Nae maiden lays her skaith to me,
 I never loved but you.
For you alone I ride the ring,
 For you I wear the blue;

For you alone I strive to sing,
　O tell me how to woo!
　　Then tell me how to woo thee, Love;
　　O tell me how to woo thee!
　　For thy dear sake nae care I'll take
　　Tho' ne'er another trow me.

JAMES BEATTIE

1735–1803

An Epitaph

ESCAPED the gloom of mortal life, a soul
　Here leaves its mouldering tenement of clay,
Safe—where no cares their whelming billows
　　roll,
　No doubts bewilder, and no hopes betray.

Like thee, I once have stemm'd the sea of life;
　Like thee, have languish'd after empty joys;
Like thee, have labour'd in the stormy strife,
　Been grieved with trifles, and amused with
　　toys.

Yet for a while, 'gainst passion's threatful blast,
　Let steady reason urge the struggling oar;
Shot through the dreary gloom, the morn, at
　　last,
　Gives to thy longing eye the blissful shore.

Forget my frailties—thou art also frail;
　Forgive my lapses, for thyself may'st fall;
Nor read unmoved my artless, tender tale—
　I was a friend, oh man, to thee, to all!

MICHAEL BRUCE
1746–67

From *Elegy: In Spring*

Now Spring returns: but not to me returns—
  The vernal joy my better years have known;
Dim in my breast life's dying taper burns,
  And all the joys of life with health are flown.

Starting and shivering in th' inconstant wind,
  Meagre and pale—the ghost of what I was,
Beneath some blasted tree I lie reclined,
  And count the silent moments as they pass—

The wingéd moments, whose unstaying speed
  No art can stop, or in their course arrest;—
Whose flight shall shortly count me with the dead,
  And lay me down in peace with them that rest.

Oft morning dreams presage approaching fate;—
  And morning dreams, as poets tell, are true:
Led by pale ghosts, I enter Death's dark gate,
  And bid the realms of light and life adieu.

I hear the helpless wail, the shriek of woe;
  I see the muddy wave, the dreary shore,
The sluggish streams that slowly creep below,
  Which mortals visit—and return no more.

Farewell, ye blooming fields! ye cheerful plains!
  Enough for me the churchyard's lonely mound,
Where Melancholy with still Silence reigns,
  And the rank grass waves o'er the cheerless
    ground.

There let me wander at the shut of eve,
　　When Sleep sits dewy on the labourer's eyes,—
The world and all its busy follies leave,
　　And talk with Wisdom where my Daphnis lies.

There let me sleep forgotten in the clay,
　　When Death shall shut these weary aching
　　　　eyes,—
Rest in the hopes of an eternal day,
　　Till the long night is gone, and the last morn
　　　　arise.

JOHN LOGAN
1748–88

To the Cuckoo

HAIL, beauteous stranger of the grove!
　　Thou messenger of Spring!
Now Heaven repairs thy rural seat,
　　And woods thy welcome sing.

What time the daisy decks the green,
　　Thy certain voice we hear:
Hast thou a star to guide thy path,
　　Or mark the rolling year?

Delightful visitant, with thee
　　I hail the time of flowers;
And hear the sound of music sweet
　　From birds among the bowers.

The schoolboy, wandering through the wood,
　　To pull the primrose gay,
Starts the new voice of Spring to hear,
　　And imitates thy lay.

What time the pea puts on the bloom,
  Thou fliest thy vocal vale—
An annual guest, in other lands,
  Another Spring to hail.

Sweet bird! thy bower is ever green,
  Thy sky is ever clear;
Thou hast no sorrow in thy song.
  No winter in thy year!

Alas! sweet bird! not so my fate;
  Dark scowling skys I see
Fast gathering round, and fraught with woe
  And ninety years to me.

O could I fly, I'd fly with thee!
  We'd make, with joyful wing,
Our annual visit o'er the globe—
  Companions of the Spring.

The Braes of Yarrow

THY braes were bonny, Yarrow stream,
When first on them I met my lover;
Thy braes how dreary, Yarrow stream,
When now thy waves his body cover!
For ever now, O Yarrow stream!
Thou aar to me a stream of sorrow;
For never on thy banks shall I
Behold my love, the flower of Yarrow.

He promised me a milk-white steed,
To bear me to his father's bowers;
He promised me a little page,
To squire me to his father's towers;
He promised me a wedding-ring,—
The wedding-day was fix'd to-morrow:
Now he is wedded to his grave,
Alas! his watery grave in Yarrow.

Sweet were his words when last we met;
My passion I as freely told him:
Clasp'd in his arms, I little thought
That I should never more behold him!
Scarce was he gone, I saw his ghost;
It vanish'd with a shriek of sorrow:
Thrice did the water-wraith ascend,
And gave a doleful groan thro' Yarrow.

His mother from the window look'd,
With all the longing of a mother;
His little sister weeping walk'd
The greenwood path to meet her brother:
They sought him east, they sought him west,
They sought him all the Forest thorough;
They only saw the cloud of night,
They only heard the roar of Yarrow.

No longer from thy window look—
Thou hast no son, thou tender mother!
No longer walk, thou little maid;
Alas! thou hast no more a brother.
No longer seek him east or west,
And search no more the Forest thorough;
For, wandering in the night so dark,
He fell a lifeless corpse in Yarrow.

The tear shall never leave my cheek,
No other youth shall be my marrow—
I'll seek thy body in the stream,
And then with thee I'll sleep in Yarrow.
—The tear did never leave her cheek,
No other youth became her marrow;
She found his body in the stream,
And now with him she sleeps in Yarrow.

ROBERT FERGUSSON

1750–74

The Daft Days

Now mirk December's dowie face
Glow'rs owre the rigs¹ wi' sour grimace,
While, thro' his *minimum* o' space
      The bleer-e'ed sun,
Wi' blinkin' light and stealin' pace,
      His race doth run.

Frae naked groves nae birdie sings;
To shepherd's pipe nae hillock rings;
The breeze nae od'rous flavour brings
      Frae Borean cave;
And dwynin' Nature droops her wings,
      Wi' visage grave.

Mankind but scanty pleasure glean
Frae snawy hill or barren plain,
Whan Winter, 'midst his nippin' train,
      Wi' frozen spear,
Sends drift owre a' his bleak domain,
      And guides the weir.²

Auld Reikie! thou'rt the canty³ hole;
A bield⁴ for mony a cauldrife⁵ soul,
Wha snugly at thine ingle loll,
      Baith warm and couth⁶;
While round they gar the bicker⁷ roll,
      To weet their mouth.

---

¹ ridges in a ploughed field.   ² war.   ³ cosy.
⁴ shelter.   ⁵ chilly.   ⁶ comfortable.   ⁷ wooden drinking vessel.

Whan merry Yule-day comes, I trow,
You'll scantlins find a hungry mou;
Sma' are our cares, our stamacks fou
   O' gusty[1] gear,
And kickshaws, strangers to our view
   Sin' fairn-year.[2]

Ye browster wives! now busk ye braw,
And fling your sorrows far awa;
Then, come and gie's the tither blaw
   O' reaming[3] ale,
Mair precious than the Well o' Spa,
   Our hearts to heal.

Then, tho' at odds wi' a' the warl',
Amang oursels we'll never quarrel;
Tho' Discord gie a canker'd snarl,
   To spoil our glee,
As lang's there's pith into the barrel,
   We'll drink and gree.

Fiddlers! your pins in temper fix,
And roset[4] weel your fiddlesticks;
But banish vile Italian tricks
   Frae out your quorum;
Nor fortes wi' pianos mix;—
   Gie's Tullochgorum.

For nought can cheer the heart sae weel,
As can a canty Highland reel;
It even vivifies the heel
   To skip and dance:
Lifeless is he wha canna feel
   Its influence.

[1] tasty.   [2] yester-year.   [3] foaming.   [4] resin.

Let mirth abound; let social cheer
Invest the dawnin' o' the year;
Let blithesome Innocence appear,
        To crown our joy:
Nor Envy, wi' sarcastic sneer,
          Our bliss destroy.

And thou, great god of *Aquavitæ!*
Wha sways the empire o' this city;—
When fou, we're sometimes capernoity[1];—
        Be thou prepar'd
To hedge us frae that black banditti,
        The City Guard.

Braid Claith

YE wha are fain to hae your name
Wrote i' the bonny book o' Fame,
Let merit nae pretension claim
        To laurell'd wreath,
But hap[2] ye weel, baith back and wame,[3]
        In gude Braid Claith.

He that some ells o' this may fa',[4]
And slae-black hat on pow like snaw,
Bids bauld to bear the gree[5] awa,
        Wi' a' this graith,[6]
Whan bienly[7] clad wi' shell fu' braw
        O' gude Braid Claith.

Waesuck[8] for him wha has nae feck[9] o't!
For he's a gowk[10] they're sure to geck[11] at,

---

[1] muddled. [2] cover. [3] belly. [4] obtain. [5] prize.
[6] equipment. [7] comfortably. [8] alas. [9] abundance.
[10] fool. [11] mock.

A chiel that ne'er will be respeckit
           While he draws breath,
Till his four quarters are bedeckit
           Wi' gude Braid Claith.

On Sabbath-days the barber spark,
Whan he has done wi' scrapin' wark,
Wi' siller broachie[1] in his sark,[2]
           Gangs trigly,[3] faith!
Or to the Meadow, or the Park,
           In gude Braid Claith.

Weel might ye trow, to see them there,
That they to shave your haffits[4] bare,
Or curl and sleek a pickle[5] hair,
           Wad be right laith,
Whan pacing wi' a gawsy[6] air
           In gude Braid Claith.

If ony mettl'd stirrah[7] green[8]
For favour frae a lady's een,
He maunna care for being seen
           Before he sheath
His body in a scabbard clean
           O' gude Braid Claith.

For, gin he come wi' coat thread-bare,
A feg for him she winna care,
But crook her bonny mou' fu' sair,
           And scald[9] him baith.
Wooers should ay their travel spare
           Without Braid Claith.

---

[1] brooch.   [2] shirt.   [3] smartly.   [4] sides of the head.
[5] little.   [6] consequential.   [7] young fellow.   [8] long.   [9] scold.

Braid Claith lends fouk an unco heese,[1]
Maks mony kail-worms[2] butterflies,
Gives mony a doctor his degrees
        For little skaith[3]:
In short, you may be what you please
        Wi' gude Braid Claith.

For thof ye had as wise a snout on
As Shakespeare or Sir Isaac Newton,
Your judgment fouk wad hae a doubt on,
        I'll tak my aith,
Till they cou'd see ye wi' a suit on
        O' gude Braid Claith.

The Farmer's Ingle

WHAN gloamin' grey out-owre the welkin keeks;
  Whan Batie ca's his owsen to the byre;
Whan Thrasher John, sair dung,[4] his barn-door
  steeks,[5]
  And lusty lasses at the dightin'[6] tire;
What bangs fu' leal the e'enings coming cauld,
  And gars snaw-tappit Winter freeze in vain;
Gars dowie mortals look baith blithe and bauld,
  Nor fley'd[7] wi' a' the poortith o' the plain;
Begin, my Muse! and chant in hamely strain.

Frae the big stack, weel winnow't on the hill,
  Wi' divots theekit frae[8] the weet and drift;
Sods, peats, and heathery trufs the chimley fill,
  And gar their thickening smeek salute the lift.

---

[1] folk a wonderful hoist.   [2] caterpillars.   [3] trouble.
[4] overcome (by fatigue).   [5] shuts.   [6] cleaning
corn.   [7] affrighted.   [8] covered with sods as a
protection against.

The gudeman, new come hame, is blithe to find,
  Whan he out-owre the hallan[1] flings his een,
That ilka turn is handled to his mind;
  That a' his housie looks sae cosh and clean;
  For cleanly house loes he, tho' e'er sae mean.

Weel kens the gudewife, that the pleughs require
  A heartsome meltith,[2] and refreshin' synd[3]
O' nappy liquor,[4] owre a bleezin' fire:
  Sair wark and poortith downa weel be join'd.
Wi' butter'd bannocks now the girdle reeks;
  I' the far nook the bowie[5] briskly reams;
The readied kail stands by the chimley cheeks,
  And haud the riggin'[6] het wi' welcome streams,
  Whilk than the daintiest kitchen[7] nicer seems.

Frae this, lat gentler gabs a lesson lear:
  Wad they to labouring lend an eident[8] hand,
They'd rax[9] fell strang upo' the simplest fare,
  Nor find their stamacks ever at a stand.
Fu' hale and healthy wad they pass the day;
  At night, in calmest slumbers dose fu' sound;
Nor doctor need their weary life to spae,
  Nor drogs their noddle and their sense confound,
  Till death slip sleely on, and gie the hindmost wound.

On sicken[10] food has mony a doughty deed
  By Caledonia's ancestors been done;
By this did mony a wight fu' weirlike bleed
  In brulzies[11] frae the dawn to set o' sun.

---

[1] partition.   [2] meal.   [3] draught.   [4] ale.
[5] ale cask.   [6] rafters.   [7] relish.   [8] earnest.
[9] grew.   [10] such.   [11] broil, battle.

'Twas this that braced their gardies[1] stiff and
        strang;
    That bent the deadly yew in ancient days;
Laid Denmark's daring sons on yird[2] alang;
    Gar'd Scottish thristles bang the Roman bays;
    For near our crest their heads they doughtna
        raise.

The couthy cracks[3] begin whan supper's owre;
    The cheering bicker gars them glibly gash[4]
O' Simmer's showery blinks, and Winter sour,
    Whase floods did erst their mailin's[5] produce
        hash.
'Bout kirk and market eke their tales gae on;
    How Jock woo'd Jenny here to be his bride;
And there, how Marion, for a bastard son,
    Upo' the cutty-stool[6] was forced to ride;
    The waefu' scauld[7] o' our Mess John[8] to bide.

The fient[9] a cheep's amang the bairnies now;
    For a' their anger's wi' their hunger gane:
Ay maun the childer, wi' a fastin mou',
    Grumble and greet, and mak an unco mane.
In rangles[10] round, before the ingle's lowe,[11]
    Frae Gudame's mouth auld-warld tales they
        hear,
O' warlocks loupin round the wirrikow[12]:
    O' ghaists that win[13] in glen and kirkyard drear,
    Whilk touzles a' their tap,[14] and gars them
        shake wi' fear!

[1] arms.   [2] earth.   [3] chats.   [4] talk.   [5] farm.
[6] stool of repentance.   [7] scolding.   [8] parson.   [9] devil.
[10] crowds.   [11] glow.   [12] hobgoblin.   [13] dwell.
[14] makes their hair stand on end.

For weel she trows that fiends and fairies be
   Sent frae the deil to fleetch¹ us to our ill;
That kye hae tint their milk wi' evil ee;
   And corn been scowder'd² on the glowin kill.
O mock na this, my friends! but rather mourn,
   Ye in life's brawest spring wi' reason clear;
Wi' eild our idle fancies a' return,
   And dim our dolefu' days wi' bairnly fear;
     The mind's ay cradled whan the grave is near.

Yet thrift, industrious, bides her latest days,
   Tho' age her sair-dow'd³ front wi' runcles
     wave;
Yet frae the russet lap the spindle plays;
   Her e'enin stent⁴ reels she as weel's the lave.
On some feast-day, the wee things, buskit braw,
   Shall heeze⁵ her heart up wi' a silent joy,
Fu' cadgie⁶ that her head was up, and saw
   Her ain spun cleedin on a darlin oy⁷;
     Careless tho' death shou'd mak the feast her
     foy.⁸

In its auld lerroch⁹ yet the deas¹⁰ remains,
   Whare the gudeman aft streeks¹¹ him at his
     ease;
A warm and canny lean for weary banes
   O' lab'rers doil'd¹² upon the wintry leas.
Round him will baudrins¹³ and the collie come,
   To wag their tail, and cast a thankfu' ee
To him wha kindly flings them mony a crum
   O' kebbuck whang'd,¹⁴ and dainty fadge¹⁵ to
     prie;
     This a' the boon they crave, and a' the fee.

---

¹ deceive.   ² burned.   ³ faded.   ⁴ quantity of
work.   ⁵ lift.   ⁶ proud.   ⁷ grandchild.   ⁸ farewell
to life.   ⁹ place.   ¹⁰ couch.   ¹¹ stretches.   ¹² tired.
¹³ cat.   ¹⁴ cheese cut.   ¹⁵ bread.

Frae him the lads their mornin' counsel tak;
 What stacks he wants to thrash; what rigs to till;
How big a birn[1] maun lie on Bassie's back,
 For meal and mu'ter[2] to the thirlin mill.[3]
Neist, the gudewife her hirelin damsels bids
 Glow'r thro' the byre, and see the hawkies[4]
  bound;
Tak tent, 'case Crummy tak her wonted tids,[5]
 And ca' the laiglen's[6] treasure on the ground,
 Whilk spills a kebbuck nice, or yellow pound.

Then a' the house for sleep begin to grien,[7]
 Their joints to slack frae industry a-while;
The leaden god fa's heavy on their een,
 And hafflins steeks them frae their daily toil;
The cruizie[8] too can only blink and bleer;
 The restit ingle's[9] done the maist it dow;
Tacksman and cotter eke to bed maun steer,
 Upo' the cod[10] to clear their drumly[11] pow,
 Till wauken'd by the dawnin's ruddy glow.

Peace to the husbandman and a' his tribe,
 Whase care fells a' our wants frae year to year!
Lang may his sock[12] and cou'ter[13] turn the
  glybe,[14]
 And bauks o' corn bend down wi' laded ear!
May Scotia's simmers ay look gay and green;
 Her yellow har'sts frae scowry blasts decreed!
May a' her tenants sit fu' snug and bien,
 Frae the hard grip o' ails, and poortith freed;
 And a lang lasting train o' peacefu' hours
  succeed!

---

[1] burden.　　　[2] portion of meal retained by miller as
his fee.　　　[3] mill to which farmer is thirled or bound.
[4] cows.　　　[5] whims.　　　[6] milk-pail.　　　[7] long.
[8] primitive oil lamp.　　　[9] stirred up fire.　　　[10] pillow.
[11] dull.　　　[12] ploughshare.　　　[13] coulter.　　　[14] glebe.

LADY ANNE LINDSAY
1750–1825

Auld Robin Gray

WHEN the sheep are in the fauld, and the kye at
    hame,
And a' the warld to rest are gane,
The waes o' my heart fa' in showers frae my e'e,
While my gudeman lies sound by me.

Young Jamie lo'ed me weel, and sought me for
    his bride;
But saving a croun he had naething else beside:
To make the croun a pund, young Jamie gaed
    to sea;
And the croun and the pund were baith for me.

He hadna been awa' a week but only twa,
When my father brak his arm, and the cow was
    stown awa';
My mother she fell sick,—and my Jamie at the
    sea—
And auld Robin Gray came a-courtin' me.

My father couldna work, and my mother couldna
    spin;
I toil'd day and night, but their bread I couldna
    win;
Auld Rob maintain'd them baith, and wi' tears
    in his e'e
Said, 'Jennie, for their sakes, O, marry me!'

My heart it said nay; I look'd for Jamie back;
But the wind it blew high, and the ship it was
    a wrack;
His ship it was a wrack—Why didna Jamie dee?
Or why do I live to cry, Wae's me!

My father urged me sair: my mother didna speak;
But she look'd in my face till my heart was like to
  break:
They gi'ed him my hand, tho' my heart was in
  the sea;
Sae auld Robin Gray he was gudeman to me.

I hadna been a wife a week but only four,
When mournfu' as I sat on the stane at the door,
I saw my Jamie's wraith,—for I couldna think
  it he,
Till he said, 'I'm come hame to marry thee.'

O sair, sair did we greet, and muckle did we say;
We took but ae kiss, and we tore ourselves away:
I wish that I were dead, but I'm no like to dee;
And why was I born to say, Wae's me!

I gang like a ghaist, and I carena to spin;
I daurna think on Jamie, for that wad be a sin;
But I'll do my best a gude wife aye to be,
For auld Robin Gray he is kind unto me.

JOHN MAYNE

1759–1836

Logan's Braes

By Logan's streams that rin sae deep,
Fu' aft wi' glee I've herded sheep;
Herded sheep, or gathered slaes,
Wi' my dear lad, on Logan braes.
But wae's my heart! thae days are gane,
And I, wi' grief, may herd alane;
While my dear lad maun face his faes,
Far, far frae me and Logan braes.

Nae mair at Logan kirk will he
Atween the preachings meet wi' me;
Meet wi' me, or when it's mirk,
Convoy me hame frae Logan kirk.
I weel may sing thae days are gane—
Frae kirk an' fair I come alane,
While my dear lad maun face his faes,
Far, far frae me and Logan braes!

At e'en, when hope amaist is gane,
I dauner out, or sit alane,
Sit alane beneath the tree
Where aft he kept his tryst wi' me.
O! could I see thae days again,
My lover skaithless, and my ain!
Belov'd by frien's, rever'd by faes,
We'd live in bliss on Logan braes.

ROBERT BURNS

1759–96

Robin

I

THERE was a lad was born in Kyle,
But whatna day o' whatna style,
I doubt it's hardly worth the while
  To be sae nice wi' Robin.

  Robin was a rovin' boy,
    Rantin rovin', rantin rovin';
  Robin was a rovin' boy,
    Rantin rovin' Robin!

II

Our monarch's hindmost year but ane
Was five and twenty days begun,
'Twas then a blast o' Janwar win'
    Blew hansel in on Robin.

III

The gossip keekit in his loof,[1]
Quo' she, wha lives will see the proof,
This waly[2] boy will be nae coof—[3]
    I think we'll ca' him Robin.

IV

He'll hae misfortunes great and sma',
But aye a heart aboon them a';
He'll be a credit till us a',
    We'll a' be proud o' Robin.

V

But sure as three times three mak nine,
I see, by ilka score and line,
This chap will dearly like our kin',
    So leeze me on[4] thee, Robin.

VI

Guid faith, quo' she, I doubt ye gar
The bonnie lasses lie aspar,
But twenty fauts ye may hae waur,
    So blessin's on thee, Robin.

    Robin was a rovin' boy,
        Rantin rovin', rantin rovin';
    Robin was a rovin' boy,
        Rantin rovin' Robin!

---

[1] peeped in his palm.   [2] big, fine.   [3] ninny.   [4] commend me to.

Epistle to William Simpson, Ochiltree

May 1785.

I GAT your letter, winsome Willie;
Wi' gratefu' heart I thank you brawlie;
Tho' I maun say't, I wad be silly,
   And unco vain,
Should I believe, my coaxin' billie,[1]
    Your flatterin' strain.

But I'se believe ye kindly meant it,
I sud be laith to think ye hinted
Ironic satire, sidelins sklented[2]
    On my poor Musie;
Tho' in sic phraisin'[3] terms ye've penn'd it,
    I scarce excuse ye.

My senses wad be in a creel,
Should I but dare a hope to speel,
Wi' Allan,[4] or wi' Gilbertfield,[5]
    The braes o' fame;
Or Fergusson, the writer chiel,[6]
    A deathless name.

(O Fergusson! thy glorious parts
Ill suited law's dry, musty arts!
My curse upon your whunstane hearts,
    Ye E'nbrugh gentry!
The tythe o' what ye waste at cartes[7]
    Wad stow'd[8] his pantry!)

---

[1] fellow.   [2] turned sidelong.   [3] flattering.
[4] Ramsay.   [5] Hamilton of Gilbertfield.   [6] lawyer-
fellow.   [7] cards.   [8] would have stored.

Yet when a tale comes i' my head,
Or lasses gie my heart a screed,[1]
As whiles they're like to be my dead[2]
      (O sad disease!)
I kittle[3] up my rustic reed;
        It gies me ease.

Auld Coila,[4] now, may fidge fu' fain,[5]
She's gotten poets o' her ain,
Chiels wha their chanters winna hain,[6]
      But tune their lays,
Till echoes a' resound again
        Her weel-sung praise.

Nae poet thought her worth his while,
To set her name in measur'd style;
She lay like some unkenned-of isle
      Beside New Holland,
Or whare wild-meeting oceans boil
      Besouth Magellan.

Ramsay an' famous Fergusson
Gied Forth an' Tay a lift aboon;
Yarrow an' Tweed, to mony a tune,
      Owre Scotland rings,
While Irwin, Lugar, Ayr, an' Doon,
      Naebody sings.

Th' Illissus, Tiber, Thames, an' Seine,
Glide sweet in mony a tunefu' line!
But, Willie, set your fit to mine,
      An' cock your crest!
We'll gar our streams and burnies shine
      Up wi' the best.

---

[1] tear, rent.   [2] death.   [3] tickle.   [4] Kyle, district in Ayrshire.   [5] tingle with delight.   [6] will not spare their pipes.

We'll sing Auld Coila's plains an' fells,
Her moors red-brown wi' heather bells,
Her banks an' braes, her dens an' dells,
   Where glorious Wallace
Aft bare the gree,[1] as story tells,
   Frae Southron billies.

At Wallace' name, what Scottish blood
But boils up in a spring-tide flood!
Oft have our fearless fathers strode
   By Wallace' side,
Still pressing onward, red-wat shod,
   Or glorious died.

O, sweet are Coila's haughs[2] an' woods,
When lintwhites[3] chant amang the buds,
And jinkin[4] hares, in amorous whids,[5]
   Their loves enjoy,
While thro' the braes the cushat croods
   With wailfu' cry!

Ev'n winter bleak has charms to me
When winds rave thro' the naked tree;
Or frosts on hills of Ochiltree
   Are hoary gray:
Or blinding drifts wild-furious flee,
   Dark'ning the day!

O Nature! a' thy shews an' forms,
To feeling, pensive hearts hae charms!
Whether the summer kindly warms,
   Wi' life an' light,
Or winter howls, in gusty storms,
   The lang, dark night!

---

[1] prize. [2] hollows. [3] linnets. [4] dodging.
[5] gambols.

The Muse, nae poet ever fand her,
Till by himsel he learn'd to wander
Adown some trotting burn's meander,
      An' no think lang;
O sweet to stray an' pensive ponder
      A heart-felt sang!

The war'ly race may drudge an' drive
Hog-shouther,[1] jundie,[2] stretch, an' strive—
Let me fair Nature's face descrive,
      And I, wi' pleasure,
Shall let the busy, grumbling hive
      Bum owre their treasure.

Fareweel, my rhyme-composing brither!
We've been owre lang unkenn'd to ither:
Now let us lay our heads thegither,
      In love fraternal;
May Envy wallop in a tether,[3]
      Black fiend, infernal!

While Highlandmen hate tolls an' taxes;
While moorlan' herds like guid fat braxies,[4]
While terra firma on her axis
      Diurnal turns,
Count on a friend, in faith an' practice,
      In ROBERT BURNS.

Tam o' Shanter

WHEN chapman billies[5] leave the street,
And drouthy[6] neebors neebors meet;
As market-days are wearin late,
An' folk begin to tak the gate[7];

[1] push.   [2] elbow.   [3] dangle in a rope.   [4] sheep that have died of disease.   [5] pedlar fellows.   [6] thirsty.
[7] road.

While we sit sousing at the nappy,[1]
An' gettin' fou[2] and unco[3] happy,
We think na on the lang Scots miles,
The mosses,[4] waters, slaps,[5] and styles,
That lie between us and our hame,
Whare sits our sulky, sullen dame,
Gathering her brows like gathering storm,
Nursing her wrath to keep it warm.

This truth fand honest Tam o' Shanter,
As he frae Ayr ae night did canter
(Auld Ayr, wham ne'er a town surpasses,
For honest men an' bonny lasses).

O Tam! hadst thou but been sae wise,
As ta'en thy ain wife Kate's advice!
She tauld thee weel thou wast a skellum,[6]
A bletherin',[7] blusterin', drunken blellum[8];
That frae November till October,
Ae market-day thou was na sober;
That ilka melder,[9] wi' the miller,
Thou sat as lang as thou had siller[10];
That ev'ry naig was ca'd[11] a shoe on,
The smith and thee gat roarin' fou on;
That at the Lord's house, ev'n on Sunday,
Thou drank wi' Kirkton Jean till Monday.
She prophesy'd that, late or soon,
Thou wad be found, deep drown'd in Doon!
Or catch'd wi' warlocks in the mirk,
By Alloway's auld, haunted kirk.
Ah, gentle dames! it gars me greet
To think how mony counsels sweet,
How mony lengthen'd, sage advices,
The husband frae the wife despises!

---

[1] ale. [2] drunk. [3] wonderfully. [4] bogs. [5] breeches.
[6] worthless fellow. [7] chattering. [8] idle fellow.
[9] meal-grinding. [10] money. [11] put.

But to our tale:—Ae market night,
Tam had got planted unco right;
Fast by an ingle, bleezing finely,
Wi' reaming swats,[1] that drank divinely;
An' at his elbow, Souter Johnie,
His ancient, trusty, drouthy crony;
Tam lo'ed him like a vera brither;
They had been fou for weeks thegither!
The night drave on wi' sangs an' clatter;
An' aye the ale was growing better:
The landlady and Tam grew gracious,
Wi' favours secret, sweet, and precious;
The Souter tauld his queerest stories;
The landlord's laugh was ready chorus:
The storm without might rair and rustle—
Tam didna mind the storm a whistle.

Care, mad to see a man sae happy,
E'en drown'd himsel amang the nappy!
As bees flee hame wi' lades o' treasure,
The minutes wing'd their way wi' pleasure:
Kings may be blest, but Tam was glorious,
O'er a' the ills o' life victorious!

But pleasures are like poppies spread,
You seize the flow'r, its bloom is shed!
Or like the snowfall in the river,
A moment white—then melts for ever;
Or like the borealis race,
That flit ere you can point their place;
Or like the rainbow's lovely form,
Evanishing amid the storm.—
Nae man can tether time or tide;
The hour approaches Tam maun ride;

[1] foaming new ale.

That hour, o' night's black arch the key-
    stane,
That dreary hour he mounts his beast in;
An' sic a night he taks the road in,
As ne'er poor sinner was abroad in.

The wind blew as 'twad blawn its last;
The rattling show'rs rose on the blast;
The speedy gleams the darkness swallow'd;
Loud, deep, and lang, the thunder bellow'd:
That night, a child might understand,
The Deil had business on his hand.

Weel mounted on his grey mare, Meg—
A better never lifted leg—
Tam skelpit on thro' dub¹ an' mire,
Despising wind, an' rain, an' fire;
Whiles holding fast his guid blue bonnet;
Whiles crooning o'er some auld Scots sonnet;
Whiles glow'ring round wi' prudent cares,
Lest bogles catch him unawares;
Kirk-Alloway was drawing nigh,
Where ghaists an' houlets nightly cry.

By this time he was cross the foord,
Whare in the snaw the chapman smoor'd²;
An' past the birks and meikle stane,
Whare drunken Charlie brak 's neck-bane;
An' thro' the whins, an' by the cairn,
Whare hunters fand the murder'd bairn;
An' near the thorn, aboon the well,
Whare Mungo's mither hang'd hersel.
Before him Doon pours a' his floods;
The doublin' storm roars thro' the woods;
The lightnings flash frae pole to pole;
Near and more near the thunders roll;

---

¹ puddle.   ² smothered.

When, glimmerin' thro' the groanin trees,
Kirk-Alloway seem'd in a bleeze;
Thro' ilka bore[1] the beams were glancin';
An' loud resounded mirth and dancin'.

Inspirin' bold John Barleycorn!
What dangers thou canst mak us scorn!
Wi' tippenny,[2] we fear nae evil;
Wi' usquabae[3] we'll face the Devil!
The swats sae ream'd in Tammie's noddle,
Fair play, he car'd na deils a boddle.
But Maggie stood, right sair astonish'd,
'Till, by the heel an' hand admonish'd,
She ventur'd forward on the light;
An', wow! Tam saw an unco sight!
Warlocks an' witches in a dance;
Nae cotillion brent new frae France,
But hornpipes, jigs, strathspeys, an' reels
Put life an' mettle in their heels:
At winnock-bunker[4] in the east,
There sat auld Nick, in shape o' beast;
A towzie[5] tyke, black, grim, an' large,
To gie them music was his charge;
He screw'd the pipes and gart them skirl,[6]
Till roof and rafters a' did dirl.[7]
Coffins stood round, like open presses[8];
That shaw'd the dead in their last dresses;
And (by some dev'lish cantraip sleight[9])
Each in its cauld hand held a light:
By which heroic Tam was able
To note upon the haly table,
A murderer's banes in gibbet airns;
Twa span-lang, wee, unchristen'd bairns;

---

[1] chink.   [2] ale.   [3] whisky.   [4] window-seat.
[5] shaggy.   [6] squeal.   [7] ring.   [8] cupboards.   [9] magic
trick.

A thief, new-cutted frae a rape—
Wi' his last gasp his gab[1] did gape;
Five tomahawks, wi' bluid red-rusted,
Five scimitars, wi' murder crusted;
A garter, which a babe had strangled;
A knife, a father's throat had mangled,
Whom his ain son o' life bereft,
The grey hairs yet stack to the heft;
Wi' mair o' horrible an' awfu',
Which ev'n to name wad be unlawfu'.

As Tammie glowr'd, amaz'd, an' curious,
The mirth an' fun grew fast an' furious:
The piper loud an' louder blew,
The dancers quick an' quicker flew;
They reel'd, they set, they cross'd, they cleekit,[2]
'Till ilka carlin swat and reekit,[3]
An' coost her duddies[4] to the wark,
An' linket[5] at it in her sark!

Now Tam! O Tam! had thae been queans
A' plump an' strappin' in their teens;
Their sarks, instead o' creeshie[6] flannen,
Been snaw-white seventeen hunder linen!
Thir breeks o' mine, my only pair,
That ance were plush, o' guid blue hair,
I wad hae gi'en them aff my hurdies,
For ae blink o' the bonnie burdies![7]

But withered beldams, auld an' droll,
Rigwoodie[8] hags, wad spean[9] a foal,
Lowping an' flinging on a crummock,[10]
I wonder didna turn thy stomach.

---

[1] mouth. [2] took hands. [3] beldam sweated and
steamed. [4] clothes. [5] tripped. [6] greasy. [7] girls.
[8] lean, ancient. [9] wean. [10] staff.

But Tam kenn'd what was what fu' brawlie,
There was ae winsome wench an' walie,[1]
That night enlisted in the core[2]
(Lang after kenn'd on Carrick shore;
For mony a beast to dead she shot,
An' perish'd many a bonnie boat,
An' shook baith meikle corn an' bear,
An' kept the country-side in fear),
Her cutty sark,[3] o' Paisley harn,[4]
That, while a lassie, she had worn,
In longitude tho' sorely scanty,
It was her best, an' she was vauntie.[5]

Ah! little kenn'd thy reverend Grannie,
That sark she coft[6] for her wee Nannie,
Wi' twa pund Scots ('twas a' her riches),
Wad ever grac'd a dance of witches!

But here my Muse her wing maun cour[7];
Sic flights are far beyond her pow'r;
To sing how Nannie lap an' flang
(A souple jade she was, an' strang),
An' how Tam stood, like ane bewitch'd,
An' thought his very een enrich'd;
Ev'n Satan glowr'd, an' fidg'd fu' fain,
An' hotched an' blew wi' might an' main:
'Till first ae caper, syne anither,
Tam tint[8] his reason a' thegither,
An' roars out, 'Weel done, Cutty-sark!'
An' in an instant a' was dark:
An' scarcely had he Maggie rallied,
When out the hellish legion sallied.

As bees bizz out wi' angry fyke,[9]
When plunderin' herds assail their byke[10];

---

[1] jolly.   [2] corps.   [3] short shift.   [4] coarse cloth.
[5] proud.   [6] bought.   [7] stoop.   [8] lost.   [9] fuss.   [10] hive.

As open pussie's¹ mortal foes,
When, pop! she starts before their nose;
As eager runs the market-crowd,
When 'Catch the thief!' resounds aloud;
So Maggie runs, the witches follow,
Wi' mony an eldritch² screech an' hollow.

Ah, Tam! ah, Tam! thou 'lt get thy fairin',
In hell they'll roast thee like a herrin'!
In vain thy Kate awaits thy comin'!
Kate soon will be a woefu' woman!
Now, do thy speedy utmost, Meg,
An' win the key-stane o' the brig;
There, at them thou thy tail may toss,
A running stream they darena cross;
But ere the key-stane she could make,
The fient³ a tail she had to shake!
For Nannie, far before the rest,
Hard upon noble Maggie prest,
An' flew at Tam wi' furious ettle⁴;
But little wist she Maggie's mettle—
Ae spring brought off her master hale,
But left behind her ain grey tail:
The carlin claught⁵ her by the rump,
An' left poor Maggie scarce a stump.

Now, wha this tale o' truth shall read,
Ilk man and mother's son take heed:
Whane'er to drink you are inclin'd,
Or cutty-sarks run in your mind,
Think! ye may buy the joys o'er dear—
Remember Tam o' Shanter's meare.

---

¹ the hare's.   ² unearthly.   ³ devil.   ⁴ aim.
⁵ seized.

Whistle o'er the Lave o't

FIRST when Maggy was my care,
Heaven, I thought, was in her air;
Now we're married—spier[1] nae mair—
    Whistle o'er the lave o't.[2]—
Meg was meek, and Meg was mild,
Bonnie Meg was Nature's child;
Wiser men than me's beguil'd—
    Whistle o'er the lave o't.

How we live, my Meg and me,
How we love, and how we 'gree,
I care na by how few may see;
    Whistle o'er the lave o't.—
Wha I wish were maggots' meat,
Dish'd up in her winding sheet,
I could write—but Meg wad see't—
    Whistle o'er the lave o't.

Macpherson's Farewell

I

FAREWELL, ye dungeons dark and strong,
    The wretch's destinie!
Macpherson's time will not be long
    On yonder gallows-tree.

    Sae rantingly, sae wantonly,
        Sae dauntingly gaed he;
    He play'd a spring,[3] and danc'd it round,
        Below the gallows-tree.

---

[1] ask.   [2] rest of it.   [3] dance-tune.

II

Oh! what is death but parting breath?—
  On mony a bloody plain
I've dar'd his face, and in this place
  I scorn him yet again!

III

Untie these bands from off my hands,
  And bring to me my sword!
And there's no a man in all Scotland
  But I'll brave him at a word.

IV

I've liv'd a life of sturt[1] and strife;
  I die by treacherie:
It burns my heart I must depart,
  And not avengèd be.

V

Now arewell light—thou sunshine bright,
  And all beneath the sky!
May coward shame distain his name,
  The wretch that dares not die!

See the smoking bowl before us

SEE the smoking bowl before us!
  Mark our jovial ragged ring!
Round and round take up the chorus,
  And in raptures let us sing.

Chorus

A fig for those by law protected!
  Liberty's a glorious feast!
Courts for cowards were erected,
  Churches built to please the priest.

[1] trouble.

What is title? what is treasure?
  What is reputation's care?
If we lead a life of pleasure,
  'Tis no matter how or where!
                    A fig, etc.

With the ready trick and fable,
  Round we wander all the day;
And at night, in barn or stable,
  Hug our doxies on the hay.
                    A fig, etc.

Does the train-attended carriage
  Thro' the country lighter rove?
Does the sober bed of marriage
  Witness brighter scenes of love?
                    A fig, etc.

Life is all a variorum,
  We regard not how it goes;
Let them cant about decorum
  Who have characters to lose.
                    A fig, etc.

Here's to budgets, bags, and wallets!
  Here's to all the wandering train!
Here's our ragged brats and callets![1]
  One and all cry out—Amen!

Chorus
A fig for those by law protected!
  Liberty's a glorious feast!
Courts for cowards were erected,
  Churches built to please the priest.

                    (From *The Jolly Beggars*.)

[1] wenches.

Lines from The Vision

THE sun had clos'd the winter day,
The curlers quat their roaring play,
An' hunger'd maukin[1] ta'en her way
      To kail-yards green,
While faithless snaws ilk step betray
      Whare she has been.

The thresher's weary flingin'-tree[2]
The lee-lang day had tirèd me;
And when the day had clos'd his e'e,
      Far i' the west,
Ben i' the spence,[3] right pensivelie,
      I gaed to rest.

There, lanely, by the ingle-cheek,[4]
I sat and e'ed the spewing reek,[5]
That fill'd, wi' hoast-provoking[6] smeek,[7]
      The auld clay biggin[8];
And heard the restless rattons[9] squeak
      About the riggin.[10]

All in this mottie,[11] misty clime,
I backward mus'd on wasted time,
How I had spent my youthfu' prime,
      And done naething,
But stringin' blethers up in rhyme,
      For fools to sing.

Had I to guid advice but harkit,
I might, by this, hae led a market,
Or strutted in a bank an' clerkit
      My cash account:
While here, half-mad, half-fed, half-sarkit,
      Is a' th' amount.

(The Vision, stanzas 1–5.)

[1] hare.   [2] flail.   [3] within, in the parlour.   [4] fireside.
[5] volleying smoke.   [6] cough-provoking.   [7] drift.
[8] building.   [9] rats.   [10] roof-tree.   [11] dusty.

A Winter Night

WHEN biting Boreas, fell and doure,[1]
Sharp shivers thro' the leafless bow'r;
When Phœbus gies a short-liv'd glow'r[2]
    Far south the lift,[3]
Dim-dark'ning through the flaky show'r,
    Or whirling drift:

Ae night the storm the steeples rocked,
Poor labour sweet in sleep was locked,
While burns, wi' snawy wreaths up-choked,
    Wild-eddying swirl,
Or thro' the mining outlet bocked,[4]
    Down headlong hurl.

List'ning the doors an' winnocks rattle,
I thought me on the ourie[5] cattle,
Or silly sheep, wha bide this brattle[6]
    O' winter war,
And thro' the drift, deep-lairing sprattle,[7]
    Beneath a scaur.[8]

Ilk happing bird, wee, helpless thing!
That, in the merry months o' spring,
Delighted me to hear thee sing,
    What comes o' thee?
Whare wilt thou cow'r thy chittering wing,
    An' close thy e'e?

Ev'n you, on murd'ring errands toil'd,
Lone from your savage homes exil'd,
The blood-stain'd roost, and sheep-cote spoil'd
    My heart forgets,
While pitiless the tempest wild
    Sore on you beats.

    (*A Winter Night*, stanzas 1–5.)

[1] hard.   [2] stare.   [3] sky.   [4] vomited.   [5] shivering.
[6] noisy onset.   [7] scramble.   [8] cliff.

To a Mouse

On turning her up in her nest with the plough,
November 1785

Wee, sleekit, cow'rin', tim'rous beastie,
Oh, what a panic's in thy breastie!
Thou need na start awa sae hasty,
   Wi' bickering brattle![1]
I wad be laith[2] to rin an' chase thee,
   Wi' murd'ring pattle![3]

I'm truly sorry man's dominion
Has broken nature's social union,
An' justifies that ill opinion
   Which makes thee startle
At me, thy poor earth-born companion,
   An' fellow-mortal!

I doubt na, whyles, but thou may thieve;
What then? poor beastie, thou maun live!
A daimen icker[4] in a thrave[5]
   'S a sma' request:
I'll get a blessin' wi' the lave,[6]
   And never miss't!

Thy wee bit housie, too, in ruin!
Its silly wa's the win's are strewin'!
An' naething, now, to big[7] a new ane,
   O' foggage[8] green!
An' bleak December's winds ensuin',
   Baith snell[9] and keen!

---

[1] hurrying scamper.   [2] loth.   [3] plough-staff.
[4] odd ear.   [5] twenty-four sheaves.   [6] remainder.
[7] build.   [8] coarse grass.   [9] bitter.

Thou saw the fields laid bare an' waste,
An' weary winter comin' fast,
An' cozie here, beneath the blast,
　　　　　　Thou thought to dwell,
'Till crash! the cruel coulter past
　　　　　Out thro' thy cell.

That wee bit heap o' leaves an' stibble
Has cost thee mony a weary nibble!
Now thou's turn'd out, for a' thy trouble,
　　　　　　But[1] house or hald,
To thole the winter's sleety dribble,
　　　　　An' cranreuch[2] cauld!

But, Mousie, thou art no thy lane,
In proving foresight may be vain:
The best-laid schemes o' mice an' men,
　　　　　　Gang aft agley,[3]
An' lea'e us nought but grief and pain
　　　　　For promis'd joy!

Still thou art blest, compar'd wi' me!
The present only toucheth thee:
But, och! I backward cast my ee,
　　　　　　On prospects drear!
An' forward, tho' I canna see,
　　　　　I guess an' fear!

Epistle to James Smith

DEAR SMITH, the slee'st, paukie thief,
That e'er attempted stealth or rief,[4]
Ye surely hae some warlock-breef[5]
　　　　　　Owre human hearts;
For ne'er a bosom yet was prief
　　　　　Against your arts.

---

[1] without.　　[2] hoar-frost.　　[3] askew.　　[4] robbery or plunder.　　[5] wizard-spell.

For me, I swear by sun an' moon,
And ev'ry star that blinks aboon,
Ye've cost me twenty pair of shoon
        Just gaun to see you;
And ev'ry ither pair that's done,
        Mair ta'en I'm wi' you.

That auld capricious carlin, Nature,
To mak amends for scrimpit[1] stature,
She's turn'd you aff, a human creature
        On her first plan;
And in her freaks, on every feature
        She's wrote, 'The Man'.

Just now I've ta'en the fit o' rhyme,
My barmie noddle's[2] working prime,
My fancy yerkit up sublime
        Wi' hasty summon:
Hae ye a leisure moment's time
        To hear what's comin'?

Some rhyme a neibor's name to lash;
Some rhyme (vain thought!) for needfu' cash;
Some rhyme to court the countra clash,[3]
        An' raise a din;
For me, an aim I never fash[4];
        I rhyme for fun.

The star that rules my luckless lot,
Has fated me the russet coat,
An' damn'd my fortune to the groat;
        But in requit,
Has blest me wi' a random shot
        O' countra wit.

---

[1] stunted.   [2] seething brain.   [3] gossip.   [4] bother.

This while my notion's ta'en a sklent,[1]
To try my fate in guid, black prent;
But still, the mair I'm that way bent,
        Something cries 'Hoolie!'[2]
I rede you, honest man, tak tent![3]
        Ye'll shaw your folly.

'There's ither poets much your betters,
Far seen in Greek, deep men o' letters,
Hae thought they had ensur'd their debtors,
        A' future ages;
Now moths deform in shapeless tatters
        Their unknown pages.'

Then fareweel hopes o' laurel-boughs,
To garland my poetic brows!
Henceforth I'll rove where busy ploughs
        Are whistling thrang,[4]
An' teach the lanely heights an' howes[5]
        My rustic sang.

I'll wander on, wi' tentless[6] heed
How never-halting moments speed,
Till fate shall snap the brittle thread;
        Then, all unknown,
I'll lay me with th' inglorious dead,
        Forgot and gone!

But why o' death begin a tale?
Just now we're living sound and hale,
Then top and maintop crowd the sail,
        Heave Care o'er side!
And large, before Enjoyment's gale,
        Let 's tak the tide.

---

[1] turn.   [2] softly.   [3] heed.   [4] crowded on all sides.
[5] hollows.   [6] careless.

This life, sae far's I understand,
Is a' enchanted fairy-land,
Where Pleasure is the magic wand,
          That, wielded right,
Maks hours like minutes, hand in hand,
          Dance by fu' light.

The magic wand then let us wield;
For, ance that five-and-forty's speel'd,[1]
See crazy, weary, joyless Eild,[2]
          Wi' wrinkled face,
Comes hoastin',[3] hirplin',[4] owre the field,
          Wi' creepin' pace.

When ance life's day draws near the gloamin',
Then fareweel vacant careless roamin';
An' fareweel cheerfu' tankards foamin',
          An' social noise;
An' fareweel, dear deluding Woman!
          The joy of joys!

O Life! how pleasant is thy morning,
Young Fancy's rays the hills adorning!
Cold-pausing Caution's lesson scorning,
          We frisk away,
Like school-boys, at th' expected warning,
          To joy an' play.

We wander there, we wander here,
We eye the rose upon the brier,
Unmindful that the thorn is near,
          Among the leaves;
And tho' the puny wound appear,
          Short while it grieves.

---

[1] climbed.   [2] Age.   [3] coughing.   [4] limping.

Some, lucky, find a flow'ry spot,
For which they never toil'd nor swat;
They drink the sweet and eat the fat,
                    But[1] care or pain;
And, haply, eye the barren hut
                    With high disdain.

With steady aim some Fortune chase;
Keen Hope does ev'ry sinew brace;
Thro' fair, thro' foul, they urge the race,
                    And seize the prey:
Then cannie,[2] in some cozie place,
                    They close the day.

And others, like your humble servan',
Poor wights! nae rules nor roads observin';
To right or left, eternal swervin',
                    They zigzag on;
Till curst with age, obscure an' starvin',
                    They aften groan.

Alas! what bitter toil an' straining—
But truce with peevish, poor complaining!
Is fortune's fickle Luna waning?
                    E'en let her gang!
Beneath what light she has remaining,
                    Let's sing our sang.

My pen I here fling to the door,
And kneel, ye Pow'rs! and warm implore,
'Tho' I should wander terra o'er,
                    In all her climes,
Grant me but this, I ask no more,
                    Ay rowth[3] o' rhymes.

---

[1] without.   [2] quietly.   [3] abundance.

'Gie dreeping[1] roasts to countra lairds,
Till icicles hing frae their beards;
Gie fine braw claes to fine life-guards,
                    And maids of honour!
And yill[2] an' whiskey gie to cairds,[3]
                    Until they sconner.[4]

'A title, Dempster merits it;
A garter gie to Willie Pitt;
Gie wealth to some be-ledger'd cit,
                    In cent. per cent.,
But gie me real, sterling wit,
                    And I'm content.

'While ye are pleas'd to keep me hale,
I'll sit down o'er my scanty meal,
Be't water-brose, or muslin-kail,[5]
                    Wi' cheerfu' face,
As lang's the Muses dinna fail
                    To say the grace.'

An anxious e'e I never throws
Behint my lug,[6] or by my nose;
I jouk[7] beneath Misfortune's blows
                    As weel's I may;
Sworn foe to sorrow, care, and prose,
                    I rhyme away.

O ye douce folk, that live by rule,
Grave, tideless-blooded, calm an' cool,
Compar'd wi' you—O fool! fool! fool!
                    How much unlike!
Your hearts are just a standing pool,
                    Your lives a dyke!

[1] dripping.   [2] ale.   [3] tinkers.   [4] grow squeamish.
[5] broth made without meat.   [6] ear.   [7] duck.

Nae hair-brain'd, sentimental traces,
In your unletter'd, nameless faces!
In arioso trills and graces
                Ye never stray,
But, gravissimo, solemn basses
                Ye hum away.

Ye are sae grave, nae doubt ye're wise;
Nae ferly[1] tho' ye do despise
The hairum-scairum, ram-stam boys,
                The rattling squad:
I see you upward cast your eyes—
                Ye ken the road.

Whilst I—but I shall haud me there—
Wi' you I'll scarce gang onywhere:
Then, Jamie, I shall say nae mair,
                But quit my sang,
Content wi' you to mak a pair,
                Whare'er I gang.

Contented wi' Little

CONTENTED wi' little, and cantie[2] wi' mair,
Whene'er I forgather wi' sorrow and care,
I gie them a skelp,[3] as they're creeping alang,
Wi' a cog[4] o' sweet swats,[5] and an auld Scottish
    sang.

I whyles[6] claw the elbow o' troublesome thought;
But man is a sodger, and life is a faught[7];
My mirth and guid humour are coin in my pouch,
And my freedom's my lairdship nae monarch
    dare touch.

---

[1] wonder.   [2] happy.   [3] smack.   [4] wooden vessel.
[5] new ale.   [6] sometimes.   [7] fight.

A towmond[1] o' trouble, should that be my fa',[2]
A night o' guid fellowship sowthers[3] it a':
When at the blithe end o' our journey at last,
Wha the deil ever thinks o' the road he has past?

Blind chance, let her snapper and stoyte[4] on her
    way;
Be't to me, be't frae me, e'en let the jade gae:
Come ease, or come travail; come pleasure or
    pain;
My warst word is,—'Welcome, and welcome
    again!'

O merry hae I been teethin' a heckle

O MERRY hae I been teethin' a heckle,[5]
    And merry hae I been shapin' a spoon;
And merry hae I been cloutin[6] a kettle,
    And kissin' my Katie when a' was done.
O a' the lang day I ca'[7] at my hammer,
    An' a' the lang day I whistle and sing,
A' the lang night I cuddle my kimmer,[8]
    An' a' the lang night as happy's a king.

Bitter in dool[9] I lickit my winnins[10]
    O' marrying Bess, to gie her a slave:
Blest be the hour she cool'd in her linnens,
    And blithe be the bird that sings on her grave!
Come to my arms, my Katie, my Katie,
    An' come to my arms and kiss me again!
Drunken or sober, here's to thee, Katie!
    And blest be the day I did it again.

---

[1] twelvemonth.   [2] lot.   [3] solders.   [4] stumble
and stagger.   [5] hackling-comb.   [6] patching.   [7] work
with.   [8] sweetheart.   [9] sorrow.   [10] earnings.

The Rigs o' Barley

It was upon a Lammas night,
  When corn rigs[1] are bonnie,
Beneath the moon's unclouded light,
  I held awa to Annie:
The time flew by wi' tentless[2] heed,
  Till 'tween the late and early,
Wi' sma' persuasion she agreed
  To see me thro' the barley.

The sky was blue, the wind was still,
  The moon was shining clearly;
I set her down, wi' right good will,
  Amang the rigs o' barley:
I kent her heart was a' my ain;
  I lov'd her most sincerely:
I kiss'd her owre and owre again,
  Amang the rigs o' barley.

I lock'd her in my fond embrace!
  Her heart was beating rarely:
My blessings on that happy place,
  Amang the rigs o' barley!
But by the moon and stars so bright,
  That shone that hour so clearly!
She aye shall bless that happy night,
  Amang the rigs o' barley.

I hae been blithe wi' comrades dear;
  I hae been merry drinking,
I hae been joyfu' gath'rin' gear;
  I hae been happy thinking:

---

[1] ridges. [2] careless.

But a' the pleasures e'er I saw,
   Tho' three times doubl'd fairly,
That happy night was worth them a',
   Amang the rigs o' barley.

Chorus

Corn rigs an' barley rigs,
   An' corn rigs are bonnie:
I'll ne'er forget that happy night,
   Amang the rigs wi' Annie.

I'll aye ca' in by yon town

I'LL aye ca'[1] in by yon town,[2]
   And by yon garden green, again;
I'll aye ca' in by yon town,
   And see my bonnie Jean again.
There's nane sall ken, there's nane sall guess,
   What brings me back the gate[3] again;
But she my fairest faithfu' lass,
   And stownlins[4] we sall meet again.

She'll wander by the aiken[5] tree,
   When trystin'-time draws near again;
And when her lovely form I see,
   O haith,[6] she's doubly dear again!
I'll aye ca' in by yon town,
   And by yon garden green again;
I'll aye ca' in by yon town,
   And see my bonnie Jean again.

---

[1] call.   [2] group of cottages.   [3] this way.   [4] by stealth.
[5] oak.   [6] faith.

A Red, Red Rose

O, MY luve's like a red, red rose,
 That's newly sprung in June:
O, my luve's like the melodie
 That's sweetly played in tune.

As fair art thou, my bonnie lass,
 So deep in luve am I;
And I will luve thee still, my dear,
 Till a' the seas gang dry.

Till a' the seas gang dry, my dear,
 And the rocks melt wi' the sun:
And I will luve thee still, my dear,
 While the sands o' life shall run.

And fare thee well, my only luve!
 And fare thee well a while!
And I will come again, my luve,
 Though it were ten thousand mile.

O were my love yon lilac fair

O WERE my love yon lilac fair,
 Wi' purple blossoms to the spring;
And I a bird to shelter there,
 When wearied on my little wing,

How I wad mourn, when it was torn,
 By autumn wild, and winter rude!
But I wad sing, on wanton wing,
 When youthfu' May its bloom renew'd.

O gin my love were yon red rose,
 That grows upon the castle wa',
And I mysel a drap o' dew,
 Into her bonnie breast to fa'!

O! there beyond expression blest,
    I'd feast on beauty a' the night;
Seal'd on her silk-saft faulds to rest,
    Till fley'd[1] awa by Phœbus' light!

The Lea Rig

WHEN o'er the hill the eastern star
    Tells bughtin-time[2] is near, my jo[3];
And owsen frae the furrow'd field
    Return sae dowf[4] and weary, O;
Down by the burn, where scented birks
    Wi' dew are hanging clear, my jo;
I'll meet thee on the lea-rig,[5]
    My ain kind dearie, O!

In mirkest glen, at midnight hour,
    I'd rove, and ne'er be eerie, O!
If thro' that glen I gaed to thee,
    My ain kind dearie, O!
Altho' the night were ne'er sae wild,
    And I were ne'er sae wearie, O,
I'd meet thee on the lea-rig,
    My ain kind dearie, O!

The hunter lo'es the morning sun,
    To rouse the mountain deer, my jo;
At noon the fisher seeks the glen,
    Along the burn to steer, my jo;
Gie me the hour o' gloamin' grey,
    It makes my heart sae cheery, O,
To meet thee on the lea-rig,
    My ain kind dearie, O!

[1] scared.   [2] folding-time.   [3] sweetheart.   [4] dull.
[5] grassy ridge.

Ae Fond Kiss

AE fond kiss, and then we sever;
Ae farewell, and then, for ever!
Deep in heart-wrung tears I'll pledge thee,
Warring sighs and groans I'll wage thee.
Who shall say that fortune grieves him,
While the star of hope she leaves him?
Me, nae cheerfu' twinkle lights me:
Dark despair around benights me.

I'll ne'er blame my partial fancy,
Naething could resist my Nancy!
But to see her was to love her;
Love but her, and love for ever.
Had we never lov'd sae kindly,
Had we never lov'd sae blindly,
Never met—or never parted—
We had ne'er been broken-hearted.

Fare thee weel, thou first and fairest!
Fare thee weel, thou best and dearest!
Thine be ilka¹ joy and treasure,
Peace, Enjoyment, Love, and Pleasure!
Ae fond kiss, and then we sever;
Ae farewell, alas! for ever!
Deep in heart-wrung tears I'll pledge thee,
Warring sighs and groans I'll wage thee!

My Bonnie Mary

Go fetch to me a pint o' wine,
    An' fill it in a silver tassie²;
That I may drink, before I go,
    A service to my bonnie lassie;

¹ every.   ² goblet.

The boat rocks at the pier o' Leith;
  Fu' loud the wind blaws frae the ferry;
The ship rides by the Berwick-Law,
  And I maun leave my bonnie Mary.

The trumpets sound, the banners fly,
  The glittering spears are rankèd ready;
The shouts o' war are heard afar,
  The battle closes thick and bloody!
It's not the roar o' sea or shore
  Wad make me langer wish to tarry;
Nor shout o' war that's heard afar—
  It's leaving thee, my bonnie Mary.

The banks of Doon

YE flowery banks o' bonnie Doon,
  How can ye bloom sae fair;
How can ye chant, ye little birds,
  And I sae fu' o' care?

Thou'll break my heart, thou bonnie bird,
  That sings upon the bough;
Thou minds me o' the happy days
  When my fause luve was true.

Thou'll break my heart, thou bonnie bird,
  That sings beside thy mate;
For sae I sat, and sae I sang,
  And wist na o' my fate.

Aft hae I rov'd by bonnie Doon,
    To see the woodbine twine,
And ilka[1] bird sang o' its luve,
    And sae did I o' mine.

Wi' lightsome heart I pu'd a rose,
    Frae off its thorny tree;
And my fause luver staw the rose,
    But left the thorn wi' me.

Bess and her Spinning-wheel

O LEEZE[2] me on my spinning-wheel,
And leeze me on my rock[3] and reel;
Frae tap to tae that cleeds[4] me bien,[5]
And haps me fiel[6] and warm at e'en!
I'll set me down and sing and spin,
While laigh descends the simmer sun,
Blest wi' content, and milk and meal—
O leeze me on my spinning-wheel!

On ilka[7] hand the burnies trot,
And meet below my theekit[8] cot;
The scented birk and hawthorn white,
Across the pool their arms unite,
Alike to screen the birdie's nest,
And little fishes' caller[9] rest:
The sun blinks kindly in the biel',[10]
Where blithe I turn my spinning-wheel.

On lofty aiks[11] the cushats wail,
And echo cons the doolfu' tale;
The lintwhites[12] in the hazel braes,
Delighted, rival ither's lays:

[1] each.   [2] commend me to.   [3] distaff.   [4] clothes.
[5] comfortably.   [6] well.   [7] either.   [8] thatched.
[9] cool.   [10] shelter.   [11] oaks.   [12] linnets.

The craik[1] amang the clover hay,
The paitrick[2] whirrin' o'er the ley,[3]
The swallow jinkin'[4] round my shiel,[5]
Amuse me at my spinning-wheel.

Wi' sma' to sell, and less to buy,
Aboon distress, below envy,
O wha would leave this humble state,
For a' the pride of a' the great?
Amid their flaring, idle toys,
Amid their cumbrous, dinsome[6] joys,
Can they the peace and pleasure feel
Of Bessie at her spinning-wheel?

Tam Glen

My heart is a-breaking, dear Tittie![7]
  Some counsel unto me come len',
To anger them a' is a pity,
  But what will I do wi' Tam Glen?

I'm thinking, wi' sic a braw fallow,
  In poortith[8] I might mak a fen'![9]
What care I in riches to wallow,
  If I mauna marry Tam Glen?

There's Lowrie the laird o' Drumeller,
  'Guid day to you, brute!' he comes ben:
He brags and he blaws o' his siller,
  But when will he dance like Tam Glen?

My minnie[10] does constantly deave[11] me,
  And bids me beware o' young men;
They flatter, she says, to deceive me,
  But wha can think sae o' Tam Glen?

---

[1] corn-crake. [2] partridge. [3] meadow. [4] darting. [5] cot. [6] noisy. [7] sister. [8] poverty. [9] shift. [10] mother. [11] deafen.

My daddie says, gin I'll forsake him,
   He'll gie me guid hunder marks ten:
But, if it's ordain'd I maun take him,
   O wha will I get but Tam Glen?

Yestreen at the Valentines' dealing,
   My heart to my mou' gied a sten[1];
For thrice I drew ane without failing,
   And thrice it was written—Tam Glen.

The last Halloween I lay waukin—
   My droukit[2] sark-sleeve, as ye ken;
His likeness cam up the house staukin
   And the very grey breeks o' Tam Glen!

Come counsel, dear Tittie! don't tarry—
   I'll gie you my bonnie black hen,
Gif ye will advise me to marry
   The lad I loe dearly, Tam Glen.

Somebody

My heart is sair—I darena tell—
   My heart is sair for Somebody;
I could wake a winter night
   For the sake o' Somebody.
      Ohon! for Somebody!
      O-hey! for Somebody!
I could range the world around,
   For the sake o' Somebody!

Ye Powers that smile on virtuous love,
   O, sweetly smile on Somebody!
Frae ilka[3] danger keep him free,
   And send me safe my Somebody.

     [1] leap.   [2] dripping.   [3] every.

Ohon! for Somebody!
O-hey! for Somebody!
I wad do—what wad I not?
For the sake o' Somebody!

Duncan Gray

DUNCAN GRAY cam here to woo,
    Ha, ha, the wooing o't,
On blythe Yule night when we were fou,
    Ha, ha, the wooing o't.
Maggie coost her head fu' high,
Look'd asklent[1] and unco skeigh,[2]
Gart[3] poor Duncan stand abeigh[4];
    Ha, ha, the wooing o't.

Duncan fleech'd,[5] and Duncan pray'd,
    Ha, ha, the wooing o't;
Meg was deaf as Ailsa Craig,
    Ha, ha, the wooing o't.
Duncan sigh'd baith out and in,
Grat[6] his een baith bleer't and blin',
Spak o' lowpin[7] o'er a linn[8];
    Ha, ha, the wooing o't.

Time and chance are but a tide;
    Ha, ha, the wooing o't;
Slighted love is sair to bide[9];
    Ha, ha, the wooing o't.
Shall I, like a fool, quoth he,
For a haughty hizzie die?
She may gae to—France for me!
    Ha, ha, the wooing o't.

---

[1] askance.   [2] very skittish.   [3] made.   [4] off.
[5] wheedled.   [6] wept.   [7] jumping.   [8] waterfall.
[9] sore to endure.

How it comes let doctors tell;
    Ha, ha, the wooing o't;
Meg grew sick—as he grew hale;
    Ha, ha, the wooing o't.
Something in her bosom wrings,
For relief a sigh she brings;
And O, her een, they spak sic things!
    Ha, ha, the wooing o't.

Duncan was a lad o' grace;
    Ha, ha, the wooing o't;
Maggie's was a piteous case;
    Ha, ha, the wooing o't.
Duncan could na be her death,
Swelling pity smoor'd[1] his wrath;
Now they're crouse[2] and canty[3] baith;
    Ha, ha, the wooing o't.

O, for ane-and-twenty

Chorus

AN' O, for ane-and-twenty, Tam!
    And hey, sweet ane-and-twenty, Tam!
I'll learn my kin a rattlin' sang,
    An I saw ane-and-twenty, Tam.

They snool[4] me sair, and haud me down,
    And gar[5] me look like bluntie,[6] Tam;
But three short years will soon wheel roun'—
    And then comes ane-and-twenty, Tam.

A gleib[7] o' lan', a claut o' gear,[8]
    Was left me by my auntie, Tam;
At kith or kin I need na spier,[9]
    An I saw ane-and-twenty, Tam.

---

[1] smothered.   [2] cheerful.   [3] merry.   [4] snub.   [5] make.
[6] stupid.   [7] glebe.   [8] handful of money.   [9] ask.

They'll hae me wed a wealthy coof,[1]
  Tho' I mysel hae plenty, Tam:
But hear'st thou, laddie—there's my loof[2]—
  I'm thine at ane-and-twenty, Tam.

O whistle, and I'll come to ye, my lad

O WHISTLE, and I'll come to ye, my lad!
O whistle, and I'll come to ye, my lad!
Tho' father and mither and a' should gae mad,
O whistle, and I'll come to ye, my lad!

But warily tent,[3] when ye come to court me,
And come na unless the back-yett[4] be a-jee[5];
Syne[6] up the back-stile, and let naebody see,
And come as ye were na comin' to me,
And come as ye were na comin' to me!

At kirk, or at market, whene'er ye meet me,
Gang by me as tho' that ye car'd na a flie;
But steal me a blink o' your bonnie black e'e,
Yet look as ye were na lookin' at me,
Yet look as ye were na lookin' at me!

Aye vow and protest that ye care na for me,
And whyles ye may lightly[7] my beauty a wee;
But court na anither, tho' jokin' ye be,
For fear that she wyle[8] your fancy frae me,
For fear that she wyle your fancy frae me!

O whistle, and I'll come to ye, my lad!
O whistle, and I'll come to ye, my lad!
Tho' father and mither and a' should gae mad,
O whistle, and I'll come to ye, my lad!

---

[1] ninny.   [2] palm.   [3] take heed.   [4] gate.   [5] ajar.
[6] then.   [7] slight.   [8] entice.

The Farewell

It was a' for our rightfu' king,
　　We left fair Scotland's strand;
It was a' for our rightfu' king,
　　We e'er saw Irish land, my dear,
　　We e'er saw Irish land.

Now a' is done that men can do,
　　And a' is done in vain;
My love and native land farewell,
　　For I maun cross the main, my dear,
　　For I maun cross the main.

He turned him right, and round about,
　　Upon the Irish shore;
And gae his bridle-reins a shake,
　　With adieu for evermore, my dear,
　　With adieu for evermore.

The sodger from the wars returns,
　　The sailor frae the main;
But I hae parted frae my love,
　　Never to meet again, my dear,
　　Never to meet again.

When day is gane, and night is come,
　　And a' folk bound to sleep;
I think on him that's far awa,
　　The lee-lang night, and weep, my dear,
　　The lee-lang night, and weep.

Auld Lang Syne

I

Should auld acquaintance be forgot,
　　And never brought to mind?
Should auld acquaintance be forgot,
　　And auld lang syne?

For auld lang syne, my dear,
  For auld lang syne,
We'll tak a cup o' kindness yet
  For auld lang syne!

II

And surely you'll be[1] your pint-stoup,
  And surely I'll be mine;
And we'll tak a cup o' kindness yet
  For auld lang syne!

III

We twa hae run about the braes,
  And pu'd the gowans[2] fine;
But we've wandered mony a weary fit[3]
  Sin auld lang syne.

IV

We twa hae paidl'd in the burn,
  Frae morning sun till dine[4];
But seas between us braid hae roar'd
  Sin auld lang syne!

V

And there's a hand, my trusty fiere,[5]
  And gie's a hand o' thine;
And we'll tak a right guid-willie waught[6]
  For auld lang syne.

For auld lang syne, my dear,
  For auld lang syne,
We'll tak a cup o' kindness yet
  For auld lang syne!

[1] pay for. [2] daisies. [3] foot. [4] noon. [5] comrade.
[6] draught.

LADY NAIRNE
1766–1845

The Laird o' Cockpen

THE Laird o' Cockpen, he 's proud an' he 's great,
His mind is ta'en up wi' things o' the State:
He wanted a wife, his braw house to keep;
But favour wi' wooin' was fashous[1] to seek.

Down by the dyke-side a lady did dwell;
At his table-head he thought she'd look well—
McClish's ae daughter o' Claverse-ha' Lee,
A penniless lass wi' a lang pedigree.

His wig was weel pouther'd and as gude as new;
His waistcoat was white, his coat it was blue:
He put on a ring, a sword, and cock'd hat,—
And wha could refuse the Laird wi' a' that?

He took the grey mare, and rade cannily,
An' rapp'd at the yett[2] o' Claverse-ha' Lee:
'Gae tell Mistress Jean to come speedily ben,—
She 's wanted to speak to the Laird o' Cockpen.'

Mistress Jean was makin' the elder-flower wine:
'And what brings the Laird at sic a like time?'
She put aff her apron and on her silk goun,
Her mutch[3] wi' red ribbons, and gaed awa doun.

An' when she cam' ben he bow'd fu' low;
An' what was his errand he soon let her know.
Amazed was the Laird when the lady said 'Na';—
And wi' a laigh curtsey she turn'd awa.

---

[1] troublesome. [2] gate. [3] cap.

Dumbfounder'd was he; nae sigh did he gie,
He mounted his mare, he rade cannily;
And aften he thought as he gaed thro' the glen,
'She's daft to refuse the Laird o' Cockpen!'

And, now that the Laird his exit had made,
Mistress Jean she reflected on what she had said:
'Oh, for ane I'll get better, it's waur I'll get ten!
I was daft to refuse the Laird o' Cockpen.'

Next time that the Laird and the lady were seen
They were gaun arm-in-arm to the kirk on the
    green:
Now she sits in the ha', like a weel-tappit[1] hen;
But as yet there's nae chickens appear'd at
    Cockpen.

(The last two stanzas were written by Miss Susan Ferrier.)

JAMES HOGG
1770–1835

Lock the Door, Lariston

'LOCK the door, Lariston, lion of Liddesdale;
Lock the door, Lariston, Lowther comes on;
    The Armstrongs are flying,
    The widows are crying,
The Castletown's burning, and Oliver's gone!

'Lock the door, Lariston—high on the weather-
    gleam
See how the Saxon plumes bob on the sky—
    Yeomen and carbineer,
    Billman and halberdier,
Fierce is the foray, and far is the cry!

---

[1] crested.

'Bewcastle brandishes high his broad scimitar;
Ridley is riding his fleet-footed grey;
  Hidley and Howard there,
  Wandale and Windermere;
Lock the door, Lariston; hold them at bay.

'Why dost thou smile, noble Elliot of Lariston?
Why does the joy-candle gleam in thine eye?
  Thou bold Border ranger,
  Beware of thy danger;
Thy foes are relentless, determined, and nigh.'

Jack Elliot raised up his steel bonnet and lookit,
His hand grasp'd the sword with a nervous
  embrace;
  'Ah, welcome, brave foemen,
  On earth there are no men
More gallant to meet in the foray or chase!

'Little know you of the hearts I have hidden here;
Little know you of our moss-troopers' might—
  Linhope and Sorbie true,
  Sundhope and Milburn too,
Gentle in manner, but lions in fight!

'I have Mangerton, Ogilvie, Raeburn, and
  Netherbie,
Old Sim of Whitram, and all his array;
  Come all Northumberland,
  Teesdale and Cumberland,
Here at the Breaken tower end shall the fray!'

Scowled the broad sun o'er the links of green
  Liddesdale,
Red as the beacon-light tipped he the wold;
  Many a bold martial eye
  Mirror'd that morning sky,
Never more oped on his orbit of gold.

Shrill was the bugle's note, dreadful the warrior's
    shout,
Lances and halberds in splinters were borne;
      Helmet and hauberk then
      Braved the claymore in vain,
Buckler and armlet in shivers were shorn.

See how they wane—the proud files of the
    Windermere!
Howard! ah, woe to thy hopes of the day!
      Hear the wide welkin rend,
      While the Scots' shouts ascend—
'Elliot of Lariston, Elliot for aye!'

The Witch o' Fife

HURRAY, hurray, the jade's away,
    Like a rocket of air with her bandalet!
I'm up in the air on my bonnie grey mare,
    But I see her yet, I see her yet.
I'll ring the skirts o' the gowden wain
    Wi' curb an' bit, wi' curb an' bit:
An' catch the Bear by the frozen mane—
    An' I see her yet, I see her yet.

Away, away, o'er mountain an' main,
    To sing at the morning's rosy yett;
An' water my mare at its fountain clear—
    But I see her yet, I see her yet.
Away, thou bonnie witch o' Fife,
    On foam of the air to heave an' flit,
An' little reck thou of a poet's life,
    For he sees thee yet, he sees thee yet!

A Boy's Song

WHERE the pools are bright and deep,
Where the grey trout lies asleep,
Up the river and o'er the lea,
That's the way for Billy and me.

Where the blackbird sings the latest,
Where the hawthorn blooms the sweetest,
Where the nestlings chirp and flee,
That's the way for Billy and me.

Where the mowers mow the cleanest,
Where the hay lies thick and greenest;
There to trace the homeward bee,
That's the way for Billy and me.

Where the hazel bank is steepest,
Where the shadow falls the deepest,
Where the clustering nuts fall free,
That's the way for Billy and me.

Why the boys should drive away
Little sweet maidens from the play,
Or love to banter and fight so well,
That's the thing I never could tell,

But this I know, I love to play
Through the meadow, among the hay;
Up the water and o'er the lea,
That's the way for Billy and me.

Bonny Kilmeny gaed up the glen

BONNY Kilmeny gaed up the glen,
But it wasna to meet Duneira's men,
Nor the rosy monk of the isle to see,
For Kilmeny was pure as pure could be.
It was only to hear the yorlin[1] sing,
And pu' the cress-flower round the spring;
The scarlet hypp and the hindberrye,[2]
And the nut that hung frae the hazel tree;
For Kilmeny was pure as pure could be.
But lang may her minny look o'er the wa',
And lang may she seek i' the green-wood shaw;
Lang the laird of Duneira blame,
And lang, lang greet or Kilmeny come hame!

When many a day had come and fled,
When grief grew calm, and hope was dead,
When mass for Kilmeny's soul had been sung,
When the bedes-man had prayed, and the dead
    bell rung,
Late, late in a gloamin' when all was still,
When the fringe was red on the westlin hill,
The wood was sere, the moon i' the wane,
The reek o' the cot hung over the plain,
Like a little wee cloud in the world its lane;
When the ingle lowed with an eiry leme,[3]
Late, late in the gloamin' Kilmeny came
    hame!
'Kilmeny, Kilmeny, where have you been?
Lang hae we sought baith holt and dean;
By linn, by ford, and green-wood tree,
Yet you are halesome and fair to see.

---

[1] yellow-hammer.   [2] raspberry.   [3] fire glowed with
an uncanny light.

Where gat you that joup[1] o' the lily schene?
That bonny snood[2] of the birk sae green?
And these roses, the fairest that ever were seen?
Kilmeny, Kilmeny, where have you been?'

Kilmeny looked up with a lovely grace,
But nae smile was seen on Kilmeny's face;
As still was her look, and as still was her ee,
As the stillness that lay on the emerant lea,
Or the mist that sleeps on a waveless sea.
For Kilmeny had been she knew not where,
And Kilmeny had seen what she could not
    declare;
Kilmeny had been where the cock never crew,
Where the rain never fell, and the wind never
    blew;
But it seemed as the harp of the sky had rung,
And the airs of heaven played round her tongue,
When she spake of the lovely forms she had seen,
And a land where sin had never been;
A land of love, and a land of light,
Withouten sun, or moon, or night;
Where the river swa'd a living stream,
And the light a pure celestial beam:
The land of vision it would seem,
A still, an everlasting dream. . . .
When seven lang years had come and fled;
When grief was calm, and hope was dead;
When scarce was remembered Kilmeny's name,
Late, late in a gloamin' Kilmeny came hame!

(*Kilmeny*, ll. 1–51 and 276–9.)

[1] bodice, loose jacket.   [2] ribbon, fillet.

The Skylark

BIRD of the wilderness,
Blithesome and cumberless,
Sweet be thy matin o'er moorland and lea!
Emblem of happiness,
Blest is thy dwelling-place—
Oh, to abide in the desert with thee!

Wild is thy lay and loud,
Far in the downy cloud,
Loves gives it energy, love gave it birth.
Where, on thy dewy wing,
Where art thou journeying?
Thy lay is in heaven, thy love is on earth.

O'er fell and fountain sheen,
O'er moor and mountain green,
O'er the red streamer that heralds the day,
Over the cloudlet dim,
Over the rainbow's rim,
Musical cherub, soar, singing, away!

Then, when the gloaming comes,
Low in the heather blooms
Sweet will thy welcome and bed of love be!
Emblem of happiness,
Blest is thy dwelling-place—
Oh, to abide in the desert with thee!

SIR WALTER SCOTT
1771–1832

Scotland

LAND of brown heath and shaggy wood,
Land of the mountain and the flood,
Land of my sires! what mortal hand
Can e'er untie the filial band,
That knits me to thy rugged strand!
Still as I view each well-known scene,
Think what is now, and what hath been,
Seems as, to me, of all bereft,
Sole friends thy woods and streams were left;
And thus I love them better still,
Even in extremity of ill.
By Yarrow's stream still let me stray,
Though none should guide my feeble way;
Still feel the breeze down Ettrick break,
Although it chill my wither'd cheek;
Still lay my head by Teviot Stone,
Though there, forgotten and alone,
The Bard may draw his parting groan.

(Lay of the Last Minstrel, Canto VI, stanza 2.)

November in Ettrick Forest

NOVEMBER's sky is chill and drear,
November's leaf is red and sear:
Late, gazing down the steepy linn,
That hems our little garden in,
Low in its dark and narrow glen
You scarce the rivulet might ken,
So thick the tangled greenwood grew,
So feeble trill'd the streamlet through:

Now, murmuring hoarse, and frequent seen
Through bush and brier, no longer green,
An angry brook, it sweeps the glade,
Brawls over rock and wild cascade,
And, foaming brown with doubled speed,
Hurries its waters to the Tweed.

No longer Autumn's glowing red
Upon our Forest hills is shed;
No more beneath the evening beam
Fair Tweed reflects their purple gleam;
Away hath pass'd the heather-bell
That bloom'd so rich on Needpathfell;
Sallow his brow; and russet bare
Are now the sister-heights of Yair.
The sheep, before the pinching heaven,
To shelter'd dale and down are driven,
Where yet some faded herbage pines,
And yet a watery sunbeam shines:
In meek despondency they eye
The wither'd sward and wintry sky,
And far beneath their summer hill,
Stray sadly by Glenkinnon's rill:
The shepherd shifts his mantle's fold,
And wraps him closer from the cold;
His dogs no merry circles wheel,
But shivering follow at his heel;
A cowering glance they often cast,
As deeper moans the gathering blast.

(*Marmion*, Introduction to Canto I.)

Nelson, Pitt, and Fox

To mute and to material things
New life revolving summer brings;
The genial call dead Nature hears,
And in her glory reappears.
But oh! my country's wintry state
What second spring shall renovate?
What powerful call shall bid arise
The buried warlike and the wise;
The mind that thought for Britain's weal,
The hand that grasp'd the victor steel?
The vernal sun new life bestows
Even on the meanest flower that blows;
But vainly, vainly may he shine
Where glory weeps o'er NELSON's shrine;
And vainly pierce the solemn gloom,
That shrouds, O PITT, thy hallowed tomb!

Deep grav'd in every British heart,
O never let those names depart!
Say to your sons,—Lo, here his grave,
Who victor died on Gadite wave.
To him, as to the burning levin,
Short, bright, resistless course was given.
Where'er his country's foes were found,
Was heard the fated thunder's sound,
Till burst the bolt on yonder shore,
Roll'd, blaz'd, destroy'd,—and was no more.

Nor mourn ye less his perish'd worth
Who bade the conqueror go forth,
And launch'd that thunderbolt of war
On Egypt, Hafnia, Trafalgar;
Who, born to guide such high emprize,
For Britain's weal was early wise;

Alas! to whom the Almighty gave,
For Britain's sins, an early grave!
His worth who, in his mightiest hour,
A bauble held the pride of power,
Spurn'd at the sordid lust of pelf,
And serv'd his Albion for herself;
Who, when the frantic crowd amain
Strain'd at subjection's bursting rein,
O'er their wild mood full conquest gain'd,
The pride, he would not crush, restrain'd,
Show'd their fierce zeal a worthier cause,
And brought the freeman's arm to aid the free-
    man's laws.

Had'st thou but liv'd, though stripp'd of power,
A watchman on the lonely tower,
Thy thrilling trump had rous'd the land,
When fraud or danger were at hand;
By thee, as by the beacon-light,
Our pilots had kept course aright;
As some proud column, though alone,
Thy strength had propp'd the tottering throne:
Now is the stately column broke,
The beacon-light is quench'd in smoke,
The trumpet's silver sound is still,
The warder silent on the hill!

Oh think, how to his latest day,
When Death, just hovering, claim'd his prey,
With Palinure's unalter'd mood,
Firm at his dangerous post he stood;
Each call for needful rest repell'd,
With dying hand the rudder held,
Till, in his fall, with fateful sway,
The steerage of the realm gave way!

Then, while on Britain's thousand plains,
One unpolluted church remains,
Whose peaceful bells ne'er sent around
The bloody tocsin's maddening sound,
But still, upon the hallow'd day,
Convoke the swains to praise and pray;
While faith and civil peace are dear,
Grace this cold marble with a tear,—
He, who preserved them, PITT, lies here!

Nor yet suppress the generous sigh,
Because his rival slumbers nigh;
Nor be thy *requiescat* dumb,
Lest it be said o'er Fox's tomb.
For talents mourn, untimely lost,
When best employ'd, and wanted most;
Mourn genius high, and lore profound,
And wit that lov'd to play, not wound;
And all the reasoning powers divine,
To penetrate, resolve, combine;
And feelings keen, and fancy's glow,—
They sleep with him who sleeps below:
And, if thou mourn'st they could not save
From error him who owns this grave,
Be every harsher thought suppress'd,
And sacred be the last long rest.
Here, where the end of earthly things
Lays heroes, patriots, bards, and kings;
Where stiff the hand, and still the tongue,
Of those who fought, and spoke, and sung;
Here, where the fretted aisles prolong
The distant notes of holy song,
As if some angel spoke agen,
'All peace on earth, good-will to men';

If ever from an English heart,
O, *here* let prejudice depart,
And, partial feeling cast aside,
Record, that Fox a Briton died!
When Europe crouch'd to France's yoke,
And Austria bent, and Prussia broke,
And the firm Russian's purpose brave,
Was barter'd by a timorous slave,
Even then dishonour's peace he spurn'd,
The sullied olive-branch return'd,
Stood for his country's glory fast,
And nail'd her colours to the mast!
Heaven, to reward his firmness, gave
A portion in this honour'd grave,
And ne'er held marble in its trust
Of two such wondrous men the dust.

With more than mortal powers endow'd,
How high they soar'd above the crowd!
Theirs was no common party race,
Jostling by dark intrigue for place;
Like fabled Gods, their mighty war
Shook realms and nations in its jar;
Beneath each banner proud to stand,
Look'd up the noblest of the land,
Till through the British world were known
The names of PITT and Fox alone.
Spells of such force no wizard grave
E'er fram'd in dark Thessalian cave,
Though his could drain the ocean dry,
And force the planets from the sky.
These spells are spent, and, spent with these,
The wine of life is on the lees;
Genius, and taste, and talent gone,
For ever tomb'd beneath the stone,

Where—taming thought to human pride!—
The mighty chiefs sleep side by side.
Drop upon Fox's grave the tear,
'Twill trickle to his rival's bier;
O'er PITT's the mournful requiem sound,
And Fox's shall the notes rebound.
The solemn echo seems to cry,
'Here let their discord with them die.
Speak not for those a separate doom,
Whom Fate made Brothers in the tomb;
But search the land of living men,
Where wilt thou find their like agen?'

Rest, ardent Spirits! till the cries
Of dying Nature bid you rise;
Not even your Britain's groans can pierce
The leaden silence of your hearse.

(*Marmion*, Introduction to Canto 1.)

March, march, Ettrick and Teviotdale

MARCH, march, Ettrick and Teviotdale,
  Why the deil dinna ye march forward in
    order?
March, march, Eskdale and Liddesdale,
  All the Blue Bonnets are bound for the Border.
      Many a banner spread,
      Flutters above your head,
    Many a crest that is famous in story.
      Mount and make ready then,
      Sons of the mountain glen,
    Fight for the Queen and the old Scottish
      glory.

Come from the hills where your hirsels are
    grazing,
  Come from the glen of the buck and the roe;
Come to the crag where the beacon is blazing,
  Come with the buckler, the lance, and the bow.
       Trumpets are sounding,
       War-steeds are bounding,
   Stand to your arms then, and march in good
    order;
       England shall many a day
       Tell of the bloody fray,
  When the Blue Bonnets came over the
    Border.

               (*The Monastery*, Chapter xxv.)

Harlaw

'THE herring loves the merry moonlight,
  The mackerel loves the wind,
But the oyster loves the dredging sang,
  For they come of a gentle kind.'

  .   .   .   .   .   .

Now haud your tongue, baith wife and carle,
  And listen, great and sma',
And I will sing of Glenallan's Earl
  That fought on the red Harlaw.

The cronach's cried on Bennachie,
  And doun the Don and a',
And hieland and lawland may mournfu' be
  For the sair field of Harlaw.

They saddled a hundred milk-white steeds,
  They hae bridled a hundred black,
With a chafron of steel on each horse's head,
  And a good knight upon his back.

They hadna ridden a mile, a mile,
　A mile, but barely ten,
When Donald came branking down the brae
　Wi' twenty thousand men.

Their tartans they were waving wide,
　Their glaives were glancing clear,
The pibrochs rung frae side to side,
　Would deafen ye to hear.

The great Earl in his stirrups stood,
　That Highland host to see;
'Now here a knight that's stout and good
　May prove a jeopardie:

'What would'st thou do, my squire so gay,
　That rides beside my reyne,
Were ye Glenallan's Earl the day,
　And I were Roland Cheyne?

'To turn the rein were sin and shame,
　To fight were wond'rous peril;
What would ye do now, Roland Cheyne,
　Were ye Glenallan's Earl?'

'Were I Glenallan's Earl this tide,
　And ye were Roland Cheyne,
The spur should be in my horse's side,
　And the bridle upon his mane.

'If they hae twenty thousand blades,
　And we twice ten times ten,
Yet they hae but their tartan plaids,
　And we are mail-clad men.

'My horse shall ride through ranks sae rude,
   As through the moorland fern,—
Then ne'er let the gentle Norman blude
   Grow cauld for Highland kerne.'

           (*The Antiquary*, Chapter xl.)

Bannockburn

UNFLINCHING foot 'gainst foot was set,
Unceasing blow by blow was met;
   The groans of those who fell
Were drown'd amid the shriller clang
That from the blades and harness rang,
   And in the battle-yell.
Yet fast they fell, unheard, forgot,
Both Southern fierce and hardy Scot;
And O! amid that waste of life,
What various motives fired the strife!
The aspiring Noble bled for fame,
The Patriot for his country's claim;
This Knight his youthful strength to prove,
And that to win his lady's love;
Some fought from ruffian thirst of blood,
From habit some, or hardihood.
But ruffian stern, and soldier good,
   The noble and the slave,
From various cause the same wild road,
On the same bloody morning, trode,
   To that dark inn, the Grave!

    (*The Lord of the Isles*, Canto vi, stanza 26.)

Flodden

By this, though deep the evening fell,
Still rose the battle's deadly swell,
For still the Scots, around their King,
Unbroken, fought in desperate ring.
Where's now their victor vaward wing,
    Where Huntly, and where Home?—
O, for a blast of that dread horn,
On Fontarabian echoes borne,
    That to King Charles did come,
When Rowland brave, and Olivier,
And every paladin and peer,
    On Roncesvalles died!
Such blast might warn them, not in vain,
To quit the plunder of the slain,
And turn the doubtful day again,
    While yet on Flodden side,
Afar, the Royal Standard flies,
And round it toils, and bleeds, and dies,
    Our Caledonian pride!
In vain the wish—for far away,
While spoil and havoc mark their way,
Near Sybil's Cross the plunderers stray.
'O, Lady,' cried the Monk, 'away!'
    And plac'd her on her steed,
And led her to the chapel fair,
    Of Tilmouth upon Tweed.
There all the night they spent in prayer,
And at the dawn of morning, there
She met her kinsman, Lord Fitz-Clare.

But as they left the dark'ning heath,
More desperate grew the strife of death.

The English shafts in volleys hail'd,
In headlong charge their horse assail'd;
Front, flank, and rear, the squadrons sweep
To break the Scottish circle deep,
   That fought around their King.
But yet, though thick the shafts as snow,
Though charging knights like whirlwinds go.
Though bill-men ply the ghastly blow,
   Unbroken was the ring;
The stubborn spear-men still made good
Their dark impenetrable wood,
Each stepping where his comrade stood,
   The instant that he fell.
No thought was there of dastard flight;
Link'd in the serried phalanx tight,
Groom fought like noble, squire like knight,
   As fearlessly and well;
Till utter darkness closed her wing
O'er their thin host and wounded King.
Then skilful Surrey's sage commands
Led back from strife his shatter'd bands;
   And from the charge they drew,
As mountain-waves, from wasted lands,
   Sweep back to ocean blue.
Then did their loss his foemen know;
Their King, their Lords, their mightiest low,
They melted from the field as snow,
When streams are swoln and south winds
    blow,
   Dissolves in silent dew.
Tweed's echoes heard the ceaseless plash,
   While many a broken band,
Disorder'd, through her currents dash,
   To gain the Scottish land;
To town and tower, to town and dale,

To tell red Flodden's dismal tale,
And raise the universal wail.
Tradition, legend, tune, and song,
Shall many an age that wail prolong:
Still from the sire the son shall hear
Of the stern strife, and carnage drear,
   Of Flodden's fatal field,
Where shiver'd was fair Scotland's spear,
   And broken was her shield!

Day dawns upon the mountain's side:
There, Scotland! lay thy bravest pride,
Chiefs, knights, and nobles, many a one:
The sad survivors all are gone.
View not that corpse mistrustfully,
Defac'd and mangled though it be;
Nor to yon Border castle high,
Look northward with upbraiding eye;
   Nor cherish hope in vain,
That, journeying far on foreign strand,
The Royal Pilgrim to his land
   May yet return again.
He saw the wreck his rashness wrought;
Reckless of life, he desperate fought,
   And fell on Flodden plain:
And well in death his trusty brand,
Firm clench'd within his manly hand,
   Beseem'd the monarch slain.
But, O! how changed since yon blithe night!
Gladly I turn me from the sight,
   Unto my tale again.

               (*Marmion*, Canto VI, stanzas 33–5.)

Coronach

He is gone on the mountain,
    He is lost to the forest,
Like a summer-dried fountain,
    When our need was the sorest.
The font, reappearing,
    From the rain-drops shall borrow,
But to us comes no cheering,
    To Duncan no morrow!

The hand of the reaper
    Takes the ears that are hoary,
But the voice of the weeper
    Wails manhood in glory.
The autumn winds rushing
    Waft the leaves that are searest,
But our flower was in flushing,
    When blighting was nearest.

Fleet foot on the correi,
    Sage counsel in cumber,
Red hand in the foray,
    How sound is thy slumber!
Like the dew on the mountain,
    Like the foam on the river,
Like the bubble on the fountain,
    Thou art gone, and for ever!

(*The Lady of the Lake*, Canto III, stanza 16.)

Hymn for the Dead

Nought of the bridal will I tell,
Which after in short space befell;
Nor how brave sons and daughters fair
Bless'd Teviot's Flower, and Cranstoun's heir:

After such dreadful scene, 'twere vain
To wake the note of mirth again.
　　More meet it were to mark the day
　　　Of penitence, and prayer divine,
　　When pilgrim-chiefs, in sad array,
　　　Sought Melrose' holy shrine.

With naked foot, and sackcloth vest,
And arms enfolded on his breast,
　　Did every pilgrim go;
The standers-by might hear uneath,
Footstep, or voice, or high-drawn breath,
　　Through all the lengthen'd row:
No lordly look, nor martial stride;
Gone was their glory, sunk their pride,
　　Forgotten their renown;
Silent and slow, like ghosts they glide
To the high altar's hallow'd side,
　　And there they knelt them down:
Above the suppliant chieftains wave
The banners of departed brave;
Beneath the letter'd stones were laid
The ashes of their fathers dead;
From many a garnish'd niche around,
Stern saints and tortur'd martyrs frown'd.

And slow up the dim aisle afar,
With sable cowl and scapular,
And snow-white stoles, in order due,
The holy Fathers, two and two,
　　In long procession came;
Taper and host, and book they bare,
And holy banner, flourish'd fair
　　With the Redeemer's name.
Above the prostrate pilgrim band
The mitred Abbot stretch'd his hand,

And bless'd them as they kneel'd;
With holy cross he sign'd them all,
And pray'd they might be sage in hall,
    And fortunate in field.
Then mass was sung, and prayers were said,
And solemn requiem for the dead;
And bells toll'd out their mighty peal,
For the departed spirit's weal;
And ever in the office close
The hymn of intercession rose;
And far the echoing aisles prolong
The awful burthen of the song,—
    Dies iræ, dies illa,
    Solvet sæclum in favilla,—
While the pealing organ rung.
    Were it meet with sacred strain
    To close my lay, so light and vain,
Thus the holy Fathers sung:

That day of wrath, that dreadful day,
When heaven and earth shall pass away,
What power shall be the sinner's stay?
How shall he meet that dreadful day?

When, shriveling like a parched scroll,
The flaming heavens together roll;
When louder yet, and yet more dread,
Swells the high trump that wakes the dead!

Oh! on that day, that wrathful day,
When man to judgment wakes from clay,
Be THOU the trembling sinner's stay,
Though heaven and earth shall pass away!

(*The Lay of the Last Minstrel*, Canto VI, stanzas 28–31.)

Love

AND said I that my limbs were old,
And said I that my blood was cold,
And that my kindly fire was fled,
And my poor wither'd heart was dead,
    And that I might not sing of love?—
How could I to the dearest theme,
That ever warm'd a minstrel's dream,
    So foul, so false a recreant prove!
How could I name love's very name,
Nor wake my heart to notes of flame!

In peace, Love tunes the shepherd's reed;
In war, he mounts the warrior's steed;
In halls, in gay attire is seen;
In hamlets, dances on the green.
Love rules the court, the camp, the grove,
And men below, and saints above;
For love is heaven, and heaven is love.

(*The Lay of the Last Minstrel*, Canto III, stanzas 1 and 2.)

To a Lady

With Flowers from the Roman Wall

TAKE these flowers which, purple waving,
    On the ruin'd rampart grew,
Where, the sons of freedom braving,
    Rome's imperial standards flew.

Warriors from the breach of danger
    Pluck no longer laurels there;
They but yield the passing stranger
    Wild-flower wreaths for Beauty's hair.

Rosabelle

O LISTEN, listen, ladies gay!
  No haughty feat of arms I tell;
Soft is the note, and sad the lay,
  That mourns the lovely Rosabelle.

—'Moor, moor the barge, ye gallant crew!
  And, gentle ladye, deign to stay!
Rest thee in Castle Ravensheuch,
  Nor tempt the stormy firth to-day.

'The blackening wave is edg'd with white:
  To inch and rock the sea-mews fly;
The fishers have heard the Water-Sprite,
  Whose screams forebode that wreck is nigh.

'Last night the gifted Seer did view
  A wet shroud swathed round ladye gay;
Then stay thee, Fair, in Ravensheuch:
  Why cross the gloomy firth to-day?'

''Tis not because Lord Lindesay's heir
  To-night at Roslin leads the ball,
But that my ladye-mother there
  Sits lonely in her castle-hall.

''Tis not because the ring they ride,
  And Lindesay at the ring rides well,
But that my sire the wine will chide,
  If 'tis not fill'd by Rosabelle.'

O'er Roslin all that dreary night
  A wondrous blaze was seen to gleam;
'Twas broader than the watch-fire's light,
  And redder than the bright moonbeam.

It glar'd on Roslin's castled rock,
  It ruddied all the copse-wood glen;
'Twas seen from Dryden's groves of oak,
  And seen from cavern'd Hawthornden.

Seem'd all on fire that chapel proud,
  Where Roslin's chiefs uncoffin'd lie,
Each Baron, for a sable shroud,
  Sheath'd in his iron panoply.

Seem'd all on fire within, around,
  Deep sacristy and altar's pale;
Shone every pillar foliage-bound,
  And glimmer'd all the dead men's mail.

Blaz'd battlement and pinnet high,
  Blaz'd every rose-carved buttress fair—
So still they blaze when fate is nigh
  The lordly line of high St. Clair.

There are twenty of Roslin's barons bold
  Lie buried within that proud chapelle;
Each one the holy vault doth hold—
  But the sea holds lovely Rosabelle!

And each St. Clair was buried there,
  With candle, with book, and with knell;
But the sea-caves rung, and the wild winds sung,
  The dirge of lovely Rosabelle.

        (*The Lay of the Last Minstrel*, Canto VI, stanza 23.)

A weary lot is thine

'A WEARY lot is thine, fair maid,
  A weary lot is thine!
To pull the thorn thy brow to braid,
  And press the rue for wine!

A lightsome eye, a soldier's mien,
   A feather of the blue,
A doublet of the Lincoln green,—
   No more of me you knew,
                My love!
   No more of me you knew.

This morn is merry June, I trow,
   The rose is budding fain;
But she shall bloom in winter snow,
   Ere we two meet again.'
He turn'd his charger as he spake,
   Upon the river shore,
He gave his bridle-reins a shake,
   Said, 'Adieu for evermore,
                My love!
   And adieu for evermore.'

                (*Rokeby*, Canto III, stanza 28.)

It was an English ladye bright

IT was an English ladye bright,
   (The sun shines fair on Carlisle wall,)
And she would marry a Scottish knight,
   For Love will still be lord of all.

Blithely they saw the rising sun,
   When he shone fair on Carlisle wall;
But they were sad ere day was done,
   Though Love was still the lord of all.

Her sire gave brooch and jewel fine,
   Where the sun shines fair on Carlisle wall;
Her brother gave but a flask of wine,
   For ire that Love was lord of all.

For she had lands, both meadow and lea,
  Where the sun shines fair on Carlisle wall;
And he swore her death ere he would see
  A Scottish knight the lord of all!

That wine she had not tasted well,
  (The sun shines fair on Carlisle wall,)
When dead in her true love's arms she fell,
  For Love was still the lord of all!

He pierc'd her brother to the heart,
  Where the sun shines fair on Carlisle wall:
So perish all would true love part,
  That Love may still be lord of all!

And then he took the cross divine,
  (Where the sun shines fair on Carlisle wall,)
And died for her sake in Palestine;
  So Love was still the lord of all.

Now all ye lovers that faithful prove,
  (The sun shines fair on Carlisle wall,)
Pray for their souls who died for love,
  For Love shall still be lord of all!

(*The Lay of the Last Minstrel*, Canto VI, stanzas 11 and 12.)

Lochinvar

O, YOUNG Lochinvar is come out of the west,
Through all the wide Border his steed was the
    best;
And save his good broadsword he weapons had
    none,
He rode all unarm'd, and he rode all alone.
So faithful in love, and so dauntless in war,
There never was knight like the young Lochinvar.

He staid not for brake, and he stopp'd not for
    stone,
He swam the Eske river where ford there was
    none;
But ere he alighted at Netherby gate,
The bride had consented, the gallant came late:
For a laggard in love, and a dastard in war,
Was to wed the fair Ellen of brave Lochinvar.

So boldly he enter'd the Netherby Hall,
Among bride's-men, and kinsmen, and brothers,
    and all:
Then spoke the bride's father, his hand on his
    sword,
(For the poor craven bridegroom said never a
    word,)
'O come ye in peace here, or come ye in war,
Or to dance at our bridal, young Lord Lochin-
    var?'

'I long woo'd your daughter, my suit you
    denied;—
Love swells like the Solway, but ebbs like its
    tide—
And now am I come, with this lost love of mine,
To lead but one measure, drink one cup of wine.
There are maidens in Scotland more lovely by
    far,
That would gladly be bride to the young Lochin-
    var.'

The bride kiss'd the goblet: the knight took it up,
He quaff'd off the wine, and he threw down the
    cup.
She look'd down to blush, and she look'd up to
    sigh,
With a smile on her lips, and a tear in her eye.

He took her soft hand, ere her mother could
    bar,—
'Now tread we a measure!' said young Lochinvar.

So stately his form, and so lovely her face,
That never a hall such a galliard did grace;
While her mother did fret, and her father did
    fume,
And the bridegroom stood dangling his bonnet
    and plume;
And the bride-maidens whisper'd, "Twere better
    by far,
To have match'd our fair cousin with young
    Lochinvar.'

One touch to her hand, and one word in her ear,
When they reach'd the hall-door, and the charger
    stood near;
So light to the croupe the fair lady he swung,
So light to the saddle before her he sprung!
'She is won! we are gone, over bank, bush, and
    scaur;
They'll have fleet steeds that follow,' quoth
    young Lochinvar.

There was mounting 'mong Græmes of the
    Netherby clan;
Forsters, Fenwicks, and Musgraves, they rode
    and they ran:
There was racing and chasing on Cannobie Lee,
But the lost bride of Netherby ne'er did they
    see.
So daring in love, and so dauntless in war,
Have ye e'er heard of gallant like young Lochin-
    var?

               (*Marmion*, Canto v, stanza 12.)

Cleveland's Song

FAREWELL! Farewell! the voice you hear
  Has left its last soft tone with you;
Its next must join the seaward cheer,
  And shout among the shouting crew.

The accents which I scarce could form
  Beneath your frown's controlling check,
Must give the word, above the storm,
  To cut the mast, and clear the wreck.

The timid eye I dared not raise,
  The hand that shook when press'd to thine,
Must point the guns upon the chase—
  Must bid the deadly cutlass shine.

To all I love, or hope, or fear,
  Honour, or own, a long adieu!
To all that life has soft and dear,
  Farewell! save memory of you!

(*The Pirate*, Chapter XXIII.)

Proud Maisie

PROUD Maisie is in the wood,
  Walking so early;
Sweet Robin sits on the bush,
  Singing so rarely.

'Tell me, thou bonny bird,
  When shall I marry me?'
'When six braw gentlemen
  Kirkward shall carry ye.'

'Who makes the bridal bed,
    Birdie, say truly?'
'The grey-headed sexton
    That delves the grave duly.

'The glow-worm o'er grave and stone
    Shall light thee steady.
The owl from the steeple sing,
    "Welcome, proud lady".'

(*The Heart of Midlothian*, Chapter XL.)

Lucy Ashton's Song

Look not thou on beauty's charming,
Sit thou still when kings are arming,
Taste not when the wine-cup glistens,
Speak not when the people listens,
Stop thine ear against the singer,
From the red gold keep thy finger;
Vacant heart and hand and eye,
Easy live and quiet die.

(*The Bride of Lammermoor*, Chapter III.)

David Gellatley's Song

Young men will love thee more fair and more
        fast;
    Heard ye so merry the little bird sing?
Old men's love the longest will last,
    And the throstle-cock's head is under his wing.

The young man's wrath is like light straw on fire;
    Heard ye so merry the little bird sing?
But like red-hot steel is the old man's ire,
    And the throstle-cock's head is under his wing.

The young man will brawl at the evening board;
  Heard ye so merry the little bird sing?
But the old man will draw at the dawning the
      sword,
  And the throstle-cock's head is under his wing.

                              (*Waverley*, Chapter XIV.)

Sweet Teviot! on thy silver tide

I

SWEET Teviot! on thy silver tide
  The glaring bale-fires blaze no more;
No longer steel-clad warriors ride
  Along thy wild and willow'd shore;
Where'er thou wind'st, by dale or hill,
All, all is peaceful, all is still,
  As if thy waves, since Time was born,
Since first they roll'd upon the Tweed,
Had only heard the shepherd's reed,
  Nor started at the bugle-horn.

II

Unlike the tide of human time,—
  Which, though it change in ceaseless flow,
Retains each grief, retains each crime
  Its earliest course was doom'd to know;
And, darker as it downward bears,
Is stain'd with past and present tears.

(*The Lay of the Last Minstrel*, Canto IV, stanzas 1 and 2.)

The Sun upon the Weirdlaw Hill

THE sun upon the Weirdlaw Hill,
  In Ettrick's vale, is sinking sweet;
The westland wind is hush and still,
  The lake lies sleeping at my feet.

Yet not the landscape to mine eye
 Bears those bright hues that once it bore;
Though evening, with her richest dye,
 Flames o'er the hills of Ettrick's shore.

With listless look along the plain,
 I see Tweed's silver current glide,
And coldly mark the holy fane
 Of Melrose rise in ruin'd pride.
The quiet lake, the balmy air,
 The hill, the stream, the tower, the tree,—
Are they still such as once they were?
 Or is the dreary change in me?

Alas, the warp'd and broken board,
 How can it bear the painter's dye!
The harp of strain'd and tuneless chord,
 How to the minstrel's skill reply!
To aching eyes each landscape lowers,
 To feverish pulse each gale blows chill;
And Araby's or Eden's bowers
 Were barren as this moorland hill.

The Gipsy's Dirge

WASTED, weary, wherefore stay,
Wrestling thus with earth and clay?
From the body pass away;—
 Hark! the mass is singing.

From thee doff thy mortal weed,
Mary Mother be thy speed,
Saints to help thee at thy need;—
 Hark! the knell is ringing.

Fear not snowdrift driving fast,
Sleet, or hail, or levin blast;
Soon the shroud shall lap thee fast,
And the sleep be on thee cast
  That shall ne'er know waking.

Haste thee, haste thee, to be gone,
Earth flits fast, and time draws on,—
Gasp thy gasp, and groan thy groan,
  Day is near the breaking.

     (*Guy Mannering*, Chapter XXVII.)

And you shall deal the funeral dole

AND you shall deal the funeral dole;
 Ay, deal it, mother mine,
To weary body, and to heavy soul,
 The white bread and the wine.

And you shall deal my horses of pride;
 Ay, deal them, mother mine;
And you shall deal my lands so wide,
 And deal my castles nine.

But deal not vengeance for the deed,
 And deal not for the crime;
The body to its place, and the soul to Heaven's
 grace,
 And the rest in God's own time.

     (*The Pirate*, Chapter XXIII.)

Donald Caird[1]

DONALD CAIRD's come again!
Donald Caird's come again!
Tell the news in brugh[2] and glen,
Donald Caird's come again!

  [1] caird signifies tinker. [2] burgh.

Donald Caird can lilt and sing,
Blithely dance the Hieland fling,
Drink till the gudeman be blind,
Fleech till the gudewife be kind;
Hoop a leglin,[1] clout a pan,
Or crack a pow[2] wi' ony man;—
Tell the news in brugh and glen,
Donald Caird's come again.

    Donald Caird's come again!
    Donald Caird's come again!
    Tell the news in brugh and glen,
    Donald Caird's come again.

Donald Caird can wire a maukin,[3]
Kens the wiles o' dun-deer staukin',
Leisters kipper,[4] makes a shift
To shoot a muir-fowl in the drift;
Water-bailiffs, rangers, keepers,—
He can wauk when they are sleepers;
Nor for bountith or rewaird
Dare ye mell wi'[5] Donald Caird.

    Donald Caird's come again!
    Donald Caird's come again!
    Gar the bagpipes hum amain,
    Donald Caird's come again.

Donald Caird can drink a gill
Fast as hostler-wife can fill;
Ilka ane that sells gude liquor
Kens how Donald bends a bicker;
When he's fou he's stout and saucy,
Keeps the cantle o' the causey[6];
Hieland chief and Lawland laird
Maun gie room to Donald Caird!

[1] milk-pail.   [2] head.   [3] hare.   [4] spears fish.
[5] meddle with.   [6] crown of the causeway.

Donald Caird's come again!
Donald Caird's come again!
Tell the news in brugh and glen,
Donald Caird's come again.

Steek the amrie,[1] lock the kist,[2]
Else some gear may weel be mis't;
Donald Caird finds orra[3] things
Where Allan Gregor fand the tings[4];
Dunts of kebbuck, taits o' woo,[5]
Whiles a hen and whiles a sow,
Webs or duds frae hedge or yaird—
'Ware the wuddie,[6] Donald Caird!

Donald Caird's come again!
Donald Caird's come again!
Dinna let the Shirra ken
Donald Caird's come again.

On Donald Caird the doom was stern,
Craig[7] to tether, legs to airn;
But Donald Caird, wi' mickle study,
Caught the gift to cheat the wuddie;
Rings of airn, and bolts of steel,
Fell like ice frae hand and heel!
Watch the sheep in fauld and glen,
Donald Caird's come again!

Donald Caird's come again!
Donald Caird's come again!
Dinna let the Justice ken,
Donald Caird's come again.

[1] cupboard.   [2] chest.   [3] odd.   [4] tongs.   [5] slices
of cheese and hanks of wool.   [6] gallows.   [7] neck.

THOMAS CAMPBELL
1777–1844

Ode to Winter

WHEN first the fiery-mantled sun
His heavenly race began to run;
Round the earth and ocean blue,
His children four the Seasons flew.
First, in green apparel dancing,
   The young Spring smiled with angel grace;
Rosy Summer next advancing,
   Rush'd into her sire's embrace—
Her bright-hair'd sire, who bade her keep
   For ever nearest to his smiles,
On Calpe's olive-shaded steep,
   On India's citron-cover'd isles:
More remote and buxom-brown,
   The Queen of vintage bow'd before his throne;
A rich pomegranate gemm'd her crown,
   A ripe sheaf bound her zone.

But howling Winter fled afar,
To hills that prop the polar star,
And loves on deer-borne car to ride,
With barren darkness by his side.
Round the shores where loud Lofoden
   Whirls to death the roaring whale,
Round the hall where Runic Odin
   Howls his war-song to the gale;
Save when adown the ravaged globe
   He travels on his native storm,
Deflowering Nature's grassy robe,
   And trampling on her faded form:—

Till light's returning lord assume
  The shaft that drives him to his polar field,
Of power to pierce his raven plume,
  And crystal-cover'd shield.

O, sire of storms! whose savage ear
The Lapland drum delights to hear,
When Frenzy with her blood-shot eye
Implores thy dreadful deity—
Archangel! power of desolation!
  Fast descending as thou art,
Say, hath mortal invocation
  Spells to touch thy stony heart?
Then, sullen Winter! hear my prayer,
  And gently rule the ruin'd year;
Nor chill the wanderer's bosom bare,
  Nor freeze the wretch's falling tear;—
To shuddering Want's unmantled bed,
  Thy horror-breathing agues cease to lend,
And gently on the orphan head
  Of innocence descend.—

But chiefly spare, O king of clouds!
The sailor on his airy shrouds;
When wrecks and beacons strew the steep,
And spectres walk along the deep.
Milder yet thy snowy breezes
  Pour on yonder tented shores,
Where the Rhine's broad billow freezes,
  Or the dark-brown Danube roars.
Oh winds of Winter! list ye there
  To many a deep and dying groan;
Or start, ye demons of the midnight air,
  At shrieks and thunders louder than your
    own.

Alas! e'en your unhallow'd breath
  May spare the victim fallen low;
But man will ask no truce to death,—
  No bounds to human woe.

Freedom and Love

How delicious is the winning
Of a kiss at love's beginning,
When two mutual hearts are sighing
For the knot there's no untying!

Yet remember, 'midst your wooing,
Love has bliss, but Love has ruing;
Other smiles may make you fickle,
Tears for other charms may trickle.

Love he comes, and Love he tarries,
Just as fate or fancy carries;
Longest stays, when sorest chidden;
Laughs and flies, when press'd and bidden.

Bind the sea to slumber stilly,
Bind its odour to the lily,
Bind the aspen ne'er to quiver,
Then bind Love to last for ever.

Love's a fire that needs renewal
Of fresh beauty for its fuel:
Love's wing moults when caged and captured,
Only free, he soars enraptured.

Can you keep the bee from ranging
Or the ringdove's neck from changing?
No! nor fetter'd Love from dying
In the knot there's no untying.

Florine

Could I bring back lost youth again
   And be what I have been,
I'd court you in a gallant strain,
   My young and fair Florine.

But mine's the chilling age that chides
   Devoted rapture's glow,
And Love—that conquers all besides—
   Finds Time a conquering foe.

Farewell! we're severed by our fate
   As far as night from noon;
You came into the world too late,
   And I depart so soon.

The River of Life

The more we live, more brief appear
   Our life's succeeding stages:
A day to childhood seems a year,
   And years like passing ages.

The gladsome current of our youth,
   Ere passion yet disorders,
Steals lingering like a river smooth
   Along its grassy borders.

But as the careworn cheek grows wan,
   And sorrow's shafts fly thicker,
Ye stars, that measure life to man,
   Why seem your courses quicker?

When joys have lost their bloom and breath,
   And life itself is vapid,
Why, as we reach the Falls of death,
   Feel we its tide more rapid?

It may be strange—yet who would change
    Time's course to slower speeding,
When one by one our friends have gone
    And left our bosoms bleeding?

Heaven gives our years of fading strength
    Indemnifying fleetness;
And those of youth, a seeming length,
    Proportion'd to their sweetness.

The Last Man

ALL worldly shapes shall melt in gloom,
    The Sun himself must die,
Before this mortal shall assume
    Its Immortality!
I saw a vision in my sleep,
That gave my spirit strength to sweep
    Adown the gulf of Time!
I saw the last of human mould,
That shall Creation's death behold,
    As Adam saw her prime!

The Sun's eye had a sickly glare,
    The earth with age was wan,
The skeletons of nations were
    Around that lonely man!
Some had expired in fight,—the brands
Still rusted in their bony hands;
    In plague and famine some!
Earth's cities had no sound nor tread;
And ships were drifting with the dead
    To shores where all was dumb!

Yet, prophet-like, that lone one stood,
  With dauntless words and high,
That shook the sere leaves from the wood
  As if a storm pass'd by,
Saying, We are twins in death, proud Sun,
Thy face is cold, thy race is run,
  'Tis Mercy bids thee go.
For thou ten thousand thousand years
Hast seen the tide of human tears,
  That shall no longer flow.

What though beneath thee man put forth
  His pomp, his pride, his skill,
And arts that made fire, flood, and earth,
  The vassals of his will;—
Yet mourn I not thy parted sway,
Thou dim discrownèd king of day:
  For all those trophied arts
And triumphs that beneath thee sprang,
Heal'd not a passion or a pang
  Entail'd on human hearts.

Go, let oblivion's curtain fall
  Upon the stage of men,
Nor with thy rising beams recall
  Life's tragedy again.
Its piteous pageants bring not back
Nor waken flesh, upon the rack
  Of pain anew to writhe,
Stretch'd in disease's shapes abhorr'd
Or mown in battle by the sword,
  Like grass beneath the scythe.

Even I am weary in yon skies
   To watch thy fading fire;
Test of all sumless agonies,
   Behold not me expire.
My lips that speak thy dirge of death—
Their rounded gasp and gurgling breath
   To see thou shalt not boast.
The eclipse of Nature spreads my pall,—
The majesty of Darkness shall
   Receive my parting ghost!

This spirit shall return to Him
   That gave its heavenly spark;
Yet think not, Sun, it shall be dim
   When thou thyself art dark!
No! it shall live again, and shine
In bliss unknown to beams of thine,
   By him recall'd to breath,
Who captive led captivity,
Who robb'd the grave of Victory,—
   And took the sting from Death!

Go, Sun, while Mercy holds me up
   On Nature's awful waste
To drink this last and bitter cup
   Of grief that man shall taste—
Go, tell the night that hides thy face,
Thou saw'st the last of Adam's race,
   On Earth's sepulchral clod,
The darkening universe defy
To quench his Immortality,
   Or shake his trust in God!

ALLAN CUNNINGHAM
1784-1842

The sun rises bright in France

THE sun rises bright in France,
    And fair sets he;
But he has tint[1] the blythe blink he had
    In my ain countree.

O, it's nae my ain ruin
    That saddens aye my e'e,
But the dear Marie I left ahin'
    Wi' sweet bairnies three.

My lanely hearth burn'd bonnie,
    And smiled my ain Marie;
I've left a' my heart behin'
    In my ain countree.

The bud comes back to summer,
    And the blossom to the bee;
But I'll win back, O never,
    To my ain countree.

O, I am leal to high Heaven,
    Where soon I hope to be,
An' there I'll meet ye a' soon
    Frae my ain countree!

Hame, Hame, Hame

HAME, hame, hame, O hame fain wad I be—
    O hame, hame, hame, to my ain countree!

---

[1] lost.

When the flower is i' the bud and the leaf is on
    the tree,
The larks shall sing me hame in my ain countree;
Hame, hame, hame, O hame fain wad I be—
O hame, hame, hame, to my ain countree!

The green leaf o' loyaltie's beginning for to fa',
The bonnie White Rose it is withering an' a';
But I'll water 't wi' the blude of usurping tyran-
    nie,
An' green it will graw in my ain countree.

O, there's nocht now frae ruin my country can
    save,
But the keys o' kind heaven, to open the grave;
That a' the noble martyrs wha died for loyaltie
May rise again an' fight for their ain countree.

The great now are gane, a' wha ventured to save,
The new grass is springing on the tap o' their
    grave;
But the sun through the mirk blinks blythe in
    my e'e,
'I'll shine on ye yet in your ain countree.'

Hame, hame, hame, O hame fain wad I be—
O hame, hame, hame, to my ain countree!

The Spring of the Year

GONE were but the winter cold,
    And gone were but the snow,
I could sleep in the wild woods
    Where primroses blow.

Cold's the snow at my head,
    And cold at my feet;
And the finger of death's at my e'en,
    Closing them to sleep.

Let none tell my father
    Or my mother so dear,—
I'll meet them both in heaven
    At the spring of the year.

ANONYMOUS

Canadian Boat Song

FAIR these broad meads—these hoary woods are
    grand;
But we are exiles from our fathers' land.

Listen to me, as when you heard our father
    Sing long ago the song of other shores—
Listen to me, and then in chorus gather
    All your deep voices, as ye pull your oars.

From the lone sheiling of the misty island
    Mountains divide us, and the waste of
        seas—
Yet still the blood is strong, the heart is Highland,
    And we in dreams behold the Hebrides.

We ne'er shall tread the fancy-haunted valley,
    Where 'tween the dark hills creeps the
        small clear stream,
In arms around the patriarch banner rally,
    Nor see the moon on royal tombstones
        gleam.

When the bold kindred, in the time long vanish'd,
    Conquered the soil and fortified the
      keep,—
No seer foretold the children would be banish'd
    That a degenerate lord might boast his
      sheep.

Come foreign rage—let Discord burst in slaughter!
    O then for clansmen true, and stern clay-
      more—
The hearts that would have given their blood
    like water,
    Beat heavily beyond the Atlantic roar.

JOHN GIBSON LOCKHART
1794–1854

When youthful faith hath fled

WHEN youthful faith hath fled,
    Of loving take thy leave;
Be constant to the dead—
    The dead cannot deceive.

Sweet modest flowers of spring,
    How fleet your balmy day!
And man's brief year can bring
    No secondary May,

No earthly burst again
    Of gladness out of gloom,
Fond hope and vision vain,
    Ungrateful to the tomb.

But 'tis an old belief
    That on some solemn shore,
Beyond the sphere of grief,
    Dear friends shall meet once more.

Beyond the sphere of time,
    And Sin and Fate's control,
Serene in endless prime
    Of body and of soul.

That creed I fain would keep,
    That hope I'll not forgo,
Eternal be the sleep
    Unless to waken so.

GEORGE OUTRAM

1805–56

The Annuity

I GAED to spend a week in Fife—
    An unco week it proved to be—
For there I met a waesome wife
    Lamentin' her viduity.
Her grief brak out sae fierce and fell,
I thought her heart wad burst the shell;
And—I was sae left to mysel'—
    I sell't her an annuity.

The bargain lookit fair enough—
    She just was turned o' saxty-three;
I couldna guessed she'd prove sae teugh,
    By human ingenuity.
But years have come, and years have gane,
And there she's yet as stieve[1]'s a stane—
The limmer[2]'s growin' young again,
    Since she got her annuity.

She's crined[3] awa' to bane an' skin,
    But that it seems is nought to me;
She's like to live—although she's in
    The last stage o' tenuity.

[1] firm.   [2] jade.   [3] shrivelled.

She munches wi' her wizened gums,
An' stumps about on legs o' thrums,[1]
But comes—as sure as Christmas comes—
    To ca' for her annuity.

She jokes her joke, an' cracks her crack,
    As spunkie[2] as a growin' flea—
An' there she sits upon my back,
    A livin' perpetuity.
She hurkles[3] by her ingle side,
An' toasts an' tans her wrunkled hide—
Lord kens how lang she yet may bide
    To ca' for her annuity!

I read the tables drawn wi' care
    For an Insurance Company;
Her chance o' life was stated there,
    Wi' perfect perspicuity.
But tables here or tables there,
She's lived ten years beyond her share,
An's like to live a dizzen mair,
    To ca' for her annuity.

I gat the loon that drew the deed—
    We spelled it o'er right carefully;—
In vain he yerked his souple head,
    To find an ambiguity;
It's dated—tested—a' complete—
The proper stamp—nae word delete—
And diligence, as on decreet,
    May pass for her annuity.

Last Yule she had a fearfu' hoast[4]—
    I thought a kink[5] might set me free;
I led her out, 'mang snaw and frost,
    Wi' constant assiduity.

---

[1] threads.   [2] spirited.   [3] crouches.   [4] cold.   [5] cough.

But Deil ma' care—the blast gaed by,
  And missed the auld anatomy;
It just cost me a tooth, forbye
    Discharging her annuity.

I thought that grief might gar her quit—
  Her only son was lost at sea—
But aff her wits behuved to flit,
    An' leave her in fatuity!
She threeps,[1] an' threeps, he's living yet,
For a' the tellin' she can get;
But catch the doited runt forget
    To ca' for her annuity!

If there's a sough o' cholera
  Or typhus—wha sae gleg[2] as she?
She buys up baths, an' drugs, an' a',
    In siccan superfluity!
She doesna need—she's fever proof—
The pest gaed o'er her very roof;
She tauld me sae—an' then her loof
    Held out for her annuity.

Ae day she fell—her arm she brak—
  A compound fracture as could be;
Nae leech the cure wad undertak,
    Whate'er was the gratuity.
It's cured!—She handles't like a flail—
It does as weel in bits as hale;
But I'm a broken man mysel'
    Wi' her and her annuity.

Her broozled flesh, and broken banes,
  Are weel as flesh an' banes can be.
She beats the taeds that live in stanes,
    An' fatten in vacuity!

<hr>

[1] maintains.   [2] lively.

They die when they're exposed to air—
They canna thole[1] the atmosphere;
But her! expose her onywhere—
   She lives for her annuity.

If mortal means could nick her thread,
   Sma' crime it wad appear to me;
Ca't murder, or ca't homicide—
   I'd justify't,—an' do it tae.
But how to fell a withered wife
That's carved out o' the tree o' life—
The timmer limmer daurs the knife
   To settle her annuity.

I'd try a shot.—But whar's the mark?—
   Her vital parts are hid frae me;
Her back-bane wanders through her sark
   In an unkenn'd corkscrewity.
She's palsified—an' shakes her head
Sae fast about, ye scarce can see't;
It's past the power o' steel or lead
   To settle her annuity.

She might be drowned;—but go she'll not
   Within a mile o' loch or sea;—
Or hanged—if cord could grip a throat
   O' siccan exiguity.
It's fitter far to hang the rope—
It draws out like a telescope;
'Twad tak a dreadfu' length o' drop
   To settle her annuity.

Will puzion do't?—It has been tried;
   But, be't in hash or fricassee,
That's just the dish she can't abide,
   Whatever kind o' *goût* it hae.

---

[1] endure.

It's needless to assail her doubts,—
She gangs by instinct—like the brutes—
An' only eats an' drinks what suits
 Hersel' an' her annuity.

The Bible says the age o' man
 Threescore an' ten perchance may be;
She's ninety-four;—let them wha can
 Explain the incongruity.
She should hae lived afore the Flood—
She's come o' Patriarchal blood—
She's some auld Pagan, mummified
 Alive for her annuity.

She's been embalmed inside and out—
 She's sauted to the last degree—
There's pickle in her very snout
 Sae caper-like an' cruety;
Lot's wife was fresh compared to her;
They've Kyanised[1] the useless knir[2]—
She canna decompose—nae mair
 Than her accursed annuity.

The water-drap wears out the rock
 As this eternal jaud wears me;
I could withstand the single shock,
 But no the continuity.
It's pay me here—an' pay me there—
An' pay me, pay me, evermair;
I'll gang demented wi' despair—
 I'm *charged* for her annuity!

---

[1] preserved in corrosive sublimate.   [2] knot of wood.

WILLIAM BELL SCOTT
1811–90

The Witch's Ballad

O I hae come from far away,
　From a warm land far away,
A southern land across the sea,
With sailor-lads about the mast,
Merry and canny, and kind to me.

And I hae been to yon town
　To try my luck in yon town;
Nort, and Mysie, Elspie too.
Right braw we were to pass the gate,
Wi' gowden clasps on girdles blue.

Mysie smiled wi' miminy[1] mouth,
　Innocent mouth, miminy mouth;
Elspie wore a scarlet gown,
Nort's grey eyes were unco' gleg,[2]
My Castile comb was like a crown.

We walk'd abreast all up the street,
　Into the market up the street;
Our hair with marigolds was wound,
Our bodices with love-knots laced,
Our merchandise with tansy bound.

Nort had chickens, I had cocks,
　Gamesome cocks, loud-crowing cocks;
Mysie ducks, and Elspie drakes,—
For a wee groat or a pound;
We lost nae time wi' gives and takes.

　　[1] prim, demure.　　[2] bright, sharp.

—Lost nae time, for well we knew,
  In our sleeves full well we knew,
When the gloaming came that night,
Duck nor drake, nor hen nor cock
Would be found by candle-light.

And when our chaffering all was done,
  All was paid for, sold and done,
We drew a glove on ilka hand,
We sweetly curtsied, each to each,
And deftly danced a saraband.

The market-lassies look'd and laugh'd,
  Left their gear, and look'd and laugh'd;
They made as they would join the game,
But soon their mithers, wild and wud,[1]
With whack and screech they stopp'd the same.

Sae loud the tongues o' randies[2] grew,
  The flytin'[3] and the skirlin'[4] grew,
At all the windows in the place,
Wi' spoons or knives, wi' needle or awl,
Was thrust out every hand and face.

And down each stair they throng'd anon,
  Gentle, semple, throng'd anon:
Souter[5] and tailor, frowsy Nan,
The ancient widow young again,
Simpering behind her fan.

Without a choice, against their will,
  Doited,[6] dazed, against their will,
The market lassie and her mither,
The farmer and his husbandman,
Hand in hand dance a' thegither.

---

[1] mad.   [2] viragoes.   [3] scolding.   [4] shrieking.
[5] cobbler.   [6] mazed.

Slow at first, but faster soon,
  Still increasing, wild and fast,
Hoods and mantles, hats and hose,
Blindly doff'd and cast away,
Left them naked, heads and toes.

They would have torn us limb from limb,
  Dainty limb from dainty limb;
But never one of them could win
Across the line that I had drawn
With bleeding thumb a-widdershin.[1]

But there was Jeff the provost's son,
  Jeff the provost's only son;
There was Father Auld himsel',
The Lombard frae the hostelry,
And the lawyer Peter Fell.

All goodly men we singled out,
  Waled[2] them well, and singled out,
And drew them by the left hand in;
Mysie the priest, and Elspie won
The Lombard, Nort the lawyer carle,
I mysel' the provost's son.

Then, with cantrip[3] kisses seven,
  Three times round with kisses seven,
Warp'd and woven there spun we
Arms and legs and flaming hair,
Like a whirlwind on the sea.

Like a wind that sucks the sea,
  Over and in and on the sea,
Good sooth it was a mad delight;
And every man of all the four
Shut his eyes and laugh'd outright.

[1] the wrong way of the sun; or E. to W. through N.
[2] chose.   [3] magic.

Laugh'd as long as they had breath,
    Laugh'd while they had sense or breath;
And close about us coil'd a mist
Of gnats and midges, wasps and flies,
Like the whirlwind shaft it rist.

Drawn up I was right off my feet,
    Into the mist and off my feet;
And, dancing on each chimney-top,
I saw a thousand darling imps
Keeping time with skip and hop.

And on the provost's brave ridge-tile,
    On the provost's grand ridge-tile,
The Blackamoor first to master me
I saw, I saw that winsome smile,
The mouth that did my heart beguile,
And spoke the great Word over me,
In the land beyond the sea.

I call'd his name, I call'd aloud,
    Alas! I call'd on him aloud;
And then he fill'd his hand with stour,[1]
And threw it towards me in the air;
My mouse flew out, I lost my pow'r!

My lusty strength, my power, were gone;
    Power was gone, and all was gone.
He will not let me love him more!
Of bell and whip and horse's tail
He cares not if I find a store.

But I am proud if he is fierce!
    I am as proud as he is fierce;
I'll turn about and backward go,
If I meet again that Blackamoor,
And he'll help us then, for he shall know
I seek another paramour.

[1] dust.

And we'll gang once more to yon town,
　Wi' better luck to yon town;
We'll walk in silk and cramoisie,[1]
And I shall wed the provost's son
My lady of the town I'll be!

For I was born a crown'd king's child,
　Born and nursed a king's child,
King o' a land ayont the sea,
Where the Blackamoor kiss'd me first,
And taught me art and glamourie.

Each one in her wame shall hide
　Her hairy mouse, her wary mouse,
Fed on madwort and agramie,—
Wear amber beads between her breasts,
And blind-worm's skin about her knee.

The Lombard shall be Elspie's man,
　Elspie's gowden husband-man;
Nort shall take the lawyer's hand;
The priest shall swear another vow:
We'll dance again the saraband!

CHARLES MACKAY
1814–89
The Two Houses

''Twill overtask a thousand men,
　With all their strength and skill,
To build my lord ere New Year's eve
　His castle on the hill.'
'Then take two thousand!' said my lord,
　'And labour with a will.'

[1] crimson.

They wrought, these glad two thousand men,
    But long ere winter gloom,
My lord had found a smaller house,
    And dwelt in one dark room;
And one man built it in one day,
    While the bells rang ding, dong, boom!
Shut up the door! shut up the door!
    Shut up the door till doom!

Great and Small

THERE is nor great nor small in Nature's plan,
Bulk is but fancy in the mind of man;
A raindrop is as wondrous as a star,
Near is not nearest, farthest is not far;
And suns and planets in the vast serene
Are but as midges in the summer sheen,
Born in their season, and that live and die
Creatures of Time, lost in Eternity.

GEORGE MAC DONALD

1824-1905

Christmas Meditation

HE who by a mother's love
    Made the wandering world his own,
Every year comes from above,
    Comes the parted to atone,
    Binding Earth to the Father's throne.

Nay, thou comest every day!
    No, thou never didst depart!
Never hour hast been away!
    Always with us, Lord, thou art,
    Binding, binding heart to heart!

The Father's Hymn for the Mother to sing

My child is lying on my knees;
   The signs of heaven she reads:
My face is all the heaven she sees,
   Is all the heaven she needs.

And she is well, yea, bathed in bliss,
   If heaven is in my face—
Behind it, all is tenderness,
   And truthfulness and grace.

I mean her well so earnestly,
   Unchanged in changing mood;
My life would go without a sigh
   To bring her something good.

I also am a child, and I
   Am ignorant and weak;
I gaze upon the starry sky,
   And then I must not speak;

For all behind the starry sky,
   Behind the world so broad,
Behind men's hearts and souls doth lie
   The Infinite of God.

If true to her, though troubled sore,
   I cannot choose but be;
Thou, who art peace for evermore,
   Art very true to me.

If I am low and sinful, bring
   More love where need is rife;
Thou knowest what an awful thing
   It is to be a life.

Hast thou not wisdom to enwrap
  My waywardness about,
In doubting safety on the lap
  Of Love that knows no doubt?

Lo! Lord, I sit in thy wide space,
  My child upon my knee;
She looketh up unto my face,
  And I look up to thee.

Rest

I

WHEN round the earth the Father's hands
  Have gently drawn the dark;
Sent off the sun to fresher lands,
  And curtained in the lark;
'Tis sweet, all tired with glowing day,
  To fade with fading light,
And lie once more, the old weary way,
  Upfolded in the night.

If mothers o'er our slumbers bend,
  And unripe kisses reap,
In soothing dreams with sleep they blend,
  Till even in dreams we sleep.
And if we wake while night is dumb,
  'Tis sweet to turn and say,
It is an hour ere dawning come,
  And I will sleep till day.

II

There is a dearer, warmer bed,
  Where one all day may lie,
Earth's bosom pillowing the head,
  And let the world go by.

There come no watching mother's eyes,
　　The stars instead look down;
Upon it breaks, and silent dies,
　　The murmur of the town.

The great world, shouting, forward fares:
　　This chamber, hid from none,
Hides safe from all, for no one cares
　　For him whose work is done.
Cheer thee, my friend; bethink thee how
　　A certain unknown place,
Or here or there, is waiting now,
　　To rest thee from thy race.

Song of the Summer Days

A MORN of winds and swaying trees—
　　Earth's jubilance rushing out!
The birds are fighting with the breeze;
　　The waters heave about.

White clouds are swept across the sky,
　　Their shadows o'er the graves;
Purpling the green, they float and fly
　　Athwart the sunny waves.

The long grass—an earth-rooted sea—
　　Mimics the watery strife.
To boat or horse? Wild motion we
　　Shall find harmonious life.

But whither? Roll and sweep and bend
　　Suffice for Nature's part;
But motion to an endless end
　　Is needful for our heart.

Song of the Autumn Nights

So, like the corn moon-ripened last,
  Would I, weary and gray,
On golden memories ripen fast,
  And ripening pass away.

In an old night so let me die;
  A slow wind out of doors;
A waning moon low in the sky;
  A vapour on the moors;

A fire just dying in the gloom;
  Earth haunted all with dreams;
A sound of waters in the room;
  A mirror's moony gleams;

And near me, in the sinking night,
  More thoughts than move in me—
Forgiving wrong, and loving right,
  And waiting till I see.

Song of the Spring Days

BLOW on me, wind, from west and south;
  Sweet summer-spirit, blow!
Come like a kiss from dear child's mouth,
  Who knows not what I know.

The earth's perfection dawneth soon;
  Ours lingereth alway;
We have a morning, not a noon;
  Spring, but no summer gay.

Rose-blotted eve, gold-branded morn
  Crown soon the swift year's life:
In us a higher hope is born,
  And claims a longer strife.

Will heaven be an eternal spring
    With summer at the door?
Or shall we one day tell its king
    That we desire no more?

A Prayer

WHEN I look back upon my life nigh spent,
    Nigh spent, although the stream as yet flows
        on,
I more of follies than of sins repent,
    Less for offence than Love's shortcomings
        moan.
    With self, O Father, leave me not alone—
Leave not with the beguiler the beguiled;
    Besmirched and ragged, Lord, take back thine
        own:
A fool I bring thee to be made a child.

Travellers' Song

BANDS of dark and bands of light
    Lie athwart the homeward way;
Now we cross a belt of Night,
    Now a strip of shining Day!

Now it is a month of June,
    Now December's shivering hour;
Now rides high loved memories' Moon,
    Now the Dark is dense with power!

Summers, winters, days, and nights,
    Moons, and clouds, they come and go;
Joys and sorrows, pains, delights,
    Hope and fear, and *yes* and *no*.

All is well: come, girls and boys,
    Not a weary mile is vain!
Hark—dim laughter's radiant noise!
    See the windows through the rain!

Rondel

HEART, thou must learn to do without—
    That is the riches of the poor,
    Their liberty is to endure;
Wrap thou thine old cloak thee about,
And carol loud and carol stout;
    Let thy rags fly, nor wish them fewer;
Thou too must learn to do without,
    Must earn the riches of the poor!

Why should'st thou only wear no clout?
    Thou only walk in love-robes pure?
    Why should thy step alone be sure?
Thou only free of fortune's flout?
Nay, nay! but learn to go without,
    And so be humbly, richly poor.

What the Auld Fowk are thinkin

THE bairns i' their beds, worn oot wi' nae wark,
    Are sleepin, nor ever an eelid winkin;
The auld fowk lie still wi' their een starin stark,
    An' the mirk pang-fou[1] o' the things they are
    thinkin.

---

[1] dark stuffed full.

Whan oot o' ilk[1] corner the bairnies they keek,[2]
  Lauchin an' daffin,[3] airms loosin an' linkin,
The auld fowk they watch frae the warm ingle-
  cheek,[4]
  But the bairns little think what the auld fowk
  are thinkin.

Whan the auld fowk sit quaiet at the reet[5] o'
  a stook,[6]
  I' the sunlicht their washt een blinterin an'
  blinkin,
Fowk scythin, or bin'in, or shearin wi' heuk
  Carena a strae what the auld fowk are thinkin.

At the kirk, whan the minister's dreich[7] an' dry,
  His fardens as gien[8] they war gowd guineas
  chinkin,
An' the young fowk are noddin, or fidgetin sly,
  Naebody kens what the auld fowk are thinkin.

Whan the young fowk are greitin[9] aboot the bed
  Whaur like water throu san' the auld life is
  sinkin,
An' some wud say the last word was said,
  The auld fowk smile, an' ken what they're
  thinkin.

ALEXANDER SMITH

1830–67

Glasgow

SING, Poet, 'tis a merry world;
  That cottage smoke is rolled and curled
    In sport, that every moss
  Is happy, every inch of soil;—

---

[1] each.   [2] peep.   [3] teasing.   [4] side of the fire.
[5] root, foot.   [6] sheaf.   [7] dreary.   [8] if.   [9] weeping.

Before *me* runs a road of toil
  With my grave cut across.
Sing, trailing showers and breezy downs—
I know the tragic heart of towns.

City! I am true son of thine;
Ne'er dwelt I where great mornings shine
  Around the bleating pens;
Ne'er by the rivulets I strayed,
And ne'er upon my childhood weighed
  The silence of the glens.
Instead of shores where ocean beats,
I hear the ebb and flow of streets.

Black Labour draws his weary waves,
Into their secret-moaning caves;
  But with the morning light,
The sea again will overflow
With a long weary sound of woe,
  Again to faint in night.
Wave am I in that sea of woes;
Which, night and morning, ebbs and flows.

I dwelt within a gloomy court
Wherein did never sunbeam sport;
  Yet there my heart was stirr'd—
My very blood did dance and thrill,
When on my narrow window-sill,
  Spring lighted like a bird.
Poor flowers—I watched them pine for weeks,
With leaves as pale as human cheeks.

Afar, one summer, I was borne;
Through golden vapours of the morn,
  I heard the hills of sheep:
I trod with a wild ecstasy
The bright fringe of the living sea:
  And on a ruined keep

I sat, and watched an endless plain
Blacken beneath the gloom of rain.

O fair the lightly sprinkled waste,
O'er which a laughing shower has raced!
    O fair the April shoots!
O fair the woods on summer days,
While a blue hyacinthine haze
    Is dreaming round the roots!
In thee, O City! I discern
Another beauty, sad and stern.

Draw thy fierce streams of blinding ore,
Smite on a thousand anvils, roar
    Down to the harbour-bars;
Smoulder in smoky sunsets, flare
On rainy nights, with street and square
    Lie empty to the stars.
From terrace proud to alley base
I know thee as my mother's face.

When sunset bathes thee in his gold,
In wreaths of bronze thy sides are rolled,
    Thy smoke is dusky fire;
And, from the glory round thee poured,
A sunbeam like an angel's sword
    Shivers upon a spire.
Thus have I watched thee, Terror! Dream!
While the blue Night crept up the stream.

The wild Train plunges in the hills,
He shrieks across the midnight rills;
    Streams through the shifting glare,
The roar and flap of foundry fires,
That shake with light the sleeping shires;
    And on the moorlands bare,
He sees afar a crown of light
Hang o'er thee in the hollow night.

At midnight, when thy suburbs lie
As silent as a noonday sky,
    When larks with heat are mute,
I love to linger on thy bridge,
All lonely as a mountain ridge,
    Disturbed but by my foot;
While the black lazy stream beneath,
Steals from its far-off wilds of heath.

And through my heart, as through a dream,
Flows on that black disdainful stream;
    All scornfully it flows,
Between the huddled gloom of masts,
Silent as pines unvexed by blasts—
    'Tween lamps in streaming rows.
O wondrous sight! O stream of dread!
O long dark river of the dead!

Afar, the banner of the year
Unfurls: but dimly prisoned here,
    'Tis only when I greet
A dropt rose lying in my way,
A butterfly that flutters gay
    Athwart the noisy street,
I know the happy Summer smiles
Around thy suburbs, miles on miles.

All raptures of this mortal breath,
Solemnities of life and death,
    Dwell in thy noise alone:
Of me thou hast become a part—
Some kindred with my human heart.
    Lives in thy streets of stone;
For we have been familiar more
Than galley-slave and weary oar.

The beech is dipped in wine; the shower
Is burnished; on the swinging flower
　　The latest bee doth sit.
The low sun stares through dust of gold,
And o'er the darkening heath and wold
　　The large ghost-moth doth flit.
In every orchard Autumn stands,
With apples in his golden hands.

But all these sights and sounds are strange;
Then wherefore from thee should I range?
　　Thou hast my kith and kin:
My childhood, youth, and manhood brave;
Thou hast an unforgotten grave
　　Within thy central din.
A sacredness of love and death
Dwells in thy noise and smoky breath.

While o'er thy walls the darkness sails,
I lean against the churchyard rails;
　　Up in the midnight towers
The belfried spire, the street is dead,
I hear in silence overhead
　　The clang of iron hours:
It moves me not, I know her tomb
Is yonder in the shapeless gloom.

Barbara

　　On the Sabbath-day,
　　　　Through the churchyard old and gray,
Over the crisp and yellow leaves I held my rust-
　　ling way;
And amid the words of mercy, falling on my
　　soul like balms,

'Mid the gorgeous storms of music—in the
    mellow organ-calms,
'Mid the upward-streaming prayers, and the
    rich and solemn psalms,
        I stood careless, Barbara.

      My heart was otherwhere,
      While the organ shook the air,
And the priest, with outspread hands, bless'd
    the people with a prayer;
But when rising to go homeward, with a mild
    and saint-like shine
Gleam'd a face of airy beauty with its heavenly
    eyes on mine—
Gleam'd and vanish'd in a moment—O that
    face was surely thine
        Out of heaven, Barbara!

      O pallid, pallid face!
      O earnest eyes of grace!
When last I saw thee, dearest, it was in another
    place.
You came running forth to meet me with my
    love-gift on your wrist:
The flutter of a long white dress, then all was lost
    in mist—
A purple stain of agony was on the mouth I
    kiss'd,
        That wild morning, Barbara.

      I search'd, in my despair,
      Sunny noon and midnight air;
I could not drive away the thought that you
    were lingering there.
O many and many a winter night I sat when
    you were gone,

My worn face buried in my hands, beside the
    fire alone—
Within the dripping churchyard, the rain plash-
    ing on your stone,
        You were sleeping, **Barbara.**

    'Mong angels, do you think
    Of the precious golden link
I clasp'd around your happy **arm** while sitting
    by yon brink?
Or when that night of gliding dance, of laughter
    and guitars,
Was emptied of its music, and we watch'd,
    through lattice-bars,
The silent midnight heaven creeping o'er us
    with its stars,
        Till the day broke, Barbara?

    In the years I've changed;
    Wild and far my heart has ranged,
And many sins and errors now have been on me
    avenged;
But to you I have been faithful whatsoever good
    I lack'd:
I loved you, and above my life still hangs that
    love intact—
Your love the trembling rainbow, I the reckless
    cataract.
        Still I love you, Barbara.

    Yet, Love, I am unblest;
    With many doubts opprest,
I wander like the desert wind without a place of
    rest.
Could I but win you for an hour from off that
    starry shore.

The hunger of my soul were still'd; for Death
    hath told you more
Than the melancholy world doth know—things
    deeper than all lore
      You could teach me, Barbara.

      In vain, in vain, in vain!
      You will never come again.
There droops upon the dreary hills a mournful
    fringe of rain;
The gloaming closes slowly round, loud winds
    are in the tree,
Round selfish shores for ever moans the hurt
    and wounded sea;
There is no rest upon the earth, peace is with
    Death and thee—
      Barbara!

JAMES THOMSON
1834–82
To our Ladies of Death

Tired with all these, for restful death I cry.

WEARY of erring in this Desert Life,
    Weary of hoping hopes for ever vain,
Weary of struggling in all-sterile strife,
    Weary of thought which maketh nothing
    plain,
I close my eyes and calm my panting breath,
    And pray to Thee, O ever-quiet Death!
    To come and soothe away my bitter pain.

The strong shall strive,—may they be victors
    crowned;
  The wise still seek,—may they at length find
    truth;
The young still hope,—may purest love be
    found
    To make their age more glorious than their
    youth.
For me; my brain is weak, my heart is cold . . .
My hope and faith long dead; my life but bold
    In jest and laugh to parry hateful ruth.

Over me pass the days and months and years
    Like squadrons and battalions of the foe
Trampling with thoughtless thrusts and alien
    jeers
    Over a wounded soldier lying low:
He grips his teeth, or flings them words of scorn
To mar their triumph: but the while, outworn,
    Inwardly craves for death to end his woe.

Thus I in secret call, O Death! to Thee,
    Thou Youngest of the solemn Sisterhood,
Thou Gentlest of the mighty Sisters Three
    Whom I have known so well since first endued
By Love and Grief with vision to discern
What spiritual life doth throb and burn
    Through all our world, with evil powers and
    good.

The Three whom I have known so long, so well,
    By intimate communion, face to face,
In every mood, of Earth, of Heaven, of Hell,
    In every season and in every place,
That joy of life has ceased to visit me,
As one estranged by powerful witchery,
    Infatuate in a Siren's weird embrace.

First Thou, O priestess, prophetess, and queen,
   Our Lady of Beatitudes, first Thou:
Of mighty stature, of seraphic mien,
   Upon the tablet of whose broad white brow
Unvanquishable Truth is written clear,
The secret of the mystery of our sphere,
   The regnant word of the Eternal Now.

Thou standest garmented in purest white;
   But from thy shoulders wings of power half-
      spread
Invest thy form with such miraculous light
   As dawn may clothe the earth with: and
      instead
Of any jewel-kindled golden crown,
The glory of thy long hair flowing down
   Is dazzling noonday sunshine round thy head.

Upon a sword thy left hand resteth calm,
   A naked sword, two-edged and long and
      straight;
A branch of olive with a branch of palm
   Thy right hand proffereth to hostile Fate.
Thy shining plumes that clothe thy feet are
      bound
By knotted strings, as if to tread the ground
   With weary steps when thou wouldst soar
      elate.

Twin heavens uplifted to the heavens, thine eyes
   Are solemn with unutterable thought
And love and aspiration; yet there lies
   Within their light eternal sadness, wrought
By hope deferred and baffled tenderness:
Of all the souls whom thou dost love and bless,
   How few revere and love thee as they ought!

Thou leadest heroes from their warfare here
  To nobler fields where grander crowns are
    won;
Thou leadest sages from this twilight sphere
  To cloudless heavens and an unsetting sun;
Thou leadest saints into that purer air
Whose breath is spiritual life and prayer:
  Yet, lo! they seek thee not, but fear and shun!

Thou takest to thy most maternal breast
  Young children from the desert of this earth,
Ere sin hath stained their souls, or grief opprest,
  And bearest them unto an heavenly birth,
To be the Vestals of God's Fane above:
And yet their kindred moan against thy love,
  With wild and selfish moans in bitter dearth.

Most holy Spirit, first Self-conqueror;
  Thou victress over Time and Destiny
And Evil, in the all-deciding war
  So fierce, so long, so dreadful!—Would that me
Thou hadst upgathered in my life's pure morn!
Unworthy then, less worthy now, forlorn,
  I dare not, Gracious Mother, call on Thee.

Next Thou, O Sibyl, sorceress and queen,
  Our Lady of Annihilation, Thou!
Of mighty stature, of demoniac mien;
  Upon whose swarthy face and livid brow
Are graven deeply anguish, malice, scorn,
Strength ravaged by unrest, resolve forlorn
  Of any hope, dazed pride that will not bow.

Thy form is clothed with wings of iron gloom;
  But round about thee, like a chain, is rolled,
Cramping the sway of every mighty plume,
  A stark constringent serpent, fold on fold:

Of its two heads, one sting is in thy brain,
The other in thy heart; their venom-pain
   Like fire distilling through thee uncontrolled.

A rod of serpents wieldeth thy right hand;
   Thy left a cup of raging fire, whose light
Burns lurid on thyself as thou dost stand;
   Thy lidless eyes tenebriously bright;
Thy wings, thy vesture, thy dishevelled hair
Dark as the Grave; thou statue of Despair,
   Thou Night essential radiating night.

Thus have I seen thee in thine actual form;
   Not thus can see thee those whom thou dost
     sway,
Inscrutable Enchantress; young and warm,
   Pard-beautiful and brilliant, ever gay;
Thy cup the very Wine of Life, thy rod
The wand of more voluptuous spells than God
   Can wield in Heaven; thus charmest thou thy
     prey.

The selfish, fatuous, proud, and pitiless,
   All who have falsified life's royal trust;
The strong whose strength hath basked in idle-
    ness,
   The great heart given up to worldly lust,
The great mind destitute of moral faith;
Thou scourgest down to Night and utter Death,
   Or penal spheres of retribution just.

O mighty Spirit, fraudful and malign,
   Demon of madness and perversity!
The evil passions which may make me thine
   Are not yet irrepressible in me;
And I have pierced thy mask of riant youth,
And seen thy form in all its hideous truth:
   I will not, Dreadful Mother, call on Thee.

Last Thou, retired nun and throneless queen,
  Our Lady of Oblivion, last Thou:
Of human stature, of abstracted mien;
  Upon whose pallid face and drooping brow
Are shadowed melancholy dreams of Doom,
And deep absorption into silent gloom,
  And weary bearing of the heavy Now.

Thou art all shrouded in a gauzy veil,
  Sombrous and cloudlike; all, except that face
Of subtle loveliness though weirdly pale.
  Thy soft, slow-gliding footsteps leave no trace,
And stir no sound. Thy drooping hands infold
Their frail white fingers; and, unconscious, hold
  A poppy-wreath, thine anodyne of grace.

Thy hair is like a twilight round thy head;
  Thine eyes are shadowed wells, from Lethe-
      stream
With drowsy subterranean waters fed;
  Obscurely deep, without a stir or gleam;
The gazer drinks in from them with his gaze
An opiate charm to curtain all his days,
  A passive languor of oblivious dream.

Thou hauntest twilight regions, and the trance
  Of moonless nights when stars are few and
      wan:
Within black woods; or over the expanse
  Of desert seas abysmal; or upon
Old solitary shores whose populous graves
Are rocked in rest by ever-moaning waves;
  Or through vast ruined cities still and lone.

The weak, the weary, and the desolate,
  The poor, the mean, the outcast, the opprest,
All trodden down beneath the march of Fate,
  Thou gatherest, loving Sister, to thy breast,

Soothing their pain and weariness asleep;
   Then in thy hidden Dreamland hushed and deep
      Dost lay them, shrouded in eternal rest.

O sweetest Sister, and sole Patron Saint
   Of all the humble eremites who flee
From out life's crowded tumult, stunned and
     faint,
   To seek a stern and lone tranquillity
In Libyan wastes of time: my hopeless life
With famished yearning craveth rest from strife;
   Therefore, thou Restful One, I call on Thee!

Take me, and lull me into perfect sleep;
   Down, down, far-hidden in thy duskiest cave;
While all the clamorous years above me sweep
   Unheard, or, like the voice of seas that rave
On far-off coasts, but murmuring o'er my trance,
A dim, vast monotone, that shall enhance
   The restful rapture of the inviolate grave.

Upgathered thus in thy divine embrace,
   Upon mine eyes thy soft mesmeric hand,
While wreaths of opiate odour interlace
   About my pulseless brow; babe-pure and
     bland,
Passionless, senseless, thoughtless, let me dream
Some ever-slumbrous, never-varying theme,
   Within the shadow of thy Timeless Land.

That when I thus have drunk my inmost fill
   Of perfect peace, I may arise renewed;
In soul and body, intellect and will,
   Equal to cope with Life whate'er its mood;
To sway its storm and energize its calm;
Through rhythmic years evolving like a psalm
   Of infinite love and faith and sanctitude.

But if this cannot be, no less I cry,
   Come, lead me with thy terrorless control
Down to our Mother's bosom, there to die
   By abdication of my separate soul:
So shall this single, self-impelling piece
Of mechanism from lone labour cease,
   Resolving into union with the whole.

Our Mother feedeth thus our little life,
   That we in turn may feed her with our death:
The great Sea sways, one interwoven strife,
   Wherefrom the sun exhales a subtle breath,
To float the heavens sublime in form and hue,
Then turning dark and cold in order due
   Rain weeping back to swell the Sea beneath,

One part of me shall feed a little worm,
   And it a bird on which a man may feed;
One lime the mould, one nourish insect-sperm;
   One thrill sweet grass, one pulse in bitter weed;
This swell a fruit, and that evolve in air;
Another trickle to a springlet's lair,
   Another paint a daisy on the mead:

With cosmic interchange of parts for all,
   Through all the modes of being numberless
Of every element, as may befall.
   And if earth's general soul hath consciousness,
Their new life must with strange new joy be
     thrilled,
Of perfect law all perfectly fulfilled;
   No sin, no fear, no failure, no excess.

Weary of living isolated life,
   Weary of hoping hopes for ever vain,
Weary of struggling in all-sterile strife,
   Weary of thought which maketh nothing
     plain,

I close my eyes and hush my panting breath,
And yearn for Thee, divinely tranquil Death,
  To come and soothe away my bitter pain.

THOMAS DAVIDSON

1838–70

And there will I be buried

TELL me not the good and wise
  Care not where their dust reposes—
That to him in death who lies
  Rocky beds are even as roses.

I've been happy above ground;
  I can never be happy under
Out of gentle Teviot's sound—
  Part us not then, far asunder.

Lay me here where I may see
  Teviot round his meadows flowing,
And around and over me
  Winds and clouds for ever going.

Love's Last Suit

LOVE, forget me when I'm gone!
When the tree is overthrown,
Let its place be digg'd and sown
O'er with grass;—when that is grown,
The very place shall be unknown!
So court I oblivion.
So I charge thee, by our love,
Love, forget me when I'm gone!

Love of him that lies in clay
  Only maketh life forlorn—
Clouding o'er the new-born day
  With regrets of yester morn.
And what is love of him that's low,
  Or sunshine on his grave that floats?
Love nor sunshine reacheth now
  Deeper than the daisy roots!

So, when he that nigh me hovers—
Death—that spares not happy lovers—
  Comes to claim his little due,
Love—as thou art good and true—
Proudly give the churl his own,
And forget me when I'm gone!

ANDREW LANG

1844–1912

Almæ Matres

(St. Andrews, 1862.   Oxford, 1865.)

St. Andrews by the Northern Sea,
  A haunted town it is to me!
A little city, worn and grey,
  The grey North Ocean girds it round,
And o'er the rocks, and up the bay,
  The long sea-rollers surge and sound.
And still the thin and biting spray
  Drives down the melancholy street,
And still endure, and still decay,
  Towers that the salt winds vainly beat.
Ghost-like and shadowy they stand
Dim mirrored in the wet sea-sand.

St. Leonard's chapel, long ago
  We loitered idly where the tall
Fresh-budded mountain ashes blow
  Within thy desecrated wall:
The tough roots rent the tomb below,
  The April birds sang clamorous,
We did not dream, we could not know
  How hardly Fate would deal with us!

O, broken minster, looking forth
  Beyond the bay, above the town,
O, winter of the kindly North,
  O, college of the scarlet gown,
And shining sands beside the sea,
  And stretch of links beyond the sand,
Once more I watch you, and to me
  It is as if I touched his hand!

And therefore art thou yet more dear,
  O, little city, grey and sere,
Though shrunken from thine ancient pride
  And lonely by thy lonely sea,
Than these fair halls on Isis' side,
  Where Youth an hour came back to me!

A land of waters green and clear,
  Of willows and of poplars tall,
And, in the spring-time of the year,
  The white may breaking over all,
And Pleasure quick to come at call.
  And summer rides by marsh and wold,
And Autumn with her crimson pall
  About the towers of Magdalen rolled;
And strange enchantments from the past,
  And memories of the friends of old,
And strong Tradition, binding fast
  The 'flying terms' with bands of gold,—

All these hath Oxford: all are dear,
    But dearer far the little town,
The drifting surge, the wintry year,
    The college of the scarlet gown.
      St. Andrews by the Northern Sea,
        That is a haunted town to me!

Clevedon Church

WESTWARD I watch the low green hills of Wales,
    The low sky silver grey,
The turbid Channel with the wandering sails
    Moans through the winter day.
There is no colour but one ashen light
    On tower and lonely tree,
The little church upon the windy height
    Is grey as sky or sea.

But there hath he that woke the sleepless Love
    Slept through these fifty years,
There is the grave that has been wept above
    With more than mortal tears.
And far below I hear the Channel sweep
    And all his waves complain,
As Hallam's dirge through all the years must keep
    Its monotone of pain.

   .   .   .   .   .

Grey sky, brown waters, as a bird that flies,
    My heart flits forth from these
Back to the winter rose of northern skies,
    Back to the northern seas.
And lo, the long waves of the ocean beat
    Below the minster grey,
Caverns and chapels worn of saintly feet,
    And knees of them that pray.

And I remember me how twain were one
    Beside that ocean dim,
I count the years passed over since the sun
    That lights me looked on him,
And dreaming of the voice that, safe in sleep,
    Shall greet me not again,
Far, far below I hear the Channel sweep
    And all his waves complain.

Nightingale Weather

Serai-je nonnette, oui ou non?
Serai-je nonnette? je crois que non.
Derrière chez mon père
Il est un bois taillis,
Le rossignol y chante
Et le jour et la nuit.
Il chante pour les filles
Qui n'ont pas d'ami;
Il ne chante pas pour moi,
J'en ai un, Dieu merci.

        Old French.

I'LL never be a nun, I trow,
While apple bloom is white as snow,
    But far more fair to see;
I'll never wear nun's black and white
While nightingales make sweet the night
    Within the apple-tree.

Ah, listen! 'tis the nightingale,
And in the wood he makes his wail,
    Within the apple-tree;
He singeth of the sore distress
Of many ladies loverless;
    Thank God, no song for me.

For when the broad May moon is low,
A gold fruit seen where blossoms blow
    In the boughs of the apple-tree,
A step I know is at the gate;
Ah love, but is it long to wait
    Until night's noon bring thee!

Between lark's song and nightingale's
A silent space, while dawning pales,
    The birds leave still and free
For words and kisses musical,
For silence and for sighs that fall
    In the dawn, 'twixt him and me.

Romance

My Love dwelt in a northern land.
    A gray tower in a forest green
Was hers, and far on either hand
    The long wash of the waves was seen,
And leagues and leagues of yellow sand,
    The woven forest boughs between!

And through the silver northern night
    The sunset slowly died away,
And herds of strange deer, lily-white,
    Stole forth among the branches gray,
About the coming of the light,
    They fled like ghosts before the day!

I know not if the forest green
    Still girdles round that castle gray;
I know not if the boughs between
    The white deer vanish ere the day:
Above my Love the grass is green,
    My heart is colder than the clay!

A Dream

WHY will you haunt my sleep?
　　You know it may not be;
The grave is wide and deep,
　　That sunders you and me;
In bitter dreams we reap
　　The sorrow we have sown,
And I would I were asleep,
　　Forgotten and alone!

We knew and did not know—
　　We saw and did not see,
The nets that long ago
　　Fate wove for you and me;
The cruel nets that keep
　　The birds that sob and moan;
And I would we were asleep,
　　Forgotten and alone!

O Joy of love's renewing

O JOY of love's renewing,
　　Could love be born again;
Relenting for thy rueing,
　　And pitying my pain:
O joy of love's awaking,
　　Could love arise from sleep,
Forgiving our forsaking
　　The fields we would not reap!

Fleet, fleet we fly, pursuing
　　The love that fled amain,
But will he list our wooing,
　　Or call we but in vain?
Ah! vain is all our wooing,

And all our prayers are vain,
Love listeth not our suing,
Love will not wake again.

Lost Love

WHO wins his love shall lose her,
    Who loses her shall gain,
For still the spirit woos her,
    A soul without a stain;
And memory still pursues her
    With longings not in vain!

He loses her who gains her,
    Who watches day by day
The dust of time that stains her,
    The griefs that leave her gray—
The flesh that yet enchains her
    Whose grace hath passed away!

Oh, happier he who gains not
    The love some seem to gain:
The joy that custom stains not
    Shall still with him remain;
The loveliness that wanes not,
    The love that ne'er can wane.

In dreams she grows not older
    The lands of dream among;
Though all the world wax colder,
    Though all the songs be sung,
In dreams doth he behold her
    Still fair and kind and young.

Endure, my Heart

ENDURE, my heart: not long shalt thou endure
        The shame, the smart;
The good and ill are done; the end is sure;
        Endure, my heart!
There stand two vessels by the golden throne
        Of Zeus on high;
From these he scatters mirth and scatters moan,
        To men that die.
And thou of many joys hast had thy share,
        Thy perfect part;
Battle and love, and evil things and fair;
        Endure, my heart!

Fight one last greatest battle under shield,
        Wage that war well:
Then seek thy fellows in the shadowy field
        Of asphodel;
There is the knightly Hector; there the men
        Who fought for Troy;
Shall we not fight our battles o'er again?
        Were that not joy?
Though no sun shines beyond the dusky west,
        Thy perfect part
There shalt thou have of the unbroken rest;
        Endure, my heart!

Ballade of his Choice of a Sepulchre

HERE I'd come when weariest!
        Here the breast
Of the Windburg's tufted over
Deep with bracken; here his crest
        Takes the west,
Where the wide-winged hawk doth hover.

Silent here are lark and plover;
    In the cover
Deep below, the cushat best
Loves his mate, and croons above her
    O'er their nest,
Where the wide-winged hawk doth hover.

Bring me here, life's tired-out guest,
    To the blest
Bed that waits the weary rover,
Here shall failure be confessed;
    Ends my quest,
Where the wide-winged hawk doth hover!

Envoy

Friend, or stranger kind, or lover,
Ah, fulfil a last behest,
    Let me rest
Where the wide-winged hawk doth hover!

ROBERT LOUIS STEVENSON
1850–94

Blows the wind to-day

Blows the wind to-day, and the sun and the rain
    are flying,
  Blows the wind on the moors to-day and
    now,
Where about the graves of the martyrs the
    whaups are crying,
  My heart remembers how!

Grey recumbent tombs of the dead in desert
    places,
    Standing stones on the vacant wine-red moor,
Hills of sheep, and the homes of the silent vanished
      races,
    And winds, austere and pure:

Be it granted me to behold you again in dying,
    Hills of home! and to hear again the call;
Hear about the graves of the martyrs the peewees
      crying,
    And hear no more at all.

It is the season now to go

IT is the season now to go
About the country high and low,
Among the lilacs hand in hand,
And two by two in fairy land.

The brooding boy, the sighing maid,
Wholly fain and half afraid,
Now meet along the hazel'd brook
To pass and linger, pause and look.

A year ago, and blithely paired,
Their rough-and-tumble play they shared;
They kissed and quarrelled, laughed and cried,
A year ago at Eastertide.

With bursting heart, with fiery face,
She strove against him in the race;
He unabashed her garter saw,
That now would touch her skirts with awe.

Now by the stile ablaze she stops,
And his demurer eyes he drops;
Now they exchange averted sighs
Or stand and marry silent eyes.

And he to her a hero is
And sweeter she than primroses;
Their common silence dearer far
Than nightingale and mavis are.

Now when they sever wedded hands,
Joy trembles in their bosom-strands
And lovely laughter leaps and falls
Upon their lips in madrigals.

The House Beautiful

A naked house, a naked moor,
A shivering pool before the door,
A garden bare of flowers and fruit
And poplars at the garden foot:
Such is the place that I live in,
Bleak without and bare within.

YET shall your ragged moor receive
The incomparable pomp of eve,
And the cold glories of the dawn
Behind your shivering trees be drawn;
And when the wind from place to place
Doth the unmoored cloud-galleons chase,
Your garden gloom and gleam again,
With leaping sun, with glancing rain.
Here shall the wizard moon ascend
The heavens, in the crimson end
Of day's declining splendour; here
The army of the stars appear.

The neighbour hollows dry or wet,
Spring shall with tender flowers beset;
And oft the morning muser see
Larks rising from the broomy lea,
And every fairy wheel and thread
Of cobweb dew-bediamonded.
When daisies go, shall winter time
Silver the simple grass with rime;
Autumnal frosts enchant the pool
And make the cart-ruts beautiful;
And when snow-bright the moor expands,
How shall your children clap their hands!

To make this earth our hermitage,
A cheerful and a changeful page,
God's bright and intricate device
Of days and seasons doth suffice.

In the Highlands

In the highlands, in the country places,
Where the old plain men have rosy faces,
And the young fair maidens
Quiet eyes;
Where essential silence cheers and blesses,
And for ever in the hill-recesses
Her more lovely music
Broods and dies.

O to mount again where erst I haunted;
Where the old red hills are bird-enchanted,
And the low green meadows
Bright with sward;
And when even dies, the million-tinted,
And the night has come, and planets glinted,
Lo! the valley hollow
Lamp-bestarred.

O to dream, O to awake and wander
There, and with delight to take and render,
Through the trance of silence,
Quiet breath;
Lo! for there, among the flowers and grasses,
Only the mightier movement sounds and passes;
Only winds and rivers,
Life and death.

JAMES LOGIE ROBERTSON ('HUGH HALIBURTON')
1849–1922

Hughie's Advice to Dauvit to Enjoy the Fine Weather

*Gratia cum nymphis geminisque sororibus audet
ducere nuda choros.* HORACE, *Car.* iv. 7.

An' noo ance mair the Lomon'
   Has donn'd his mantle green,
An' we may gang a-roamin'
   Thro' the fields at e'en.

An' listen to the rustlin'
   O' green leaves i' the shaw,[1]
An' hear the blackbird whistlin'
   Winter weel awa'.

Sae mild 's the weather, Dauvit,
   That was but late sae bauld,
We gang withoot a grauvit[2]
   Careless o' the cauld.

An' juist the ither nicht, man,
   Twa barefit Mays[3] were seen
(It maun hae been a sicht, man!)
   Dancin' on the green.

     [1] wood.   [2] scarf.   [3] maids.

It sets a body thinkin'
   Hoo quick the moments fly,
Hoo fast the days gang linkin'!
   Spring 'ill sune be by;

Then Simmer wi' the roses,
   Then Autumn wi' the grain;
Then Winter comes an' closes
   A' thing ance again.

An' yet, tho' short her range is,
   Dame Nature's never dune;
She just repeats the changes,
   Just renews the tune.

The auld mune to her ruin
   Gangs rowin' doon the sky,
When, swith, a braw bran new ane
   Cocks her horn on high!

Alas! when oor short mornin'
   Slides doun the slope to nicht,
There's neither tide nor turnin'
   Back to life an' licht.

We fa' as fell oor faithers
   Into the narrow hame,
An' fog forgetfu' gaithers
   Owre oor very name.

But what needs a' this grievin'
   For griefs we dinna feel?
Let's leeve as lang 's we're leevin',
   Lauch as lang 's we're weel.

An' if it's gude i' gloamin'
    It's better sune than syne[1]
To rise an' gang a-roamin'
    Noo the weather's fine.

Hughie seeks to console a Brother Shepherd, over-grieving for the Loss of his Son

Non semper imbres.   HORACE, *Car.* ii. 9.

IT's no aye rainin' on the misty Achils,
    It's no aye white wi' winter on Nigour;
The winds are no sae mony sorrowing Rachels,
    That grieve, and o' their grief will no' gie owre.

Dark are Benarty slopes, an' the steep Lomon'
    Flings a lang shadow on the watter plain;
But fair Lochleven's no' for ever gloomin',
    An' Devon's no' aye dark wi' Lammas rain.

The birks tho' bare, an' the sune-naked ashes,
    Not always widowed of their leaves appear;
The oaks cry oot beneath November's lashes,
    But not for all the months that mak' the year.

Comes round a time, comes round at last tho'
        creepin',
    And green and glad again stand buss an' tree;
E'en tender gowans, thro' the young gress
        peepin',
    Rise in their weakness, and owre-rin the lea.

Thus Nature sorrows, and forgets her sorrow;
    And Reason soberly approves her way:
Why should we shut oor een against to-morrow
    Because our sky was clouded yesterday.

---

[1] sooner rather than later.

JOHN DAVIDSON
1857–1909

Greenock

I NEED
No world more spacious than the region here:
The foam-embroidered firth, a purple path
For argosies that still on pinions speed,
Or fiery-hearted cleave with iron limbs
And bows precipitous the pliant sea;
The sloping shores that fringe the velvet tides
With heavy bullion and with golden lace
Of restless pebble worn and fine spun sand;
The villages that sleep the winter through,
And, wakening with the spring, keep festival
All summer and all autumn: this grey town
That pipes the morning up before the lark
With shrieking steam, and from a hundred stalks
Lacquers the sooty sky; where hammers clang
On iron hulls, and cranes in harbours creak
Rattle and swing, whole cargoes on their necks;
Where men sweat gold that others hoard or
	spend,
And lurk like vermin in their narrow streets:
This old grey town, this firth, this further strand
Spangled with hamlets, and the wooded steeps,
Whose rocky tops behind each other press,
Fantastically carved like antique helms
High-hung in heaven's cloudy armoury,
Is world enough for me.   Here daily dawn
Burns through the smoky east; with fire-shod feet
The sun treads heaven, and steps from hill to hill
Downward before the night that still pursues
His crimson wake; here winter plies his craft,

Soldering the years with ice; here spring appears,
Caught in a leafless brake, her garland torn,
Breathless with wonder, and the tears half-dried
Upon her rosy cheek; here summer comes
And wastes his passion like a prodigal
Right royally; and here her golden gains
Free-handed as a harlot autumn spends;
And here are men to know, women to love.

(From *A Ballad in Blank Verse of the Making of a Poet.*)

In Romney Marsh

As I went down to Dymchurch Wall,
  I heard the South sing o'er the land;
I saw the yellow sunlight fall
  On knolls where Norman churches stand.

And ringing shrilly, taut and lithe,
  Within the wind a core of sound,
The wire from Romney town to Hythe
  Alone its airy journey wound.

A veil of purple vapour flowed
  And trailed its fringe along the Straits;
The upper air like sapphire glowed;
  And roses filled Heaven's central gates.

Masts in the offing wagged their tops;
  The swinging waves pealed on the shore;
The saffron beach, all diamond drops
  And beads of surge, prolonged the roar.

As I came up from Dymchurch Wall,
  I saw above the Downs' low crest
The crimson brands of sunset fall,
  Flicker and fade from out the west.

Night sank: like flakes of silver fire
   The stars in one great shower came down;
Shrill blew the wind; and shrill the wire
   Rang out from Hythe to Romney town.

The darkly shining salt sea drops
   Streamed as the waves clashed on the shore;
The beach, with all its organ stops
   Pealing again, prolonged the roar.

               (From *Ballads and Songs*.)

Vivian's Speech

I saw the blackthorn blaze
Like wreaths of moonlit snow,
Where the budded leaf delays
And the violet woodlands glow;
From Highbeach steepled tower
I heard the quarter-chime—
From the ancient and hallowed bower
Of the beautiful virgin, Time,
I heard the melodious vesper hour
And the sprightly quarter-chime.
Then the blackbird finished his song
On a penetrant, resolute note;
Though the thrush descanted long,
For he knows no tune by rote—
With sighs descanted long
Of the sorrow he aches to tell;
With sobs and shuddering moans,
Like one that sings in Hell,
He laced the phantom over-tones
Of the mellow vesper-bell:
Some terror he fain would tell,
But he never can strike the note:
So the thrush descanted long,

While the blackbird finished his song
And the woodwele's laughter ceased
In his ash-green gurgling throat
On the fringe of the tones released
By the vibrant vesper-bell—
The forest laughter ceased
In the wake of the twilight bell.
And high, so high, from the dusky sky
The last lark breathless fell.
But the nightingales sang on
Like welling founts of sound,
As the saffron sunset paler shone
And the darkness grew profound;
The nightingales sang on
And the sleepless cuckoos beat
Their dulcimers anon, anon,
In the echoing woodland street—
Their golden dulcimers anon
In every forest street.
And lo! from their secret bowers
In the shadowy depths of the chace,
With lanterns jewelled like flowers
In state at a stately pace—
The elfin-folk from their hallowed bowers
In the innermost shrine of the chace,
Came, swinging their fragrant and luminous
      flowers,
To dance in the market-place—
Came with their dances and lanterned flowers
To the forest's market-place.
And I watched them dancing for hours
In elfin pomp and state:
I saw the elves and I watched them for hours,
And therefore I come so late.

           (From *St. Mark's Eve: Holiday and Other Poems*.)

From *Good Friday*

THE patchwork sunshine nets the lea;
  The flitting shadows halt and pass;
Forlorn, the mossy humble-bee
  Lounges along the flowerless grass.

With unseen smoke as pure as dew,
  Sweeter than love or lovers are,
Wood-violets of watchet hue
  Their secret hearths betray afar.

The vanguards of the daisies come,
  Summer's crusaders sanguine-stained,
The only flowers that left their home
  When happiness in Eden reigned.

They stayed abroad, old writers tell,
  Hardy and bold, east, west, south, north:
Our guilty parents, when they fell,
  And flaming vengeance drove them forth,

Their haggard eyes in vain to God,
  To all the stars of heaven turned;
But when they saw where in the sod,
  The golden-hearted daisies burned,

Sweet thoughts that still within them dwelt
  Awoke, and tears embalmed their smart;
On Eden's daisies couched they felt
  They carried Eden in their heart.

(From *Fleet Street Eclogues, First Series.*)

London

ATHWART the sky a lowly sigh
  From west to east the sweet wind carried;
The sun stood still on Primrose Hill;
  His light in all the city tarried:

The clouds on viewless columns bloomed
Like smouldering lilies unconsumed.

'Oh sweetheart, see! how shadowy,
    Of some occult magician's rearing,
Or swung in space of heaven's grace
    Dissolving, dimly reappearing,
Afloat upon ethereal tides
St. Paul's above the city rides!'

A rumour broke through the thin smoke
    Enwreathing abbey, tower, and palace,
The parks, the squares, the thoroughfares,
    The million-peopled lanes and alleys,
And ever-muttering prisoned storm,
The heart of London beating warm.

                              (From *Ballads and Songs*.)

I haunt the hills that overlook the sea

I HAUNT the hills that overlook the sea.
Here in the Winter like a meshwork shroud
The sifted snow reveals the perished land,
And powders wisps of knotgrass dank and dead
That trail like faded locks on mouldering skulls
Unearthed from shallow burial. With the Spring
The west-wind thunders through the budding
        hedge
That stems the furrowed steep—a sound of
        drums,
Of gongs and muted cymbals; yellow breasts
And brown wings whirl in gusts, fly chaffering,
        drop,
And surge in gusts again; in wooded coombs
The hyacinth with purple diapers
The russet beechmast, and the cowslips hoard

Their virgin gold in lucent chalices;
The sombre furze, all suddenly attired
In rich brocade, the enterprise-in-chief
And pageant of the season, over-rides
The rolling land and girds the bosomed plain
That strips her green robe to a saffron shore
And steps into the surf where threads and
    scales
And arabesques of blue and emerald wave
Begin to damascene the iron sea;
While faint from upland fold and covert peal
The sheep-bell and the cuckoo's mellow chime.
Then when the sovereign light from which we
    came,
Of earth enamoured, bends most questioning
    looks,
I watch the land grow beautiful, a bride
Transfigured with desire of her great lord.
Betrothal-music of the tireless larks,
Heaven-high, heaven-wide possesses all the air,
And wreathes the shining lattice of the light
With chaplets, purple clusters, vintages
Of sound from the first fragrant breath and first
Tear-sprinkled blush of Summer to the deep
Transmuted fire, the smouldering golden moons,
The wine-stained dusk of Autumn harvest-
    ripe;
And I behold the period of Time,
When Memory shall devolve and Knowledge
    lapse
Wanting a subject, and the willing earth
Leap to the bosom of the sun to be
Pure flame once more in a new time begun:
Here, as I pace the pallid doleful hills
And serpentine declivities that creep

Unhonoured to the ocean's shifting verge,
Or where the prouder curve and greener
    sward,
Surmounting peacefully the restless tides,
The cliffed escarpment ends in stormclad
    strength.

        (From *The Testament of a Man Forbid.*)

From *The Testament of a Prime Minister*

i

FOR whether earth already to its doom
Reels orbit-slipped, or whether decades hence,
Or next year, or to-morrow, or to-day
The weight of ice amassed at either pole
Shall change our axis till a deluge wipe
The citied world away, and glacial drift
Plough up the earth and harrow it again;
Or whether flame consume us comet-struck;
Or the earth's crust fall in; or to the sun
Returning whence it sprang, our orb effete,
Enwombed in pristine fire once more, become
The brilliant seed of stars to be, we know
That men shall cease: their speech, their deeds,
    their arts,
The wonder of their being, passion, love,
Ambition, charity, transcendent thought
Shall leave no memory, token, sign, or sigh
In any speck of dust, or nook of space;
We know that here and now is Heaven-and-
    Hell;
This is the Promised Land, the Golden Age,
This, the Millennium, and the Aftertime,
The fixed, eternal moment, sounding on.

ii

Like savage wood-nymphs with their hair on
  end
The pollard-willows mocked the pleasure-boat,
Or athlete skimming in his shell of splints;
But spectral poplars in the distance kept
The secrets of the wind upgathered close;
And on the verge, where sky and suburb met,
With shadow teeming and with emerald light
The forest beckoned on the voyager.
Thither I hastened, in my waking dream
Oblivious of the way: the firmament,
In quaint mosaic ceiled, of porcelain,
Azure and gray, milky and olive-hued,
Umber and flame, close canopied the earth;
An exaltation of suburban larks
Against the lowering vault shattered their
  songs;
A ground-bee twanged across the chequered
  plain;
And then the forest took me. Evening fell.
I marked the lattice-work on swarthy boles
Of lustred chestnuts as I walked about,
And saw the trees keep up a torch-lit dance,
In noiseless chains and figures flitting past.
The cuckoos beat their golden gongs through-
  out
The echoing forest; finches, sparrows, wrens,
Blackbirds and nightingales in every bough
Descanted music fresh as garlands woven
In Arcady; in hollows where the mist
Began to hang its ghostly tapestry out,
Mistrustful creatures stole from tree to tree—
The fallow deer come from their inner haunts

To snatch a supper of the crusts and crumbs
Left by the Londoner. Bird after bird
Forbore its song as darkness crept abroad,
Till the last lark dropped breathless from the
    sky:
Only the passionate nightingales poured out
Their uninterpretable carol—wreaths
Of jewels, dewdrops, gold, chaplets of stars
That stained the ashen dust with diverse fire.

The Last Journey

I FELT the world a-spinning on its nave,
   I felt it sheering blindly round the sun;
I felt the time had come to find a grave:
   I knew it in my heart my days were done.
I took my staff in hand; I took the road,
And wandered out to seek my last abode.
        Hearts of gold and hearts of lead
        Sing it yet in sun and rain,
         'Heel and toe from dawn to dusk,
         Round the world and home again.'

Oh, long before the bere was steeped for malt,
   And long before the grape was crushed for
    wine,
The glory of the march without a halt,
   The triumph of a stride like yours and mine
Was known to folk like us, who walked about,
To be the sprightliest cordial out and out!
        Folk like us, with hearts that beat,
        Sang it too in sun and rain—
         'Heel and toe from dawn to dusk,
         Round the world and home again.'

My feet are heavy now, but on I go,
  My head erect beneath the tragic years.
The way is steep, but I would have it so;
  And dusty, but I lay the dust with tears,
Though none can see me weep: alone I climb
The rugged path that leads me out of time—
        Out of time and out of all,
          Singing yet in sun and rain,
            'Heel and toe from dawn to dusk,
            Round the world and home again.'

Farewell the hope that mocked, farewell despair
  That went before me still and made the pace.
The earth is full of graves, and mine was there
  Before my life began, my resting-place;
And I shall find it out and with the dead
Lie down for ever, all my sayings said—
        Deeds all done and songs all sung,
          While others chant in sun and rain,
            'Heel and toe from dawn to dusk,
            Round the world and home again.'

                (From *The Testament of John Davidson.*)

R. F. MURRAY
1863–93

Moonlight North and South

LOVE, we have heard together
  The North Sea sing his tune,
And felt the wind's wild feather
  Brush past our cheeks at noon,
And seen the cloudy weather
  Made wondrous with the moon.

Where loveliness is rarest
    'Tis also prized the most:
The moonlight shone her fairest
    Along that level coast
Where sands and dunes the barest
    Of beauty seldom boast.

Far from that bleak and rude land
    An exile I remain
Fixed in a fair and good land,
    A valley and a plain
Rich in fat fields and woodland,
    And watered well with rain.

Last night the full moon's splendour
    Shone down on Taunton dene,
And pasture fresh and tender,
    And coppice dusky green,
The heavenly light did render
    In one enchanted scene,

One fair unearthly vision.
    Yet soon mine eyes were cloyed,
And found those fields Elysian
    Too rich to be enjoyed.
Or was it our division
    Made all my pleasure void?

Across the window glasses
    The curtain then I drew,
And, as a sea-bird passes,
    In sleep my spirit flew
To grey and windswept grasses
    And moonlit sands—and you.

For Scotland

OH, cruel off St. Andrews Bay
  The winds are wont to blow!
They either rest or gently play,
  When there in dreams I go.

And there I wander, young again,
  With limbs that do not tire,
Along the coast to Kittock's Den,
  With whinbloom all afire.

I climb the Spindle Rock, and lie
  And take my doubtful ease,
Between the ocean and the sky,
  Derided by the breeze.

Where coloured mushrooms thickly grow,
  Like flowers of brittle stalk,
To haunted Magus Muir I go,
  By Lady Catherine's Walk.

In dreams the year I linger through,
  In that familiar town,
Where all the youth I ever knew,
  Burned up and flickered down.

There's not a rock that fronts the sea,
  There's not an inland grove,
But has a tale to tell to me
  Of friendship or of love.

    And so I keep, and ever shall,
      The best place in my heart for Scotland,
    Scotland, Scotland,
      The best place in my heart for Scotland!

SIR RONALD ROSS

1867–1932

The River

WHETHER winding idly on or roaring ravaging
    downward,
Now in heav'n-revealing pools or now in the
    passion of torment;
Whether willows while thy way or vainly-
    opposing mountains
Cast across thy calm career great avalanches of
    boulders,
River, lord of rural rest or master of turbulent
    thunder,
Pause and hear me, ling'ring near me, god of the
    golden woodland.
When from forth thy flaming floods Phœbus
    ariseth immortal,
And the beaded reeds are bladed black in the
    blaze of his glory,
And the laughing lark leapeth light to the light
    of morning—
When the starry buds of spring are bright in the
    blue of the hazels;
And under unadorned brambles blacken'd by
    winter,
Golden through a thousand vales the daffodils
    gleam in the sunlight;
By thy side when light is high, we, thy lovers of
    old time,
Wander forth to tempt and take the tyrants that
    dwell in the deep pools
Where the trembling denizens are finning the
    freshets for fear—

Old men ling'ring long; but secretly more in our
    slow hearts,
Rather to see thy pageant pass in shadow or
    shower or sunlight,
Thanking God for one more Spring and Heaven
    for Heaven on earth;
Haply rather still to see, from the dim haunts of
    the wild things,
Ere we die, the gods descend to drink of thy
    thronging waters.

When in umber eve appears, or in his mist the
    morning,
Pan and Artemis may come, Pan or Apollo,
    divine.
Swift the sudden gods descend. Husht are the
    notes of the woodland,
Husht the clarioning throstlecock clamours the
    spring no more,
And the swarming buds delay to open their eyes
    for fear.
River running slow, be still, deep in thy cavernous
    winding.

    .   .   .   .

First, at dim surprise of dawn, mid mist and the
    gurgling of waters,
When all night long thy stream, new-born of ice
    and the far stars
Runs in thunder under rocks that reel with the
    roar of its fury,
While the waned moon walketh the uttermost
    peaks of the black crags,
Pan may come. Sudden his cry. Sudden the
    moan of his music;

And the morning star shall gleam high on a hill
    with envy
And the waking kestrel shriek to hear his clamour
    outdone.
Sudden and far the music floats o'er forest and
    fir and moorland.

．　．　．　．　．　．　．

There alone in dewy dell or lost in the fume of thy
    thunder,
By thy side when light is high, I thy lover, wide-
    eyed,
May behold them there, divine, and tell of their
    wisdom and beauty—
Mortal immortality and man of immortals may
    sing;
May behold them ere for e'er I climb to the
    uttermost mountains,
May behold them there by thee ere I ascend to
    the mountains,
Ice, and eyries of the Stars, and peaks of eternal
    death.
                      (From *Lyra Modulata*.)

HAROLD MONRO
1879–1932

Midnight Lamentation

WHEN you and I go down
Breathless and cold,
Our faces both worn back
To earthly mould,
How lonely we shall be!
What shall we do,
You without me,
I without you?

I cannot bear the thought
You, first, may die,
Nor of how you will weep,
Should I.
We are too much alone;
What can we do?
To make our bodies one:
You, me; I, you?

We are most nearly born
Of one same kind;
We have the same delight,
The same true mind.
Must we then part, we part;
Is there no way
To keep a beating heart,
And light of day?

I could now rise and run
Through street on street
To where you are breathing—you,
That we might meet,
And that your living voice
Might sound above
Fear, and we two rejoice
Within our love.

How frail the body is,
And we are made
As only in decay
To lean and fade.
I think too much of death;
There is a gloom
When I can't hear your breath
Calm in some room.

O, but how suddenly
Either may droop;
Countenance be so white,
Body stoop.
Then there may be a place
Where fading flowers
Drop on a lifeless face
Through weeping hours.

Is then nothing safe?
Can we not find
Some everlasting life
In our one mind?
I feel it like disgrace
Only to understand
Your spirit through your word,
Or by your hand.

I cannot find a way
Through love and through;
I cannot reach beyond
Body, to you.
When you or I must go
Down evermore,
There'll be no more to say
—But a locked door.

INDEX OF FIRST LINES